D1570273

Understanding
JOHN McGAHERN

Understanding Modern
European and Latin American
Literature

James Hardin, *Series Editor*

volumes on

Ingeborg Bachmann
Samuel Beckett
Thomas Bernhard
Johannes Bobrowski
Heinrich Böll
Italo Calvino
Albert Camus
Elias Canetti
Camilo José Cela
Céline
Julio Cortázar
Isak Dinesen
José Donoso
Friedrich Dürrenmatt
Rainer Werner Fassbinder
Max Frisch
Federico García Lorca
John McGahern
Gabriel García Márquez
Juan Goytisolo
Günter Grass
Gerhart Hauptmann

Christoph Hein
Hermann Hesse
Eugène Ionesco
Uwe Johnson
Milan Kundera
Primo Levi
John McGahern
Boris Pasternak
Octavio Paz
Luigi Pirandello
Graciliano Ramos
Erich Maria Remarque
Alain Robbe-Grillet
Joseph Roth
Jean-Paul Sartre
W. G. Sebald
Claude Simon
Mario Vargas Llosa
Peter Weiss
Franz Werfel
Christa Wolf

UNDERSTANDING

JOHN
McGAHERN

DAVID MALCOLM

THE UNIVERSITY OF SOUTH CAROLINA PRESS

© 2007 University of South Carolina

Published by the University of South Carolina Press
Columbia, South Carolina 29208

www.sc.edu/uscpress

Manufactured in the United States of America

16 15 14 13 12 11 10 09 08 07   10 9 8 7 6 5 4 3 2 1

Library of Congress Cataloging-in-Publication Data

Malcolm, David, 1952–
    Understanding John McGahern / David Malcolm.
       p. cm. — (Understanding modern European and Latin American literature)
    Includes bibliographical references and index.
    ISBN-13: 978-1-57003-673-6 (cloth : alk. paper)
    ISBN-10: 1-57003-673-X (cloth : alk. paper)
    1. McGahern, John, 1934–2006—Criticism and interpretation. I. Title.
    PR6063.A2176Z79 2006
    823'.914—dc22

                                                                    2006032562

For Agata Miksa

Contents

Editor's Preface

Understanding Modern European and Latin American Literature has been planned as a series of guides for undergraduate and graduate students and non-academic readers. Like the volumes in its companion series *Understanding Contemporary American Literature,* these books provide introductions to the lives and writings of prominent modern authors and explicate their most important works.

Modern literature makes special demands, and this is particularly true of foreign literature, in which the reader must contend not only with unfamiliar, often arcane artistic conventions and philosophical concepts but also with the handicap of reading the literature in translation. It is a truism that the nuances of one language can be rendered in another only imperfectly (and this problem is especially acute in fiction), but the fact that the works of European and Latin American writers are situated in a historical and cultural setting quite different from our own can be as great a hindrance to the understanding of these works as the linguistic barrier. For this reason the *UMELL* series emphasizes the sociological and historical background of the writers treated. The philosophical and cultural traditions peculiar to a given culture may be particularly important for an understanding of certain authors, and these are taken up in the introductory chapter and also in the discussion of those works to which this information is relevant. Beyond this, the books treat the specifically literary aspects of the author under discussion and attempt to explain the complexities of contemporary literature lucidly. The books are conceived as introductions to the authors covered, not as comprehensive analyses. They do not provide detailed summaries of plot because they are meant to be used in conjunction with the books they treat, not as a substitute for study of the original works. The purpose of the books is to provide information and judicious literary assessment of the major works in the most compact, readable form. It is our hope that the *UMELL* series will help increase knowledge and understanding of European and Latin American cultures and will serve to make the literature of those cultures more accessible.

J. H.

Acknowledgments

I thank Zina Rohan without whose friendship and generosity this book could not have been written. I thank also the rector of the University of Gdańsk, Professor Andrzej Ceynowa, and the vice-rector of the University of Gdańsk, Professor Bernard Lammek, for providing funds that permitted research trips to the British Library. In addition, I thank Scott Burgess and Karen Beidel for their skilled editorial work on the book.

My thanks go also to William and James Malcolm for their toleration of my work. Above all, I thank Cheryl Alexander Malcolm for her help, support, advice, and much else besides.

Chronology

<table>
<tr><td>1934</td><td>November 12. John McGahern born in Dublin to Susan McManus McGahern, a schoolteacher, and Francis McGahern, a police officer. McGahern lives mostly with his mother in rural northwest Ireland. Parents live apart.</td></tr>
<tr><td>1945</td><td>McGahern's mother dies. He starts to live with his father in a police barracks in Cootehall, county Roscommon.</td></tr>
<tr><td>1954</td><td>Graduates from St Patrick's Teacher Training College, Drumcondra, Dublin. Teaches in Drogheda and studies part-time at University College, Dublin.</td></tr>
<tr><td>1955–64</td><td>Teaches in Dublin.</td></tr>
<tr><td>1957</td><td>B.A. from University College, Dublin.</td></tr>
<tr><td>1961</td><td>"The End and the Beginning of Love," an extract from an unpublished novel, published in X: A Literary Magazine in London. (Parts of this novel are included, with alterations, in The Dark.)</td></tr>
<tr><td>1962</td><td>Receives the Æ Memorial Award from the Irish Arts Council for extracts from The Barracks.</td></tr>
<tr><td>1963</td><td>The Barracks.</td></tr>
<tr><td>1964</td><td>Receives an Irish Arts Council Macauley Fellowship, which allows him to travel to Paris, Finland, and Spain. Marries the Finnish translator and theater director Annikki Laaksi. The Dark is published and is seized by Irish customs officials under the Ireland's censorship laws. McGahern loses his job as a schoolteacher and leaves Ireland.</td></tr>
<tr><td>1965–68</td><td>Works in London. Laaksi and McGahern divorce.</td></tr>
<tr><td>1968–89</td><td>Teaches as visiting professor and holds position as writer in residence at universities in the United Kingdom, the United States, Canada, and the Ireland.</td></tr>
<tr><td>1970</td><td>Nightlines (short stories).</td></tr>
<tr><td>1973</td><td>Marries Madeline Green.</td></tr>
<tr><td>1974</td><td>Settles with Green on a small farm in county Leitrim.</td></tr>
</table>

1975	*The Leavetaking.*
1978	*Getting Through* (short stories).
1979	*The Pornographer.*
1984	Revised version of *The Leavetaking* published in the United Kingdom.
1985	*High Ground* (short stories).
1989	Made Chevalier de l'Ordre des Arts et Lettres by French president.
1990	*Amongst Women.* The novel is shortlisted for the Booker Prize, and it wins the *Irish Times* / Aer Lingus Irish Fiction Prize.
1991	*The Power of Darkness,* a play, produced at the Abbey Theater, Dublin.
1992	*The Collected Stories.* The volume contains one major new story, "The Country Funeral."
2002	*That They May Face the Rising Sun.* Published in the United States as *By the Lake.*
2005	*Memoir.* Published in 2006 in the United States as *All Will Be Well: A Memoir.* In it McGahern reports his father's death (without giving the date): "When word of my father's death reached me, the intensity of the conflicting emotions—grief, loss, relief—took me unawares," he writes (270–71). In the closing paragraph of *Memoir,* McGahern imagines walking the "summer lanes" of county Leitrim with his mother (271–72).
2006	McGahern dies on March 30.

Understanding
JOHN McGAHERN

CHAPTER 1

John McGahern

Life, Career, Vision, and Technique

Biography

John McGahern's life is well documented—in interviews he has given, in essays by scholars, and in his *Memoir,* published in 2005.[1] McGahern was born on November 12, 1934, the first of seven children. His mother, Susan McManus McGahern, was a deeply religious schoolteacher, and his father, Francis McGahern, was a sergeant in the Garda (the police force of the Irish Free State and the Republic of Ireland). McGahern grew up in rural northwest Ireland, living for the most part with his mother, as his parents lived apart for work-related reasons. His mother's death in 1945 was deeply traumatic for McGahern. His father was, according to McGahern, a violent and moody man who made McGahern's childhood and youth extremely unpleasant. McGahern escaped through education, becoming a teacher in 1955.

McGahern began writing in the late 1950s and immediately found success. An extract from his first, unpublished, novel, "The End and the Beginning of Love," was published in a London literary magazine in 1961; he was awarded the Æ Memorial Award[2] for extracts from his then unpublished novel *The Barracks. The Barracks* itself was published by Faber in London in 1963. His next novel, *The Dark,* provoked bitter controversy when it appeared in 1965. The book was seized by the authorities in the Ireland under the country's censorship laws. As a result, McGahern lost his job as a schoolteacher and felt forced to leave Ireland for England. There followed a decade of wandering during which McGahern lived in London (1965–68), where he worked as a schoolteacher. He later taught at various British and North American universities, including Reading University (1968) and Colgate University in New York State (1969–70, 1972–73). In *Memoir,* McGahern also records living briefly during this period (though without giving precise dates) near Almeria in southern Spain, in Helsinki, and in Paris. He returned to Ireland in the early 1970s, settling in 1974 on a small farm in county Leitrim, near where he had lived with his mother. McGahern was married twice. His first wife was the Finnish translator and theater director Annikki Laaksi. The marriage broke up (it appears in the late 1960s), according to McGahern, because he would not live with her in Helsinki where she wished to pursue her career.[3] In 1973 McGahern married Madeline Green, an American, with whom he lived for the rest of his life and to whom *Amongst Women* and *That They May Face the Rising Sun* are dedicated.

McGahern published six novels, three volumes of short stories, a play, a volume of collected short stories, and an autobiography. The novels are *The Barracks* (1963), *The Dark* (1965), *The Leavetaking* (1974; revised edition 1984), *The Pornographer* (1979), *Amongst Women* (1990), and *That They May Face the Rising Sun* (2002). All his novels have U.S. editions, although the revised edition of *The Leavetaking* has never been published there. *That They May Face the Rising Sun* was issued in North America under the title *By the Lake*. The three short story collections are *Nightlines* (1970), *Getting Through* (1978), and *High Ground* (1990). *The Collected Stories* (which contains one major new work, "The Country Funeral") was published in 1992, and his play, *The Power of Darkness,* was published in 1991. The short story collections (but not the play) have all been published in the United States. *Memoir* appeared in 2005. Throughout his forty-year career, McGahern was loyal to his British publishers, and the London firm Faber brought out all his books. He never had an Irish publisher.

Despite the controversy over *The Dark*—a controversy that McGahern found very distressing—McGahern's career was thoroughly successful. From the 1970s there was a clear reconciliation with the cultural institutions of the Ireland. His stature was recognized by official awards. The French government made him a Chevalier de l'Ordre des Arts et des Lettres in 1989, and he received an honorary doctorate from Trinity College, Dublin, in 1991. The University of Galway likewise awarded him an honorary doctorate in 1993, as did the University of Poitiers in France in 1997. He was the recipient of a Macauley Fellowship (1964) and fellowships at the Universities of Reading (1968), Durham, and Newcastle upon Tyne (1974–75) in the United Kingdom. He held the position of writer in residence at University College, Dublin (1977–78) and at Trinity College, Dublin, (1988–89) and won an Irish American Foundation Award (1985). His novel *Amongst Women* was shortlisted for the British Booker Prize in 1990 and won the *Irish Times* / Aer Lingus Award for that year. It also brought McGahern the GPA Award in 1992. He was a member of Aosdana, the Irish Academy of Letters, and a Fellow of the Royal Society of Literature. McGahern's work has been filmed—most notably *Amongst Women,* which was produced by the BBC and Irish state TV in 1998.

McGahern's death in 2006 brought laudatory obituaries in the Ireland, Britain, and the United States.

Although McGahern has written of his distrust of self-expression in writing and of his distaste for autobiographical fiction, his biography clearly has a close relation to his work. Indeed, critics such as James Whyte have read McGahern's fiction as an outgrowth of a particular biography in a particular social and cultural context. The argument is valid. The shock of the banning of *The Dark* pushed McGahern's career in a specific direction. Would he have started writing short fiction otherwise? *The Pornographer* is a response to the scandal. In addition, the characters and created worlds of McGahern's work are based on his own family and the environments in which he grew up and spent his adolescence. Rural northwest Ireland, a religious mother who dies, a domineering patriarch, a repressive and religious social order, 1950s and 1960s Dublin—these form the compass points of much of his work. Yet McGahern's *Memoir* makes it clear how much he changed and omitted from his life when turning that life into fiction. The autobiography is full of incidents and anecdotes that the author never uses in short story or novel. The picture of his father in *Memoir* is even more unsparing and hostile than those of Reegan and Moran in *The Barracks* and *Amongst Women*, respectively. McGahern emphasizes this process of selection and transformation in an interview with Liliane Louvel, published in the *Journal of the Short Story in English* in 2003.[4]

Reception and Place in Tradition

Apart from the scandal surrounding *The Dark,* McGahern's work has always been respectfully and often positively received. He is the subject of four major studies: Denis Sampson's *Outstaring Nature's Eye* from 1993; James Whyte's *History, Myth, and Ritual in the Fiction of John McGahern* from 2002; Gerd Kampen's *Zwischen Welt und Text* from 2002; and Eamon Maher's *John McGahern: From the Local to the Universal* from 2003.[5] His short stories have been extensively written about in relevant journals, such as the *Journal of the Short Story in English.* Commentators have not stinted their praise. In an essay in 1981, Alan Warner describes his work as "compulsive reading." In 1994 Liliane Louvel calls him one of the most important Irish writers of our day. Sampson describes him as "Ireland's most important contemporary novelist," and Riana O'Dwyer names him "the premier Irish novelist of the second half of the twentieth century." The anonymous reviewer of *The Collected Stories* in the *Antioch Review* writes of McGahern that he is "the preeminent fiction

3

writer working in Ireland today," while, according to Louvel in 2003, his "work has dominated the Irish literary landscape for almost forty years." The eminent contemporary Irish novelist John Banville is always most generous in his praise of McGahern. In a review of *Amongst Women,* he writes,

> McGahern works within a narrow compass. The bulk, and perhaps the best, of his writing is set in rural Ireland, among small farmers, village policemen, teachers; even when he moves to the city it is countryfolk he writes about, those who live in digs and dingy flats and go "home" for the weekend. . . . McGahern understands these people, their loves and longings, their hatreds, their fierce loyalties, and captures in his work the harsh poetry of their lives. He neither romanticizes nor simplifies; his is an immensely subtle and sophisticated art.[6]

Critics place McGahern's work in both an Irish and a continental European context. He is seen as an eclectic author, drawing influences from a wide range of earlier writers. Sampson finds in his work echoes of W. B. Yeats, James Joyce, and Samuel Beckett, as well as of Gustave Flaubert, Anton Chekhov, and Marcel Proust. Banville similarly sees McGahern as a writer who is indebted to Proust and Beckett, reworking aspects of their novels in his fiction. Nicola Bradbury relates his work in the short story genre to that of Joyce and George Moore. All these identifications are astute. A reading from his student days that McGahern mentions to Louvel in the 2003 interview confirms his broad interest in European fiction. In addition, in an essay on Joyce's *Dubliners,* published in 1990, McGahern makes clear his regard for and debt to Joyce's collection of short stories and also his admiration for Flaubert and George Moore. The focus of his short stories on the ambiguous revelations of the quotidian harks back to Chekhov's; McGahern's fascination with memory and time clearly echoes Proust's; his stories of humble rural life draw on a short story tradition that goes back to George Moore; Flaubert's fusion of realistic conventions with metaphor, symbol, and aspects of poetry reflects McGahern's own technique; Joyce's savage dissection of Irish life and its dismal paralyses is close to McGahern's own in *The Dark* and in several short stories; and McGahern can achieve a sense of the futility of human existence that, for all the differences in the created worlds of the writers, is as intense as Beckett's. Further, in *The Barracks, The Dark,* and in many short stories, the reader has a sense of the brooding presence of Patrick Kavanagh's innovative long poem of Irish rural life, *The Great Hunger.*[7]

McGahern's work is also related to that of other, in some cases more recent, writers. Neil Corcoran compares his work to that of Joyce but also to later writers such as Sean O'Faolain and Frank O'Connor, and even to McGahern's own contemporaries Edna O'Brien and Brian Moore. This latter comparison is also taken up by James M. Cahalan, who likewise notes McGahern's interest (shared with O'Brien and Brian Moore) in motifs of growing up in small Irish provincial towns. William Trevor's short stories about rural Ireland and about the Irish in England share common ground with McGahern's fiction, while one wonders if Colm Tóibín's great novel about midcentury and contemporary Ireland, *The Heather Blazing,* would have the shape it does without McGahern's example. A comparison of McGahern's work with that of John Banville forms the substance of Gerd Kampen's study from 2003. In it the German scholar clearly distinguishes McGahern's output from that of an experimental Irish tradition that includes late works by Joyce and the novels of Flann O'Brien and Banville. (The issue of McGahern's experimentality will be dealt with in more detail below.)[8]

One of the most striking features of McGahern's reception is his success in France. His fiction has been widely translated into French, and French scholarship on McGahern is among the best there is.

Vision and Technique

There are three major issues to be considered with regard to McGahern's work as a whole. These are the relation of the individual fates his fiction presents to more general human and national Irish concerns; the pessimism or ultimate optimism that underlies his writing; and the degree to which his work can be seen as traditionally realist in orientation, or, in some measure, experimental.

There is no doubt among critics as to the coherence and cohesion of McGahern's work as a whole. Sampson puts it clearly: McGahern's fictions "circle and converge on one another, and the reader is invited to contemplate the process of making within an evolving life. Each new fiction casts light on earlier stories and novels." This coherence is seen in a negative light by Jürgen Kamm. In an essay from 1990, Kamm writes that "McGahern's oeuvre, now spanning a quarter of a century, shows little tendency to develop and expand. Thematically, the writer has turned again and again to his obsessions with death, suffering, pain, lost faith, sex and love, and the futility of life." Kamm also writes of "the irksome repetition of motifs and narrative patterns" in McGahern's writing. In his review of *The Collected Stories* in the *New York Review of Books,* Banville puts it succinctly: "McGahern is one of those rare artists (Philip Larkin is another) who do not 'develop.'"[9]

One does not have to acknowledge the static view of McGahern's fiction to accept the general tenor of these remarks. McGahern's oeuvre is coherent and cohesive without being inert. If McGahern's interests are indeed as Kamm suggests, nonetheless they are quite far reaching. In addition, throughout six novels and three collections of short stories, McGahern's work shows both continuity and development. The picture of rural Ireland shifts, within certain parameters, from the stifling imprisonment of *The Barracks* to the ambivalent acknowledgment of value in *The Pornographer* to the more benign bounds of *That They May Face the Rising Sun.* McGahern's treatment of domineering patriarchs in *The Barracks, The Dark,* and *Amongst Women* is different in complex ways. The outsiders that populate his short fiction do not all share the same fate: in *The Leavetaking* the protagonist has more than a good chance of happiness. McGahern's portraits of women, from *The Barracks* to *Amongst Women,* are subtly varied. Rose Moran is not Elizabeth Reegan; the Moran sisters are not Josephine or Nurse Brady (in *The Pornographer*).[10]

Nevertheless there is a consensus that the critical issues outlined at the start of this section are central to a coherent oeuvre. The relationship of the individual to the more general is one of these. At one critical pole is the observation of Wolfgang Schmitz that John McGahern concentrates in his short stories on the presentation of individual fates that clearly have no social reference. At the other is Whyte's study from 2002, which interprets McGahern's fictions closely in the framework of the social and political world of mid- to late-twentieth-century Ireland. McGahern himself has contributed to this debate. For example, in an interview with Patrick Godon in 1984, he declares, "I think all good writing is local in the sense of place, and I think nearly all bad writing is 'national.'" Most critics see McGahern as an intensely particular and local writer, deeply interested in individual existential experience while, at the same time, pointing beyond the particular and individual to a more general level of reference. This is Sampson's view. He writes, "Struggles within the family on the small farm in the Shannon valley, within the prison of the barracks, are seen in the terms of human nature itself and are a microcosm of the world beyond." Kamm, too, admires McGahern's achievement (in this case in *The Barracks*) of combining the individual, the Irish, and the universal. Anne Goarzin notes of McGahern's work

Quand bien même l'action des romans de McGahern a lieu dans un contexte irlandais, il serait réducteur de ne prendre en consideration que cette spécificité nationale pour en fair la bannière d'un écrivain qui souligne lui-même que son appartenance à l'Irlande, si elle est indéniable, ne constitue qu'une des facettes de son écriture.

[Although the action of McGahern's novels takes place in an Irish context, it would be reductive to take only this national specificity and make of it a banner for a writer who himself underlines that his belonging to Ireland, if it is undeniable, only constitutes one facet of his writing.]

Claude Fierobe accurately assesses the relationship of the local and particular to the general in McGahern's work when he writes of *The Barracks* and *Amongst Women:* "Ce sont deux livres de la solitude, de la désillusion personelle et nationale à la fois" (These are two books about solitude, about disillusion that is at the same time personal and national). The subtitle of Maher's monograph, *From the Local to the Universal,* makes his stance on this issue clear.[11]

Sampson, Kamm, Goarzin, Fierobe, and Maher get it right. McGahern writes about individual fates in specific locales and social contexts, but those fates are resonant of national and of universal existential concerns. Elizabeth Reegan (in *The Barracks*) must cope with her sense of the futility of things and is an Irish woman in a small provincial town in the 1950s. Moran (in *Amongst Women*) is an old man facing death and an IRA gunman who has never made it in the country he fought to make. The Ruttledges (in *That They May Face the Rising Sun*) move through a closely rendered and specific Irish community in which individual fates touch upon the great existential concerns of good living and death and the less universal, but still general, experiences of exile and emigration.

Critics differ over the question of McGahern's pessimistic vision in his fiction. McGahern himself has intelligently sidestepped the issue. In a letter to Alan Warner, he writes that "the YEA and the NAY are equal. . . . All that counts is the quality of the saying." However, the issue will not go away. One of Kampen's criticisms of Sampson's work on McGahern is that it elides the novelist's dark pessimism. Certainly Sampson sees Elizabeth Reegan (in *The Barracks*) as achieving some kind of secular redemption in her suffering. Writing in 1975 Roger Garfitt also perceives hope in McGahern's work. He notes, "It is the possibility of growth towards meaning, and the finding of a sense of freedom within what could have easily turned into a nihilist position, that makes McGahern's writing, while almost mercilessly clear-sighted, both positive and humane." However, most other commentators are of a different opinion in this matter. Cahalan calls him a "despairing existentialist," although he acknowledges he may be "ultimately affirming." Seamus Deane writes of McGahern's "crepuscular world" in which "the deep energies of life have been occluded and turned poisonous." Warner claims that "much of his fiction explores the pain of living and the purposelessness of life's journey to nowhere," and Robert Hogan declares of the short fiction that "depression is the overriding feeling that one takes away from these accounts of death, futility, and disillusionment."[12]

Much may be said on both sides. Clearly the created world of much of McGahern's fiction is a very unhappy one. Disillusionment, broken faith, utter alienation, a sense of futility, loss, transience, pain, and death—these are McGahern's central themes. Yet he has also written texts that point in other directions. *The Leavetaking* and *The Pornographer* are far from hopeless works. *Amongst Women* is desperately sad, but *That They May Face the Rising Sun,* while avoiding sentimentality, does suggest that there is dignity and humanity in certain kinds of human relations, as well as a redemptive beauty in nature. Several of the later short stories, such as "Bank Holiday" and "The Country Funeral," are far from pessimistic about the possibilities of human life, although they can not erase the desolation of earlier stories such as "Korea," "Strandhill, the Sea," "The Wine Breath," or "Swallows." McGahern's vision must be adjudged a dark one (that of most twentieth-century literature is, too), but there are moments of illumination and hope within that darkness. In this matter, as in much else, Elizabeth Reegan (in *The Barracks*) is the presiding genius of McGahern's work. She moves in pain toward the terrible void of death, trying to understand, trying to see what is rich and splendid around her. The greatness in McGahern's work lies in allowing the reader to share Reegan's perceptions as she dies. The reader is both saddened and enriched simultaneously.

Is McGahern an experimental writer? Once again, critics differ in their answers. Several deny any experimental quality in his fiction (for example, Warner and Kamm). The contrast between the experimental Banville and the traditional realist McGahern is the central thesis of Kampen's study. McGahern does not see himself as an experimental writer. Sampson quotes him as saying, "you never meet place names in Beckett's books," contrasting his own realist technique with that of the author of *Malone Dies.* He calls himself "a traditional writer" and declares, "I have no interest in experiment for experiment's sake." "I would see myself as much more a conservative or classical writer than a romantic or experimental writer," he told Kampen in 1993. Yet some critics have argued otherwise. Cahalan suggests that in McGahern's writing there is "a willingness to continually experiment with style and form." Sampson insists that McGahern's fiction is imbued with features of poetry; he is "a poet who happens to write in the medium of realistic prose." This last idea is explored successfully, with regard to McGahern's short fiction, by Wolfgang Görtschacher. Stanley van der Ziel argues forcefully that *That They May Face the Rising Sun* is an innovative novel, breaching traditional genre conventions.[13]

This is clearly a vexed issue. It is certainly a complex one, and it must be approached complexly. First, one must ask what critics mean by the term "experimental." Usually the term appears to mean self-referential (that is the text draws attention to itself as a text and does not pretend to be a transparent window on actuality or a simple transcription of the real). It also, in van der Ziel's case, means innovatory. Second, if one considers McGahern's fiction from this point of view, one comes up with complex answers. His novels are certainly intermittently imbued with poetic technique—repetitions and phonological orchestration, above all. But much that is pointed to as being part of poetic technique (Sampson's emphasis on McGahern's deployment of metaphor and image, for example) is not alien to the European realist novel. One thinks here of George Eliot and Hardy, as well as Flaubert, Zola, and Fontane. Similarly, van der Ziel overstates his case as to the innovativeness of *That They May Face the Rising Sun.* The novel lacks much of the story material of traditional fiction but otherwise operates within the conventions of the realist novel. This is the third point that must be made with regard to McGahern's fiction: it nowhere breaches the conventions that operate in, for example, George Eliot's *Middlemarch.* His fondness for the psychological novel, the story material of which carries social implications, is evidence of this. Witness *The Dark, The Leavetaking,* and *The Pornographer,* which can all best be understood as social-psychological novels. However—and here the argument becomes quite complicated—to write such technically traditional novels as *Amongst Women* and *That They May Face the Rising Sun* in the 1990s and early 2000s, in an anglophone literary world dominated by highly self-referential, metafictional texts, is itself not just bold but innovative. Fourth, it must be pointed out that, indeed, McGahern is capable of quite radical innovation in his fiction. Especially *The Dark* provides the narratologist with one of the few extended uses of a second-person narrator in English-language fiction. Provisionally, until a complete study is written on this subject, one must adhere to Terence Brown's comment: "McGahern's short stories, like his novels, occupy a middle ground between the conservative traditionalist mode and modernist experiment."[14]

Over the course of a forty-year career, John McGahern produced some of the most powerful and accomplished fiction to be written in English. He is a master of the novel and the short story. Some of his short fiction will surely endure as exemplars of the form. All his novels are extraordinary in their own ways. *The Barracks,* his first novel, is one of the greatest works of fiction written in English ever. All the rest are merely magnificent.

CHAPTER 2

The Land (I)

The Barracks (1963)

Story Material

The echoes of McGahern's early biography are obvious in *The Barracks*. The female protagonist is a dying mother, the male protagonist an Irish police officer, and the main setting a rural Irish police barracks. The novel recounts the last fifteen months in the life of its protagonist, Elizabeth Reegan. She is the second wife of Reegan (the reader never learns his given name), a sergeant in the police force of the Ireland, the Garda. His first wife died a short time before he meets Elizabeth. They live with Reegan's three children by his first marriage in a Garda barracks in a small rural community a few miles from a larger town and a few hours train journey from Dublin. The novel begins in February and concludes in the winter of the following year. As it starts, Elizabeth is already aware of the cysts in her breasts that will, along with heart disease, eventually kill her. The rest of the text charts her steady decline in health and her death, a progression that she experiences in alternations of despair and hope, attempting desperately to understand herself and her life in the face of extinction. The illness forces Elizabeth to reflect and also to see clearly the striking beauty of the natural world around her.

She was a nurse in London during the Second World War, and while there she meets and has a brief affair with an embittered doctor named Halliday (his speech appears Irish at times, but the text does not state this explicitly) who drinks to excess and dies in a car accident. Halliday, however, awakens Elizabeth's intelligence and opens her eyes and mind to literature and to a more critical and thoughtful understanding of the world. During the months of her illness, Elizabeth twice reflects at length on her time in London and her relationship with Halliday. She also recalls other moments from her past: for example, when she first met Reegan, or when she would return to her family at Christmas.[1]

However, much of the novel presents the daily activities of life in the Garda barracks. Elizabeth engages in household tasks—cooking, mending, cleaning, gathering berries for jam, fetching water, or supervising the children's homework. The text also shows Elizabeth's conversations with the other policemen attached to, but not resident in, the barracks and their wives. It consistently notes and describes the various religious festivals that mark the stages of the Christian year—Lent, Ash Wednesday, Easter, All Souls' Day, Christmas —as well as non-Christian celebrations such as Halloween and New Year's Eve. Seasonal change is also noted, as are the various kinds of plant growth, weather, and labor associated with particular times of the year. The stages of Elizabeth's disease and decline run parallel to these festivals and seasonal shifts. Her life is a circumscribed one. The novel only depicts her leaving the immediate area of the barracks on two occasions: to visit the doctor in the nearby town and to be treated in a Dublin hospital. Her one other trip away from home, to a local hospital for treatment, is summarized briefly (109–10).

As the novel proceeds, it also charts the complexities and movements of Elizabeth's relationship with her husband, her closeness to him, her love for him and yet her distance from him, and her sense of isolation. Reegan himself is a complex figure, and a substantial part of the novel concerns his feelings for his wife and his response to her illness. More space, however, is given to Reegan's embittered relations with his superiors in the police force, his distaste for his work, and his desire to become independent after some thirty years of wearing a Garda uniform. Reegan's alienation from the police force is part of his estrangement from independent Ireland. When a young man, Reegan had been a guerrilla commander in the Anglo-Irish War of 1919–22, and in 1921 had joined the police force of the new Irish Free State. However, he has never risen beyond the rank of sergeant and has to follow the orders of younger officers, men who did not fight against the British. He feels that the country for whose freedom he fought has given him little in return. The novel ends with Reegan's quitting the Garda and his and his children's imminent departure from the barracks, even though Elizabeth's illness and death have used up the savings he had put aside to buy a small farm.

Reception

This bleak novel about death and disappointment has always been very highly regarded by critics and scholars. In 1962, before the novel was published, McGahern received the prestigious Æ Memorial Award by the Irish Arts Council for sections of *The Barracks,* and extracts from the novel were published in *The Dolmen Miscellany of Irish Writing* (all the parts of the novel published before 1963 are from chapter 1). After the novel's publication, McGahern was awarded an Irish Arts Council Macauley Fellowship, which allowed him to take a year away from his teaching position. The Irish cultural establishment clearly thought highly of his work. So did the British. The novel was published by the major London firm of Faber and Faber. Anthony Burgess and David Lodge wrote positive reviews in British journals, as did the anonymous reviewer in the *Times Literary Supplement.* It has remained a much lauded text. In 1969 John Cronin wrote that *The Barracks* is "a remarkable *tour de force* for a young writer," and a *Times Literary Supplement* reviewer in 1970 writes of the novel's qualities that "place him [McGahern] almost on his own among the younger novelists." Among these are "his ability to project a world which, though richly darkened by the novelist's imagination, is yet convincingly inhabited and furnished, [and] his very delicate ear for the resources of prose rhythm." Writing in 1983, Eileen Kennedy calls *The Barracks* "so extraordinary, its tone so distinctive, and its poise so remarkable that some feel it is [McGahern's] best." Praise does not just come from anglophone critics. In 1994 the French journal *Études Irlandaises* gave over a whole issue to *The Barracks,* and in the issue's preface, Claude Fierobe calls the novel "une œuvre singulière et complexe" (a unique and complex work), which, "à la fois coup d'essai et coup de maître, atteint une plénitude de conception et une félicité d'expression qu'on ne retrouvera, me semble-t-il, que beaucoup plus tard avec *Amongst Women*" (at once a novice work and a master work, achieves a fullness of conception and a felicity of expression that one will not find, it seems to me, until much later with *Amongst Women*).[2]

Narration and Language

The Barracks is traditional in its narrative style. The anonymous narrator is third person and omniscient, one who can shift from the consciousness of one character to that of another, moving freely in time and place. For example, in the first few pages of the novel the narrator shifts from Elizabeth's point of view to that of her stepchildren (10–13) and then to Reegan's (18–19). In this opening chapter, the reader sees into the minds of minor characters, such as the policemen Casey (23) and Brennan (30). Even within one of Elizabeth's memories (of her time in London), the narrator can slip into another character's consciousness, in this case Halliday's, to provide information not accessible to Elizabeth (93). At the end of chapter 7, after Elizabeth's funeral, the narrator leaves the Reegans altogether and follows Mullins and Casey as they escape the day's sadness by setting off for an out-of-the-way pub where they can talk of lighter matters (223–25).

However, the narrator tends to adopt one of two points of view in the text, predominantly that of Elizabeth, although also extensively that of Reegan.

Indeed, Elizabeth's point of view dominates the novel. The novel focuses on her perceptions, her fears, her epiphanies, and her arguments with herself. This is clear from the early pages. For example, in chapter 1 the four paragraphs beginning "Elizabeth drifted from between them" represent the novel's narrative technique (20–21). The narrator turnes the reader's attention to Elizabeth, who is tending the fire and putting a kettle on to boil. Elizabeth feels ill and hears her husband's angry voice as he talks to the other guards. She notes the state of the scullery table and the noise of the rain on the roof. The narration drifts into free indirect speech or thought here—"sometimes it seemed as if it might never cease, the way it beat down in these western nights" (20)—placing the reader very close to Elizabeth's consciousness. More of her perceptions follow, and her desire for peace and worries about the future are given again as free indirect discourse.

> Were their days not sufficiently difficult to keep in order as they were without calling in disaster? Quirke had the heavy hand of authority behind him and Reegan could only ruin himself. And if he got the sack! What then? What then? (20–21)

Another example of this technique is during Elizabeth's stay in the hospital when she attempts to control the pain after her operation (chap. 4). Here the narration uses free direct speech at times (122), thus bringing Elizabeth's mind and feelings very close to the reader indeed.

Reegan's consciousness, too, is very prominent in *The Barracks*. The reader is never allowed to forget Reegan's vision of things and his responses to the world. It is surely Reegan's attitude to the sugary music of the sweepstakes advertisement that is given in chapter 1 (32), and certainly his response when Elizabeth first tells him she is unwell (47). In addition, throughout the novel the narrator presents his plans for the future, his resentments about the police service, and his insights into Elizabeth's unhappiness and suffering (67, 99, 109–11). His reaction to Elizabeth's death is presented in a direct and immediate fashion. The reader has a concrete sense of the depth of Reegan's feelings.

> There's nothing to lose! Nothing to lose! You just go out like a light in the end. And what you've done or didn't do doesn't matter a curse then, wore itself into Reegan's bones in the next months. (226)

Elizabeth's experience and consciousness are central to *The Barracks,* but Reegan's are important too. The narrator not only presents the characters' thoughts and feelings but also their actions, although these are frequently seen from Elizabeth's or Reegan's points of view. But regardless of whether a character's emotions or actions are being presented, the narrator's language is syntactically consistent and distinctive. Its distinctiveness lies in the frequent use of passive voice throughout the text and also in the constant employment of a very loose syntax, particularly run-on sentences. Passive forms are recurrent in the narrator's language, and this linguistic feature is established from the beginning of the novel. For example, in chapter 1, Casey and the Reegans decide to play cards: "A pack of cards was found behind a statue of St. Therese on the sideboard, the folding card table fixed in the centre of the hearth. The cards were dealt and played" (24). A short time later Brennan arrives. "From the outside the heavy porch door was shouldered open," the reader is told. Once Brennan arrives, the card game is abandoned. "They [the cards] were raked up and the green table lifted out." The conversation with Brennan begins: "'You let no grass grow under yer feet tonight, Jim?' he was asked" (25). Active voice is used in this sequence, but the frequency of the passive voice is unusually high.

Examples of the narrator's use of passive voice occur throughout the novel. Much later, for example, the immediate aftermath of Elizabeth's death is reported thus:

> After the first shock, the incredulity of the death, the women, as at a wedding, took over: the priest and doctor were sent for, the news broken to Reegan on the bog, the room tidied of its sick litter, a brown habit and whiskey and stout and tobacco and foodstuffs got from the shops at the chapel, the body washed and laid out—the eyes closed with pennies and her brown beads twined through the fingers that were joined on the breast in prayer. Her relatives and the newspapers were notified, and the black mourning diamonds sewn on Reegan's and the children's coats. (221–22)

Here almost an entire course of action (apart from "the women . . . took over") is described in the passive voice.[3]

The narrator's syntax is also marked by a remarkable looseness, and especially by a fondness for run-on sentences (parataxis). A few examples must stand for many. Note the informality and looseness of syntax in the following sentence from the later stages of the text, recounting the policemen's return to the barracks.

> As they were the days were futile enough, and the whole feeling of them seemed to gather into the late evening in December they came tipsy from the District Court, nothing obviously resolved in the pub or on the bikes

home or in the day room, and they landed finally in the kitchen, anything that'd prolong the evening so that they'd not have to go home. (171)

In this passage one should note the lack of punctuation after "As they were" and the ellipsis of the "when" conjunction after "December." One should also note the polysyndeton of the repeated "and" and "or." The closing phrase, "anything that'd prolong . . . ," is not clearly related by any part of speech to what precedes it. This is loose syntax indeed. However, with regard to the narrator's syntax, the recurrence of parataxis throughout the novel is particularly striking. This occurs when characters' thoughts are given—for example, Elizabeth's "She knew he'd go his own way, he'd heed no one, opposition would only make him more determined" (13) or her later "She couldn't bear to think about it, she'd have to show her own aging flesh to the doctor, and it was no use trying to think anything, it was too painful, it all got on the same claustrophobic road back to yourself, it was the trick always played you in the end" (55–56). The same is true of passages that give Reegan's thoughts—for example, on the morning when Elizabeth can not rise: "one look was enough to tell him she wasn't well, he thought immediately of cancer, they had discovered no cure for cancer yet" (195). The narrator, however, does not use such syntax when recounting actions.

The narrator's vocabulary is largely informal and consistent with the characters' (especially Elizabeth's and Reegan's) lexis in direct speech. Only occasionally does the narrator's language seem too formal for the characters whose thoughts and actions are being related. An isolated example is when the narrator declares that Elizabeth's "tiredness was growing into a fearful apprehension" and that she "was existing far within the recesses of the dead walls [of her body]" (57). But there are very few such passages. The narrator's language, with its intermittent contracted forms ("didn't," "she'd," and so on) and its relatively informal vocabulary, matches the characters.'

The novel's narrative strategy is central to the meaning of *The Barracks*. The reader's attention is closely focused on the minds, with all their changing movements, of Elizabeth and Reegan. Although Elizabeth's point of view is predominant, Reegan's is never ignored. The narrator's choice of parataxis in presenting thoughts and feelings both highlights those passages in which it is employed and also aims to embody the fluidity and speed of emotions and thinking. The choice of passive voice throughout the text, however, has a different and opposed function. It depersonalizes actions—things are done, the specific agents ignored, unknown, or irrelevant—and thus shifts the reader's focus from individual characters to impersonal processes and forces, such as the passing of time, disease and dying, and communal activities and rituals.

Time

This interest in depersonalized forces can be seen clearly in the novel's organization of time. The stages of Elizabeth's life and death are seen in parallel to seasonal changes and the events of the community calendar. One aspect of time setting is meticulously documented in *The Barracks*. The action begins in February, the first sentence of the novel announces (7), and chapters 2 and 3 on consecutive days in March, after the beginning of Lent, with an early Easter not far away (40). Chapter 4 moves into late March and April (107–8), when Elizabeth goes to Dublin for her operation and further treatment (111). Elizabeth spends May and June in the hospital, returning home at the end of June (128). The novel moves much more swiftly in time in chapter 5, from July through August and September to Halloween and December, and this speed is matched in chapter 6, which runs from Christmas to the end of February and Ash Wednesday (194). The passage of time is summarized in chapter 7, running through the five weeks in which Elizabeth is confined to bed to Our Lady's Eve (213) to Elizabeth's death in May (220). Chapter 6 is set as the year of Elizabeth's death is coming to a close (226).

As Elizabeth moves toward death, the novel carefully juxtaposes her decline with the seasons, seasonal change, and the work associated with different times of the year: the dark and the rain of February (7, 20); the frosts of March mornings (40); the sudden arrival of spring and the preparations for planting potatoes (107–8); the growth of plants and the cutting of turf in May (125); gathering turf, ripe blackcurrants, and jam making in July (140, 142); the rain at the end of July (152); the fallen leaves of September (160); and the return of frosts in October (168). Once Elizabeth becomes bedridden in chapter 7, references to the world beyond her sickroom and consciousness become more scanty, but the reader is still aware of Reegan's work cutting and drying turf and the weather during the month of May in which she dies (220). The novel also carefully notes the stages of the Christian year—Lent and Easter (40), Our Lady's Eve (125, 213), Halloween and All Souls' Day (168), Christmas (175), Epiphany (186), and Ash Wednesday (194).

This charting of time has several functions. First, there is often a cruel irony in the contrast between Elizabeth's disease and the life of nature. Second, Elizabeth's death comes to be seen as part of a natural transience. Time passes and she passes with it (although, of course, nature is cyclical while human life comes to a stop). Third, Elizabeth's individuality becomes submerged in the movement of nature, the work of the community, and the traditional rites and rituals of that community. She, the individual, dies, but nature and the community continue. It is notable that the novel continues after her death, just as there will be another summer, another Christmas, and another Epiphany.[4]

The novel charts time in another way as well. The reader is given the ages of two of Reegan's children (8) and knows that Elizabeth is in her forties (49) and Reegan 50 by the novel's end (192). Certain matters are left unclear, however, such as the length of time between Reegan's first wife's death and his marriage to Elizabeth (although it is surely not a long one, if Elizabeth's brother is to be believed [15]). One recurrent reference is to the length of time Reegan has been a policeman, that is, thirty years since joining the Irish Free State forces in 1921 (29, 169). This places the novel's central action in the early 1950s, although that is not the main function of such references to the thirty years that have followed independence. Rather these give Reegan's disillusionment a resonance beyond the personal; he is a man who feels he has achieved nothing in an independent Ireland and is deeply frustrated by the postindependence status quo.[5]

Place

As has been pointed out already, spatial setting in *The Barracks* is extremely restricted and restrictive. "Le huis clos est étouffant" (the enclosure is suffocating), writes Liliane Louvel, and Neil Corcoran classes the novel as one of McGahern's "intensely claustrophobic domestic fictions." Sampson sums the novel up as being limited, like much of McGahern's fiction, to "a small, largely rural world."[6] Much of the text takes place in the titular barracks, and the action rarely moves far beyond its immediate vicinity. Chapter 7 limits its action largely to Elizabeth's sickroom. It is striking that not until chapter 5 does the reader learn in any detail of the other people, the shops, and buildings of the community in which the Reegans live, and then only briefly (161–66). Elizabeth's trip to the local town to see the doctor (chap. 3) and her stay in the Dublin hospital (chap. 4) are the only excursions outside the direct locality of the barracks that are narrated in any detail. Clearly entrapment is one of the principal motifs of the novel. Yet despite the physical borders that are placed on setting, the novel's scope is not limited. Sampson indicates that he sees the barracks and its environs as a microcosm of the world at large.[7] Certainly the experiences that Elizabeth has in that restricted setting (her dealing with imminent death) could scarcely be more universal in nature. In addition, by its references to Reegan's guerrilla past and his present discontent after his years of service to an independent Ireland, the novel indicates that its action has a national focus beyond the personal and local. It is notable that the community around the barracks and even the nearby small town remain nameless, the only clear geographical marker being the reference to the Shannon River (58). The local geography thus achieves a universality, for they could be perhaps anywhere in southern Ireland, or any rural community, anywhere.

Protagonists

At the novel's center are the portraits of its two protagonists, Elizabeth and Reegan. As indicated by the narrative, the text's primary focus is Elizabeth. Critics have written extensively, and disagree forcibly, about her development throughout the novel.[8] She is certainly a complex figure whose beliefs, questions, memories, and insights are presented in detail. Her life consists of deep unhappiness. At one moment, for example, she looks at her husband, feeling his sense of failure and frustration, and reflects that her "own life had grown as desperate" (64). At times she feels "panic" at her life (49). Her fears about her illness provoke an outburst of anger that both she and Reegan find disturbing (98–99), and as she leaves him at the Dublin hospital she is "quiet with fear" (115). In chapter 4, her pain and emotional and spiritual distress both before and after her operation are presented at length (118–25). Once she returns to the barracks she feels time passing and her entrapment within that movement of time, and she grows "desperate" again (160–61). During the final stages of her illness she approaches "near madness" in her loneliness and distress (201). She is torn between a desire to be with people and a need to be alone (162, 212–13).

Her relationship with her husband is marked by lack of communication and emotional inadequacy. She feels her emotions are "starved," yet she does not want to burden herself or her husband with too much closeness (71). She can not talk to her husband as she would wish (111, 174). Toward the end of her life she wishes to tell him that she loves him but does not know how (192). Yet there are moments of love and joy in her life. Her husband is finally a stranger to her, she reflects, but she watches him "with tenderness" (64); she feels fortunate to have married him and not Halliday (153–54); Reegan and she make love passionately (181); she knows she loves him and will do so till she dies (192).

There are occasions of vivid happiness in other areas of her life, too. For example, when she first meets Reegan the glorious summer day makes her "full of longing and happiness" and renders her commonplace expression of pleasure "a prayer of praise," filled as she is with a "longing to live forever" (14–15). She feels delighted to be needed by her stepchildren (32). As she listens to the rosary she feels a sense of "sweetness" and "blessing," although she knows this emotion to be a "delusion" (73). Her religion—a love of the rituals, sights, sounds, and atmosphere of church services, especially those of Holy Week—has always brought her an intense pleasure (123). The rhythms of the rosary, although not the words' meaning, offer her beauty as she comes very close to death (220). Even as she enters the Dublin hospital for her operation she becomes aware of all the happiness she has had in life. A few moments later she is filled with fear, but she has had that brief access of joy (115). Although she recognizes her life as one of entrapment, futility, and failure (at least in part), the utter mystery of human life offers her "such a deep joy sometimes" (210–11).

Elizabeth also achieves self-understanding in her life. Her intelligence and insight give her a stature and a vigor that counterbalance the desperation and failure of her life. She knows herself without delusion. "She was Elizabeth Reegan," she notes with specific possibilities and limitations (49). Her encounter with Halliday helps her develop a sense of her own uniqueness, the wonder and intensity of her own life (87). She knows exactly what she is doing by keeping her own money: she is guaranteeing her own freedom (104). She understands her relationship to religious observances (123, 220). Although she regrets that she has not always been alive to it, she does recognize that "her life and herself were such rich and shocking gifts" (134). Elizabeth's life may be one of desperation, failure, and death, but it is illuminated by passages of joy, satisfaction, and insight, so that the reader can not feel it is an entirely empty and futile one.

Sampson describes the parts of the novel that deal with Reegan as a "subplot."[9] This is certainly true, but *The Barracks* does give a great deal of attention to Elizabeth's husband. He, too, is a complex figure and is seen as such by his wife. He desires to be alone (18) yet is fiercely committed to his family. He is changeable, desiring to be alone one minute and welcoming interruption the next (19). "He was a strange person," his wife reflects, and despite his rage and despair (19) he can achieve happiness (129). Unreflective, whereas Elizabeth speculates intensely (64), he is both distant from his wife's emotional life (158, 210) and yet capable of considerable tenderness toward her (71, 99). Above all, Reegan is driven by an impulse to rebel against the status quo and an impulse to achieve independence from authority. Throughout the text he inveighs against any established power apart from his own: against school, schoolteachers, and the clergy (17–18, 22); against the local judge and his sycophants (69); and, above all, against the police force. "He, too, was sick," Elizabeth reflects, "sick of authority and the police, sick of obeying orders" (49). His superior officer, Quirke, is the particular butt of Reegan's loathing (68–69, 168–69). Quirke represents for Reegan an independent Ireland that has never properly recognized his services as a freedom fighter against the British. In the thirty years following independence, he has never risen above the rank of sergeant and now must take orders from those who did not risk their lives for freedom (109). He desires to tear down everything around him (179) and, in the end, savagely rejects Quirke's authority and resigns from the Garda (231).

Reegan is motivated by a desire for independence. This is an important element in his rejection of authority. He is happiest when he is working on his own land without anyone telling him what to do (108). "Why should another bastard shove me about?" he exclaims to Elizabeth (69). The Garda uniform is "this slave's uniform" for him (169). The desire for independence obsesses him as the novel progresses, pushing him to take time off from his police work to gather turf and to work constantly at trying to make money which will allow him to quit the police force (126–27, 141). So ridden is he by this fierce longing for freedom that he ignores the consequences of his actions for his children and Elizabeth (126, 189). There is an impressive quality to Reegan. Elizabeth sees his willingness to start a new life in his fifties as a mark of greatness (192), and McGahern gives him a patriarchal grandeur at times—when saying goodnight to his son, for example, or receiving candies from his daughters (37, 63). He is certainly more positive than Mahoney in *The Dark* and even than Moran in *Amongst Women*. He can be honest about himself as, at the novel's end, when he rejects Mullins's attempt to make him a hero for his attack on Quirke (232). Reegan's portrait complements that of Elizabeth, and both together make *The Barracks* a complex piece of psychological fiction.

Motifs

Within and throughout the relatively restricted world of *The Barracks*, McGahern provides not just complex portraits of his protagonists but also a vision of the world that echoes beyond the novel's particular setting to encompass the nation as a whole and, indeed, human life in general. He does this through the deployment of certain motifs in the text.

Most obvious is that of the quotidian. McGahern told an interviewer in 1995 that his intention in *The Barracks* was "to write a book about boredom."[10] His central characters, and even the minor ones, too, are constantly seen in the unglamorous, day-to-day tasks of their lives: cooking, cleaning, mending, filling out reports, making patrols, attending court, waiting, and working in fields or on the bog. Their lives are consumed with the trivia of their everyday existences. A good example of such absorption in the flat prose of the commonplace can be seen in chapter 2 when Elizabeth prepares for the children's return from school for lunch, feeds them, tidies up after them, feeds the chickens, bakes, talks to the children after they have finished school, sends them off to play, looks through the newspapers while one of her husband's colleagues listens to a soccer match on the radio, oversees the children's homework, and lays the table for her husband's supper (55–63). The narrator carefully chronicles hours of a life made up of such drab, trivial actions.

These are actions, among others, that are performed every day. The motif of the repeated and the habitual runs throughout *The Barracks*. The novel begins and ends with the same moment, the lighting of the lamp and the drawing of the blinds in the Reegans' home (7–8, 232). This moment is also returned to elsewhere in the text. "The blinds were down, the lamp lit, the children at their exercises, and the night repeating itself in the same order of so many nights" (103). From the very start of the novel the reader learns that Elizabeth has married Reegan in an attempt to escape from "her repetitive days," an attempt that has failed and frustrated her as her daily duties have dragged her down (15–16). She cannot escape the repetition of "chores" that are "colourless and small" yet keep her constantly busy and fill her days, chores that can scarcely be distinguished and that no one notices or praises (21). Certain tasks recur throughout the text, for example, the preparations for Reegan's days in court (44, 46, 194). Reegan, too, is conscious of this, reflecting on the drudgery of life (32). The rosary itself, recited each evening at the Reegans', is a monotonous matter of habit to the family (33, 73, 185), and the reader is shown the same scene enacted twice in the first two chapters in order to emphasize this monotony. Elizabeth feels that her conversation with Mrs. Casey "echoed a thousand others" (51), and her afternoon spent with Casey listening to the radio is also seen as one among a thousand similar occasions (59). Reegan describes his days at court as all repetitions of each other (67). Elizabeth's life in the Dublin hospital is also one of repetition (134), and when she returns to the barracks she feels again the "quiet drift of days" that continually follow the same pattern (160). Elizabeth becomes even more desperate than before in the face of such changelessness. She even wishes that she could be "broken into the deadness of habit" as she sees happening to the others around her (188). It is her failure to do something she habitually does that alerts Reegan to the final collapse of her health (195).

The repetitive nature of Elizabeth's, Reegan's, and, indeed, all the characters' lives is echoed by the novel's time scheme, which emphasizes the recurrent changes in the seasons and the recurrent festivals of the Christian year, some of which are actually repeated within the course of the novel. Those festivals are explicitly seen as matters of repetition. Elizabeth values Holy Week for its "unchanging pattern" (123), and the narrator says even of the transfiguring Christmas meal in the novel that "it couldn't be all blind habit" (183).

Characters are trapped within a daily round of chores and within habitual actions that recur daily or at fixed points in the year. Just as the spatial setting is one of enclosure, so characters are bound in chains of habit and custom. It is worth noting that the main character, whose entrapment the reader most clearly observes, is a woman. James M. Cahalan sees an awareness of "women's problems" to be an important part of McGahern's work, and this is certainly true in *The Barracks*. It is Elizabeth whom the reader sees ground down by the sameness of her days, the grinding, repeated tasks of running a home. James Whyte is somewhat critical of McGahern's presentation of women; he argues that while McGahern shows the crushing force of a male-dominated and male-centered world, he provides no "socially liberating vision" for women. He also suggests that while McGahern successfully presents "the subjectivity of women," he leaves Elizabeth, and other female characters, within certain traditional models of female life, especially the enclosed space. Riana O'Dwyer, however, argues that McGahern goes beyond this in *The Barracks;* the novel, she feels, "represents the conventions of a woman's life, with its restrictions and frustrations, but also interrogates such conventions continually."[11]

This last observation is accurate. Elizabeth frets about the constraints that her world puts on her and is very conscious of its crushing demands and limits. Few novels have better presented the mass of small, unrecognized, but fatiguing and seemingly endless, tasks that have shaped many women's lives at various points in history. Few have better presented the response of an intelligent but rather conservative forty-year-old woman to that world and her desperate attempts to maintain a mental and emotional life in those circumstances. That Reegan is no oppressive monster but rather a fellow sufferer (although not on the same level, and his obsessive desire for freedom means he pays less attention to his partner than is her due) is evidence of the richness and complexity of the novel. In any case, one can not exaggerate the importance of the fact that Elizabeth, a female character, her rich experience, and her complex consciousness are at the center of *The Barracks*.

Part of Elizabeth's desperate response to her situation is based on her sense of the pointlessness of so much in her world. The motif of futility punctuates novel. In chapter 1 the policemen's discussions in the Reegans' kitchen go nowhere; no one's mind is changed; nothing is resolved (27–28). In this case it is Reegan who expresses the most frustration; Elizabeth responds with a weary, "Hadn't the night to pass?" (32). It is clear that the other policemen are in the Reegans' kitchen to stave off a sense of pointlessness (24). However, Elizabeth most often feels the emptiness of her life. She falls into a panic, not just because of her illness, but because she has "a life on her hands that was losing the last vestiges of its purpose and meaning" (49). Nothing seems to matter to her at times (50). "She could see no purpose, no anything" and finds it hard to continue in such futility (57). Her vision of the emptiness of existence is repeated. "Where did Main Street lead to but to Bridge Street and Bridge Street led to St. Patrick's terrace or the Dublin Road and where in the name of Jesus did they lead but to other streets and roads and towns and countries?" (84). She engages in a dialogue with herself as she returns home from her first visit to the doctor, desperately trying to find some reason for her actions, for her very existence (96–97). Elizabeth's is not the only empty life. Halliday looks vainly for purpose in his affair with Elizabeth (93). The narrator describes the lives of the other policemen's wives as an "intolerable vacuum" (106). Reegan, too, is brought to desperation by the "vision of futility" made tangible in his colleagues' conversation (174). Elizabeth, however, is the character with the strongest sense of that futility, and she repeats the word to herself as she declines toward death (187, 209, 211).[12]

Elizabeth's perception of futility stems from her awareness of death as the end of everything (72). Indeed death, illness, and transience dominate *The Barracks*. The central element in its story material is Elizabeth's movement toward death, its various stages, and its seemingly inevitable end. But the motif of death occurs throughout the novel. As Elizabeth comes downstairs in chapter 2, the house is "quiet as death" (41); Reegan's first wife has died in childbirth (47); the evening prayers in the kitchen begin with "O Jesus, I must die!" (73); Halliday sees his life "moving in a hell of loneliness between a dark birth and as dark a death" (93) and he seeks death in a car crash (94). Mullins's pig is slaughtered in chapter 5, just as Elizabeth suffers her first heart attack, and she hears its screams and imagines the stages of its death (170–71). As a corollary there are numerous references to illness. From the early pages of the novel the reader is aware of Elizabeth's fatigue and pain. She touches her breasts to feel the cysts (33). Her stepchildren's liveliness only makes her more aware of her sickness (42). The novel follows the stages of her illness: the first exploratory operation, the treatment in the Dublin hospital, her recovery and relapse, her worsening health, her heart attacks, and her eventual confinement to bed. She is almost without hope of recovery throughout it all (136); her "decline . . . seemed certain and relentless" (186).

Motifs of transience also recur in the novel. At the very beginning of the text, Elizabeth imagines the family without her after her death (35). For Elizabeth, the beautiful, fashionably dressed young women who return from the city stand for the instability of things (52). Death waits for everyone, she feels (72), and the young and the old, the ugly and the beautiful, all must face physical suffering (84). Halliday's despair is driven by his sense of the passing of time and things (93–94), while, in her sickness, Elizabeth goes back in her dreams to a vanished past, longing for lost sensations and faces (135). As she is walking with her stepson she talks of a plant turning red "because it changes, because it dies" (166). At the novel's end Casey and Mullins are in a graveyard with its memorials to the dead of two world wars. It is worth noting that that they are in the graveyard of a Protestant church, which itself becomes a metaphor of transience: the Protestants are largely gone from independent Ireland; the great house, once the seat of the local Protestant landowner, has been burned down, and its estate divided up into small farms (223–24). In addition, the novel's time scheme, which emphasizes seasonal change, and the constant references to autumn as well as to spring also foreground transience. It is notable that, although Elizabeth dies in May, the novel concludes with winter coming on and Reegan bitter at the passing of another year of his life (226).

In *The Barracks* the reader sees Elizabeth, a woman of limited education and experience of the world and a seemingly unexceptional figure, deal with a world that is entrapping, repetitive, futile, and marked by transience, illness, and death. She tries to understand and, ultimately, just to survive such a world. The problems she faces—death, transience, and the rest—carry a great deal of existential weight. They are central issues of human life, and Elizabeth meets them with a great deal of intelligence and sensitivity. She is one of the outstandingly "ordinary" figures in the English-language novel tradition—figures that include George Eliot's Maggie Tulliver, Thomas Hardy's Jude, D. H. Lawrence's Gerald Crich, Graham Greene's Pinkie Brown, and Graham Swift's George Webb—who have a deep awareness of central aspects of human existence and who struggle with their dark vision of existence. McGahern shows his central character trying to "get some grip and vision on the desperate activity of her life" (49), intensely conscious of her mortality and of the dark depths of that life (112–13) and constantly asking "the big questions" about what the point of it all is (64). Is there God? Is there nothing (59, 89, 177)? Is her life simply a "total mystery" (59)? The reader sees her wrestling in concrete terms with substantial existential issues: "the rich and shocking gifts" of her self and her life (135) and yet their inevitable passing and extinction (152), her love for other people and yet the limits of that love (192). At various times she has consoling visions—of Christ's crucifixion and resurrection (194–95), of the unspeakable mystery of things (211, 220)—but these are short lived. In the end there is the buzzing fly in the sickroom, the dragging weight of her ill body, the banal occupations of others, the last rites administered by a priest for whom she does not care, and, finally, extinction (213–20).

It would be wrong to see her entire life as empty. She has thought, she has loved, and she has seen. Her life is enlivened by moments of memory (135) and also by moments of something like ecstasy. Usually connected with the beauty of the natural world, these moments include the day when she meets Reegan (14–15), the day in the Dublin hospital when she understands the "rich and shocking gifts" of self and life (134), the mundane beauty of her journey back home in the ambulance (139), "a lovely evening both green and yellow together, held still between summer and autumn" (160–61), and a frosty morning in autumn that makes her exclaim softly "Jesus Christ" (170).

Critics differ substantially in their readings of Elizabeth's life and death. Sampson, for example, argues that the overall movement of the novel suggests hope in Elizabeth's moments of revelation and transcendence. Kennedy, too, emphasizes positive aspects of Elizabeth's life and death. The critic writes that "she has taken her existential situation and, within the limits of her freedom, has shaped her life into one of significance and meaning," and she concludes that *The Barracks* is a somber novel, but it is neither grim nor depressing." Michael Foley places the emphasis a little differently when he writes that Elizabeth's is "a life in the main a mystery without meaning or purpose but lived in the dignity of acceptance, which is love, and lit up by the flashes of joy which only acceptance can bring." Sylvie Mikowski sees the whole matter in a darker light, describing Elizabeth as "un esprit qui se bat pour ne pas se laisser détruire par l'absurdité de la contingence" (a spirit that struggles in order not to be destroyed by the absurdity of contingency). This is close to the interpretation that Cronin gives Elizabeth's experience.[13] Both camps have truth on their side. However, although McGahern is careful not to direct the reader in any crude way, the overall movement of the novel seems to emphasize extinction rather than joy, futility rather than ecstasy. Moments of rapture are precisely that—moments. Love perishes in weariness, as does intelligence. The passages that precede the description of Elizabeth's death contain none of the redeeming instants of earlier sections. It is very hard to see the purpose, meaning, or positive aspects of all this, especially as the novel stresses that life goes on, in all its complexity and banality, after Elizabeth's death.

Ireland and Realism

Two questions remain to be addressed with regard to *The Barracks:* the national dimension of the novel's action and the novel's relationship to the realist tradition of Irish and European fiction. The first has been ignored by some critics. Sampson, for example, does not mention this aspect of the novel. However, it is clear that Reegan sees his own life as closely connected with Irish history, and a large number of commentators have pointed out that the novel engages with Irish history through its male protagonist. The narrator draws the reader into the minds of the policemen (including Reegan) in the barracks recalling the days when the British had withdrawn and they were among the new men taking their places (28–29). Reegan himself recalls his ideals during the Anglo-Irish War and his disappointment in years of service to the Irish Free State and the Republic of Ireland (109). He casts up to Quirke that he (Reegan) served his country when it was dangerous to do so and now must take orders from men who did not (231). Reegan's disappointment is with independent Ireland, and while the narrator does not endorse his attitude, he certainly lets it stand forcefully in the text. There are brief references to other aspects of Irish history scattered throughout the novel: the women in the doctor's waiting room in chapter 3 come from a class whose menfolk still serve in the British army despite independence (78); Elizabeth's doctor making comments about social change in the Ireland, one of which amuses Elizabeth (82–83, 208–9). The moment when Mullins and Casey stand in the Protestant churchyard after Elizabeth's funeral captures complex trends in twentieth-century Irish history (223–24). In addition, it must always be remembered that Elizabeth is an Irish woman at a particular point and place in the country's history, with all the constraints that those specifics engender. Her life and death must, in some measure, be seen as more universally representative. *The Barracks* is not just about individual human lots but is about those as they connect with national experience.

Critics usually associate *The Barracks* with the tradition of literary realism. Sampson, for example, writes that it "seems to be a version of mid-twentieth-century realism." There are certainly many reasons to think of the novel in this way. It provides a very detailed and highly verisimilar presentation of the material and social aspects of its characters' lives. It is set in the kind of socially humble milieu that is often the focus of nineteenth- and twentieth-century realism. Yet Sampson also argues, "it would be restrictive to think of *The Barracks* as a realistic novel." Sampson's reasons have to do with the novel's interest in "personal and metaphysical" aspects of experience (which are not unknown in the canon of realist fiction), but his later references to Beckett and Proust as writers with whom McGahern, in *The Barracks,* has something in common are more telling. Mikowski also relates *The Barracks* to the work of Proust and Beckett (as well as of Flaubert), thus placing McGahern in another more experimental and self-referential fictional tradition. Kampen describes what he sees as self-referential elements in *the Barracks*—Elizabeth's reflections on knowledge, on language, on texts (read and produced), and the novel's focus on silence and the inability to communicate.[14] As is always the case with McGahern's work, *The Barracks* is ambiguous in its relationship to literary tradition. It clearly does share topical concerns with Beckett's work—waiting, silence, and death, for example. The vision of the world in *The Barracks,* at least in the more negative interpretations of it, seems close to Beckett's deep despair. But it must be remembered that McGahern's characters inhabit a world that is much more like the world of realist fiction than that of Beckett's characters. Also, in *The Barracks* at least, the narrator's language has not the same degree of self-referentiality (in the sense of drawing attention to itself as text) that Beckett's does. The linguistic configuration of the narrator's language in the novel aims to emphasize and suggest the fluidity of consciousness rather than to draw attention to itself. Nor does the novel have the metafictional focus of Beckett's work. *The Barracks* seems much closer to Flaubert's "Un cœur simple" or to Proust's studies of consciousness in *À la recherche du temps perdu* than to Beckett's *Malone Dies.*

Whatever its relation to literary tradition—and, as is suggested in the first chapter of this study, McGahern's position vis-à-vis literary tradition is always complex—*The Barracks* stands as one of the most powerful, subtle, and moving works of mid-twentieth-century fiction in English. It is a complex study of two psychologically rich figures, bound together in a complex relationship of love and incomprehension, and it presents a darkly persuasive vision of the world. Its interweaving of history and individual experience is subtle. Above all, its picture of the intricacies of a woman's consciousness hemmed in by the mundane details of life at a particular place and time remains with the reader for a long time after the book has been laid down.

CHAPTER 3

The Land (II)

The Dark (1965)

Story Material

"The idea for McGahern's second novel seems to have grown quite logically out of *The Barracks*," notes critic Jürgen Kamm. Certainly *The Dark*, which Denis Sampson calls "this harrowing account of adolescence," echoes the earlier novel in most of its settings (a small farm and its surroundings in western Ireland, sometime in the late 1950s or early 1960s), in its characters (a dominating father, whose wife has died, and his suffering family), and in some of its action (above all, the conflicts within the family).[1] The central focus of the novel, however, is not a dying female protagonist but a young male one, Mahoney, growing up under fraught domestic circumstances. It is important to note, however, that the young Mahoney in *The Dark* is as complexly in conflict with his environment as Elizabeth Reegan is with hers in *The Barracks*.

The novel's title comes from W. B. Yeats's 1932 poem "The Choice." The speaker of the poem insists that a human being must make choices in life and that if they reject a "heavenly mansion" the result is that one will remain "raging in the dark." Certain elements in Yeats's poem match those in *The Dark*, and although the nature of the choice offered ("Perfection of the life, or of the work") does not apply to young Mahoney, the poem's conclusion concerning the vanity of human aspiration does.[2]

The Dark depicts two or three years in the life of the protagonist, Mahoney (the reader never learns his first name), who grows up on a small Irish farm. His mother is dead, and the family is dominated by an unpredictable father (also known only by his surname) whose moods, worries, and violent, domineering behavior make his children's lives thoroughly unpleasant. The novel opens with the protagonist's being terrified by his father, who threatens to thrash him with a belt. In an even more sinister fashion, in chapter 3, the protagonist is sexually abused by his father. At the end of chapter 5, young Mahoney is sixteen and feels he can only "stare out at the vacancy of my life."[3] It is not clear what space of time is covered by the remainder of the novel. It details the protagonist's resistance to his father and his increasing success at school. Young Mahoney starts to consider the possibility of a career in the priesthood at this point despite his adolescent sexual desires, which lead to frequent masturbation. However, a visit to his cousin Gerald, who is a priest, turns him from such ambitions. Mahoney's sister, Joan, has found work in the home of a local shopkeeper, one of his cousin's parishioners. On his arrival Mahoney discovers that Joan is being sexually molested by her employer. Further, Mahoney is also put in a sexually ambiguous situation by his cousin, the priest, who comes to him in his bed at night. In addition the young man finds the atmosphere in the presbytery oppressive. He decides to reject the priesthood and take his sister away from her employers.

Now devoted utterly to his studies, Mahoney spends the winter and spring preparing for his state examinations. He is successful in them and wins a scholarship to university in Galway. There, however, he is seized by doubts and uncertainties and by a sense of his own inadequacy. When offered a secure clerk's job with the Electricity Supply Board in Dublin, he gives up his place at university. The novel closes with a partial reprise of the scene in chapter 3, in which Mahoney had been sexually abused by his father. Lying together in bed in a rented room in Galway, father and son go over the past and repeat their love for each other, in phrases that may be partly insincere and sentimental but are also—partly—true.

Sections of *The Dark* had been published before Faber brought the book out in London in 1965. Under the title of "The End or the Beginning of Love: Episodes from a Novel," four lengthy extracts were published in *X: A Literary Magazine* in London in April 1961. These extracts recount episodes dealt with in chapters 3, 4, 8, and 9 of the final version of *The Dark*.[4] They differ from the equivalent passages in the novel: entire paragraphs are omitted in the novel and others substituted for the omissions; the protagonist is named this time (Francie); his sister is called Josie rather than Joan; there is no mention of other siblings; dialect forms are used in characters' speech; and some events, such as Mahoney senior's writing letters to find work for his daughter, do not occur in the novel. The texts in *X* are less universal in scope (because the main character is named and through the use of Irish dialect forms), and the elder Mahoney appears less menacing in these passages than he does in the equivalent ones in the novel, humanized as he is by his woefully misplaced sense of what makes a good letter.

Reception

On its publication *The Dark* met with critical appreciation, although with notes of reservation. The anonymous reviewer in the *Times Literary Supplement* sees

The Dark as typical of contemporary Irish fiction in that "it is plotless, auto-biographical in form and about growing up," and especially because it focuses on religion as a shaping force on Irish mentality. The critic censures McGahern's failure to establish whether the Mahoneys' lives are individual or representa-tive, declares that the protagonist "remains a bit of a suffering machine," and finds the novel as a whole "slightly too repetitive about everything." However, the reviewer admires the way in which McGahern moves from "a story of studious success or failure" to "grim and terrible farce." Vivian Mercier in the *New York Review of Books* is more positive, admiring the "technique for this brief, stripped-down novel," which includes the lack of names of the principal characters, the avoidance of personal pronouns in the final chapter, and the passages that represent young Mahoney's consciousness. This, the reviewer argues, promotes objectivity and avoids sentimentality. "No work since Joyce has presented Irish adolescence with such freshness and objectivity," the arti-cle concludes. The novel has continued to attract critical commentary. John Cronin compares it unfavorably to *The Barracks,* finding the protagonist insuf-ficiently realized and, as an adolescent, not a proper focus for the "philosophy" about life in the novel. He calls the novel "so determinedly bleak." A reviewer in the *Times Literary Supplement* in 1970 echoes Cronin's view, describing *The Dark,* like *The Barracks,* as providing "a somber, sufferingly malicious view of contemporary Ireland." Much later in 2002 David W. Madden also places *The Dark* alongside *The Barracks* as a pair of "violent, brooding books that emphasize the ambushes of family life and the vulnerability of children." Neil Corcoran in 1997 notes the "hideously explicit violence of the father" in *The Dark* and comments on the title as indicating the dark "of rural Irish hatred and self-pity, that obscuring and obscurantist darkness through which all of McGahern's characters must fumble their way." He also remarks on the novel's prescience in touching on the topic of sexual irregularity "decades in advance of current revelations about domestic and ecclesiastical child abuse in Irish society."[5] The depiction of domestic violence and the text's prescience, how-ever, cost McGahern dear, and led to the novel's banning in the Ireland, as has already been discussed in the introduction to this study.

Narration

Although the subject matter of *The Dark* suggests that it is a traditional real-ist text, its narrative organization is complex and unusual for this kind of novel. The point of view in *The Dark* is almost always that of the young Mahoney. Almost nothing is shown by the novel that is not seen or heard by him. However, the text shifts from a third-person narrator to a second-person one (itself a relatively rare form of narration in English) and at one point adopts a first-person narrator. Thus chapters 1 through 4 have a third-person narrator, and chapters 5 through 7 have a second-person narrator. The novel moves between these two kinds of narrator for the next fourteen chapters: chapters 8 and 9—third-person; chapter 10—second-person; chapter 11—third-person; chapters 12 through 16—second-person; chapter 17—third-person; and chapters 18 through 21—second person. Chapters 22 and 23 stand out by using a first-person narrator. The remaining chapters alternate between third- and second-person narration, with chapters 24 through 27 being in the third person and chapters 28 through 30 being in the second. The final chapter, chapter 31, is striking because its narrative type is unresolved. Mahoney senior's actions are recounted in the third person, but Mahoney junior is not identified by "I," "you," or "he." Much of the chapter is given in the form of direct speech with no narrative intrusions. Such narrative observations as there are seem to be Mahoney junior's but can not be unambiguously designated as such.

The intricacies of the novel's narration are not summed up by the above scheme. Verb tenses shift within different kinds of narration (for example, in chapters 5, 7, and 9 there are intermittent movements into the present tense). There are extended passages of direct speech with limited narrative framing or markers. The first two pages of the novel (7–8) illustrate this, as do later passages, such as Mahoney's conversation with his cousin in chapter 16 or that with his father in chapter 17. Through most of the novel the reader meets with the young Mahoney's point of view, but, at times, the text slips to that of an older narrator with a wider perspective. Examples of this are the passage in which the narrator talks of the room in the Mahoney's house being "as lifeless as any other good example" (24) or that describing life as "the haphazard flicker between nothingness and nothingness" (69). In addition there is at least one passage where the narrative point of view is that of the older Mahoney (46) and other sections of the text that take on the form of an interior monologue (82–82) and even of free direct speech (153, 157, 165).

Narration in *The Dark* has been commented on by critics. It is presumably part of what Hedwig Schwall designates as the "slightly experimental" quality of the novel, and Gerd Kampen points out the unusualness of the "you" narrator. Neil Corcoran argues that the novel's narrative technique can be read as an attempt to make the text both "autobiographical and generic" by fusing different points of view on the protagonist. James M. Cahalan suggests that it gives the novel "a somewhat ironic undercurrent." Kamm, however, criticizes the technique, arguing that it "runs counter to the confessional mode" of the novel.[6] McGahern's narrative strategy in *The Dark* is certainly complex in its function. Although Kampen argues that it has no self-referential function, one must doubt this.[7] Such a complex narrative organization inevitably draws attention to itself and makes the novel not just a report on actuality but a complex shaping of elements in that actuality, an artistic artifact. It is typical of McGahern's fiction in that it inhabits a border land between the relatively invisible conventions of realism and the foregrounded art of other kinds of fiction. A further function of narrative strategy in *The Dark* is, however, to indicate the unstable and provisional nature of young Mahoney's personality, shifting constantly in his sense of himself and his difficulty in seeing himself in a clear, unified fashion (neither "I," "you," nor "he"). The novel's final chapter, in which the protagonist ceases to exist as an "I" except in direct speech, points toward the crushing of his individuality by an unfriendly environment and his own self-doubt. McGahern's narrative strategy in *The Dark* is a subtle and suggestive aspect of the novel.

Narrative Organization

The novel's story material is organized in an equally suggestive way. It begins abruptly, without exposition. The first ten chapters provide an episodic account of Mahoney's life from childhood into unspecified teen years. This is particularly clear in the first five chapters.[8] Chapter 1 recounts Maloney's beating from his father; chapter 2 tells of a day on the river with father and siblings; chapter 3 presents Maloney senior's abuse of his son; chapter 4 deals with Father Gerald's visit and family conflict over potato digging; and chapter 5 shows the reader young Maloney at sixteen, sexually driven, guilty, and hopeless. However, this technique continues in subsequent chapters. Chapter 6, which is set a little later than chapter 5, details a terrible act of violence on the elder Mahoney's part and his son's opposition to it and to him. Chapters 7 and 8 present, for the first time in the novel, a continuous flow of action extending over more than one chapter. They recount an episode in which Mahoney and his father go to confession. Chapters 9 and 10 are different in that, apart from Joan's departure, they detail above all the passage of time.

The remainder of the novel breaks down into three parts. Chapters 11–17 cover a period of only three days and provide an account of Mahoney's visit to his cousin the priest, his bringing Joan home, and his rejection of the church. Chapters 18–23 move from winter to summer and deal with the protagonist's dedicated studying for his exams. Chapters 24–27 form a coda to this part, recounting the period in which Mahoney waits for his examination results. In chapters 28–31 Mahoney goes to university in Galway, only to give up his studies within a week. The novel has an open ending, for, although it is clear that the protagonist will reject university and choose security in an office job in Dublin, nothing else about his future is clear.

Such an organization of the novel's story material focuses the reader's attention in specific ways. The early stages of the protagonist's life are recounted largely through single episodes that represent recurrent actions and experiences—of brutality, paternal moodiness, and sexual abuse and longing. The focus is on the searing, particular experience. The protagonist's attitude to the church and priesthood are given prominence by its presentation in two chapters with continuous action. The lack of substantial incident, however, in chapters 9 and 10 suggests that young Mahoney is somehow waiting for the central incidents in life that are to follow.

The importance of each of the novel's subsequent parts is underlined by their length and by the way in which, for the first time in this novel, action spreads over more than two chapters of text. The two days' visit to Father Gerald is clearly crucial. It is covered in seven chapters; the previous seventeen years of Mahoney's life have received only ten. The same is true of his studies. The few months of his studying for and passing his exams take up ten chapters. In comparison, the four chapters devoted to a few days in Galway emphasize the importance of this experience yet also its anticlimactic nature (after such effort, such disappointment). The novel's open ending is ambiguous. It suggests either that nothing has been resolved (Mahoney still has many possibilities before him) or that the future will lead to an even greater erosion of individuality and possibility in his life.

Language

This darker interpretation is supported, partly, by one aspect of the linguistic organization of the novel. With regard to language *The Dark* is like *The Barracks.* Both novels are marked by an extensive use of passive voice. As in the discussion of *The Barracks,* a few examples must stand for many. When young Mahoney is about to be beaten by his father, the reader learns that "the trousers were let slip down around the ankles on the floor" (9). As he and his father hunt and kill fleas, their "thumb nails were easily brought to bear" (22). When Father Gerald visits, the preparations the Mahoneys make are presented partly through the passive voice (24). At confession, newcomers are stared at "till they were recognized in the tabernacle light" (39). Mahoney's feelings of joy after confession are expressed in the passive voice (42), as are some of the preparations for the crucial exams (144) and some farmwork (150). The novel's final chapter begins in the passive voice: "the rosary was said before undressing" (189). As in *The Barracks,* this extensive use of passive voice suggests an individual powerlessness against certain forces. Things are done, irrespective of the wishes of the protagonist. In *The Dark,* however, it is not the impersonal processes of time and death that govern the novel's action but, rather, personal and social forces: the power of a father over his children, of an education system over those involved in it, and of upbringing and inculcated social expectations over individual action.

Other linguistic features of *The Dark* echo those of *The Barracks.* Once again language is informal, in both narration as well as in direct speech. For example, when Mahoney remembers his mother he recalls, "Day of sunshine he'd picked wild strawberries for her on the railway she was dying" (10). Here a prepositional phrase, for example "on the," is missing before "day." Later Corpus Christi is described as "the last feast before," omitting something like "his visit to Father Gerald" (58). There is a misplaced modifier, "She introduced them . . . shaking hands," in which the shaking hands refers to Mahoney, not to Mrs. Ryan (62). Again syntax is informal and elliptical at the beginning of chapter 15: "Ryan was selling sandals to a customer, and no sign of Joan in the shop" (90). Vocabulary, too, is informal. For example, the protagonist reflects at one point that a request "was sure to rise trouble" (112), and in a piece of interior monologue he asks himself "why had you to cursed smile" (180).

The narrator's fondness for parataxis in *The Barracks* is also echoed in *The Dark.* Indeed, this is one of the most pronounced linguistic features of the text, apparent throughout the novel from beginning to end. For example, as young Mahoney waits for his father to strike him, his thoughts are rendered thus: "He'd never imagined horror such as this, waiting naked for the leather to come down on his flesh, would it ever come, it was impossible and yet nothing could be much worse than this waiting" (9). The same loose syntax can be seen at the novel's end, when Mahoney thinks of the university. "It wasn't Brady drove you, you'd go and crawl for him if it was worth it, only a fool stood up, you could go and crawl and savage him after if you got the chance and wanted still" (181). (Note, too, the extensive use of polysyndeton here.) And later: "It was the University, you looked at it, the shambles of a dream" (186). Such loose syntax has much the same function as in *The Barracks.* It is an attempt to capture the flow of Mahoney's thoughts and feelings, although the nonstandard syntax may also suggest the protagonist's provincial and poor background. After all, the dean at Mahoney's university looks on him and his father (according to Mahoney) as "his stableboys" (188). Doubtless he would look down at their written syntax too.

Setting

Setting in *The Dark* also echoes that of *The Barracks*. While time setting is never precisely given, the novel as a whole must be set sometime in the late 1950s and early 1960s. Father Gerald talks of "forty years of freedom," which places Mahoney's visit to him in the early 1960s (65). The novel does not follow any seasonal pattern as *The Barracks* does. However, as sketched out above, it does focus on particular episodes in Mahoney's life: discrete, but presumably representative, childhood and adolescent experiences in the first ten chapters; the two days of his visit to Father Gerald; the six or seven months of his studying for his exams; and the week he spends in Galway at university. Here time setting is an integral part of the novel's meaning.

The landscape of *The Dark* is also familiar from *The Barracks*—a small farm and a market town in the west of Ireland, with one brief excursion to a larger city (in this case, Galway). Verisimilar place names are given (Knockvicar, Oakport, Elphin, Rockingham), but the important point about spatial setting is its provincial, local quality and its familiarity to the protagonist. Just before his exams Mahoney goes on the river with his sister.

> In a dream the boat went by known landmarks. The Gut at the mouth between a red navigation pan and a black, the Golden Bush good for perch, Toughran's Island, Knockvicar Island and the creamery through the trees, the three arches of Knockvicar Bridge with the scum from the creamery sewer along the sally bushes, names bedded forever in my life, as eternal. (139)

Genre

The above passage also suggests the genre of *The Dark*. The focus on the main character's identification with and feeling for the familiar landscape that surrounds him suggests that this is a psychological novel, dealing with emotional states and development of the protagonist. This is clearly true. *The Dark* shows affinities to the class of novel called the bildungsroman,[9] for it explores the shaping forces, the conflicts and the changes in Mahoney's young life. In this respect, critics have noted above all connections with James Joyce's *A Portrait of the Artist as a Young Man* (1916).[10] One can see why. Both novels depict a young Irishman growing up, rejecting his family, flirting with and finally rejecting the church, attending university, and in the end choosing a new life. Cahalan notes McGahern's novel's "striking affinities" to Joyce's but argues that the end of *The Dark* "could not more deliberately invert, subvert, and deflate the *dénouement* of *Portrait*."[11] Indeed the differences between the two novels are as remarkable as the similarities. Stephen Dedalus and Mahoney are thoroughly different characters with substantially different experiences. For example, Mahoney has none of Stephen's artistic impulses, and Stephen does not have Mahoney's childhood of physical abuse. The ends of the two novels differ radically: Stephen leaves Ireland for an undefined future in the wide world; Mahoney opts for a safe job with the Electricity Supply Board. Critics have suggested that *The Dark,* while clearly referring to *A Portrait of the Artist as a Young Man,* is more closely modeled on the stories of failure and paralysis that make up Joyce's earlier collection of short stories, *Dubliners* (1914). Cahalan compares it specifically to "A Little Cloud," although several other stories' despairing inertia is reflected in McGahern's novel.[12]

The Dark is, above all, a study of characters and their relations with each other and with a wider environment. Secondary characters are mostly dealt with superficially. The Ryans, for example, are presented as shadowy and unpleasant figures (chaps. 11–17), as is Father Gerald's enigmatic houseboy (chaps. 13–14). Most of these characters simply provide a human backdrop for the novel's main focus, which is on Mahoney and his relationship with his father. This is true even of other members of the family. Mahoney's dead mother is defined by her absence. All he remembers of her is picking wild strawberries for her (10) and that he promised her that he would become a priest (33). Mahoney's siblings are equally shadowy. Indeed, it is not even clear how many of them there are. Only two are named, Mona and Joan, and the reader learns something substantial only of Joan. This is, however, little. Joan's experience of sexual abuse is not explored, and her distress at the Ryans' functions in the novel principally to provide an opportunity for Mahoney to crystallize his low opinion of respectable society and his distaste for the church, and also to act in an independent and decisive manner (chap. 15).

Father Gerald, Mahoney's cousin, is more developed than other secondary characters. He is an ambiguous figure. On his first appearance, in chapter 4, he appears rigid, cold, even complacent. In chapter 11 he seems a thoroughly secular figure, part of his parish's bourgeoisie, a man whose neck is chafed red by his priest's collar and who shows the scars of a stomach operation to his guest. Chapter 12 shows him in a more sinister light. He joins young Mahoney in bed, puts his arm round him, and talks to him about his (Mahoney's) sexual

desires. He elicits several confessions from the boy and then refuses to recip-
rocate with his own. Reminded of his father's abuse of him and hurt that the
priest will not respond to his frankness, Mahoney is disturbed and horrified by
Father Gerald, as he is in chapter 14 by the stale respectability of the priest's
house. However, in chapter 16, when Mahoney tells him of Ryan's abuse of his
sister and of his decision not to pursue a life in the priesthood, Father Gerald
eventually responds with a striking openness. He talks of the pains of a priest's
life and of his own doubts about his role as one "who ministers to the *bourgeoisie*" (99). He also offers an unorthodox view of prayer and the individual's
relationship to God (one that he says he would deny in public). He even asks
Mahoney to pray for him. Nevertheless, when he takes Mahoney the next morning to Ryan's shop, he does not drive right up to the door (103).

However, there is a much greater degree of complexity in the novel's treatment of its two central figures, Mahoney senior and junior, and much of the
text is concerned with their fraught relationship. Mahoney senior is a deeply
complex figure. As he did with Reegan in *The Barracks,* McGahern takes pains
to win some sympathy for what seems at first a wholly negative character. In
the novel's first six chapters, Mahoney is a patriarchal monster. He torments
and humiliates his son; he is moody and changeable toward him and the other
children; he sexually abuses his son; he insults his children and complains of
their inability to do work properly and to help him; he mocks his son; he bru-
tally attacks his daughter on an insubstantial pretext. It is little wonder that
his children dislike and fear him and exclude him from their lives as much as
possible. He seems a man driven by cruelty, sexual desire, an almost insane
anger, and a tendency toward violence. Even when he ceases to be physically
violent toward his children, he is capable of emotional cruelty, as when he
mocks young Mahoney's educational ambitions (125).

However, McGahern does try to make the reader's response to Mahoney
more complex. For example, rejected by his children he plays cards by himself
sitting in an old car seat. He looks, Mahoney junior reflects, like "an infant
enclosed in its pen chair," a pathetic figure rather than a monster (50). A few
pages earlier, the narrator has, for the only moment in the novel, switched to
the father's point of view, when, after confession, he tries to come close to his
son and is rejected (46). In addition, when Mahoney junior brings home his
sister, their father does not rage but surprises his children with a warm and
sympathic reception (106–7). He embarrasses his son at later points in the
novel—in his gift of potatoes to Mahoney's teachers (119–22) and when he
takes his son out for a celebratory meal after he has received his examination
results (chap. 26)—but these seem venial faults. In one telling moment, he

reveals that he, too, was bright and successful at school but was not able to go further in his studies (123). Later his frustration with himself and his own life turns to a rage and a self-pity that is not quite maudlin. "I went to school too," he shouts. He talks of the limits of his life and how "nobody sees me but a crowd of children. . . . But it's important, it's important to me, it's the only life I've got, it's more important than anything else in the world to me. I went to school too" (128). The novel is surely asking the reader to give the father a modicum of sympathy at this point. Later still in the text, his son sees him as old, weary, and disappointed, and is filled not with hatred but with a musing tolerance (150). Mahoney senior's actions in the novel's last two chapters, in which he comes to Galway to help his son, are a mixture of self-dramatization, affection, and sense. His son is, once again, embarrassed by his father's presence, but he also identifies himself with him. The reader is left to judge the final dialogue as the two lie in bed together (189–91). How much is hypocrisy, and how much contains a modicum of truth and sincerity?

The son's relationship with his father lies at the heart of *The Dark.* It is striking that neither is given a first name, but both are known only as Mahoney, suggesting a unity between the two. Young Mahoney's feelings toward his father are, at the beginning of the novel, ones of fear and horror (chap. 1), emotional and physical loathing (chap. 3), but also defiance (26) and rebellion (36–37) as well as more hatred (37) and rejection (46). However, the son's feelings modulate at times to a different attitude toward the father. He feels he ought to love him (43) and not to exclude him from his life (45). Later in the novel, he still wants to escape and deny his father. His desire to be a priest has long been part of that (25), but so too is his desire to marry and, thus, as he says to himself, "deny and break finally your father's power" (84). Nonetheless, Mahoney's attitude toward his father becomes much more complex as the novel proceeds. He finds in him "at least the beauty of energy" (122); an argument with him makes the son want to apologize (131); and the sight of his father's boots by the fire prompts Mahoney to reflect on his parent's life and to regret his own egoism toward his father (131). After showing the father his exam papers, the son is even prepared to concede to the father that under other circumstances the older man would have done as well (145). The physical labor with his father after the examinations brings them together and gives young Mahoney satisfaction, and this interlude before the exam results come leads to a much greater degree of toleration of his father on the son's part (147–50). Embarrassment at his father's ostentatious behavior in town gives way to an indulgent "You are marvelous, my father" (160). However, in Galway "a cold and hidden fury" is the son's response to his father's genial sociability (185), although this, too, modulates into the complexity of the novel's final chapter, in which Mahoney junior expresses love and regard for his father but it is also suggested that such a profession is part of an empty exchange of banalities (191).

It is clear that young Mahoney is a complex figure, and the novel develops his character not just in relation to his father but to a wider world and to human existence itself. In chapter 3, Mahoney lies passively while his father sexually abuses him, and this passivity is an important aspect of his character throughout the novel. When asked by Father Gerald what he would like to be when grown, he answers (a formulation his father greets with approval), "Whatever I'm let be I suppose" (24). He finds himself staring inertly at "the vacancy" of his life at sixteen (33). There are several other examples of such passivity, most notably in the episode in which Father Gerald joins him in bed (chap. 12), but also at other moments when, for example, Mahoney feels a duty to love his father (43) or sees himself as inescapably linked to the community into which he was born ("This was the way your life was" [58]). When he helps Father Gerald to serve Mass, he assumes a role in a set ritual (78–79). There is an element of passive conformity here too, just as there is in the rote learning of his studying (113–14). In despair he suggests to Joan that immigration to England waits for them both and for everyone else, too (104). Mahoney can not even brave a group of mocking young people to go to his first dance but must slink away in inert failure (177–78). He allows himself to be ejected from the lecture hall although he is innocent of any offense (180–81). "Though what was the use, there was no escape," Mahoney reflects. "You were only a drifter and you'd drift" (84). This passivity on the protagonist's part leads the reviewer in the *Times Literary Supplement* in 1965 to describe Mahoney as "a bit of a suffering machine" (365).[13]

However, as has been sketched out above, Mahoney also rebels against his father and aspires to something beyond his life on the farm. His sexual desires are part of this (30–31), as are his interest in the priesthood and his studying. He sees his leaving for university in this way, too (163). Mahoney also rebels against, and rejects in angry frustration, the dusty sterility of the priest's house. Even his own home with its terrible conflicts seems more alive than it (87–88). As he gets older, Mahoney develops a more sophisticated awareness of himself and his relationship with others—with his sister (94) and with his father (131, 150). During his long conversation with Father Gerald, he realizes that life is more complicated than he thought (101) and he sees himself becoming like his father at one point, too (111). But at this stage of his life he has a sense of the absurdity of human life when viewed against the prospect of death (84).

The novel's final part, in which Mahoney goes to university and then abandons his studies, is particularly rich in complexity. Mahoney's state is from the start one of confusion (168). There is so much that is new—being on his own, an unfamiliar town, new companions, one of the few films he has ever seen (169), his first dance (176), and imagined sexual opportunities (177–78). He must also confront his own uncertainty and the undermining of his dream as to what university is and can mean for him (172–73). His decision to leave Galway is itself complex. On one hand Mahoney desires freedom in Dublin (179) and, above all, wants to make his own decision (184). Yet on the other hand, the choice of the E.S.B. is seen by the dean, and by Mahoney himself, as a failure to meet a challenge, to do more than his background has ever encouraged him to do (187–88). In the end Mahoney is left aspiring to a self-understanding, a clarity, and an ability to decide ("an authority that was simply a state of mind, a calmness even in the face of the turmoil of your own passing" [188]), although the reader can not be at all sure that he will achieve these ever.[14]

Motifs

Mahoney's physical and psychological experiences provide the main motifs of the text. Most prominent among these, and already discussed above, are those of passivity. This is, however, seen not just as a trait of the younger Mahoney but of his family and the wider community. The people in church wait passively for their turn to confess (39). "There was an even flow that carried you nearer," Mahoney notes (40). Mahoney senior is convinced that, despite one's best efforts, only the privileged will get good jobs (45). The fate of many seems to be an inevitable immigration to England, he suggests (45). Sitting in his modified car seat, the father seems like "an infant enclosed in its pen chair" (50). Joan, too, does not want to go to Ryan's but does so anyway (61), and she puts up with sexual molestation until her brother arrives (92–93). Mahoney senior argues that failure is inevitable for the likes of his son (125).[15]

Linked to passivity are motifs of repetition, in which a character follows a prescribed pattern and makes little or no choice. Thus, Mahoney plays patience (solitaire), repeating the same actions usually "to the same dead end" (50). Joan's letters follow the same empty formula (53), as do young Mahoney's penances and promises of amendment (54). "Boredom" is the word he uses of eternity (56) and prayer (66); both become matters of senseless repetition. "It seemed that the whole world must turn over in the night and howl in its boredom," the narrator remarks (reflecting, surely, young Mahoney's viewpoint) during father and son's final, partly platitudinous, conversation (191). Even the most everyday of actions provides Mahoney with material for reflecting on the absurd repetitions of life. As he takes his clothes off on the first night in Galway, he reflects that even here he has to go through the same "habitual actions of the funeral" of the day, and that this will go on forever (170–71).

In the world of the novel, there is little change to counter passivity and repetition. Mahoney stares at "the vacancy" of his life at sixteen (33); the other children talk of "their hopeless life with no sign of change" (35). Even when Father Gerald comes to take Joan away (and thus bring change), that evening is "as lifeless and as starched as always" (48). The rituals of the community never seem immutable (58), and both Mahoney and Joan endure the same patterns of abuse. In Mahoney's case, this even entails a repetition of what occurred in chapter 3. The novel ends with him and his father in bed together once more. The only changes in the novel come with aging (in the case of Mahoney senior) and in Mahoney junior's rebellion. There is also an element of change in Mahoney's emotional and intellectual development. But within the scope of the novel, even this defiance, this attempt to achieve some freedom, and this maturation lead nowhere. At the novel's end Mahoney is, in a sense, back where he always was.

In such a world, motifs of death (an event that no one, no matter how active, can escape) are appropriate. Mahoney's mother has died before the novel begins. He himself develops an acute sense of death and how it calls the purpose of all human activities into question (83, 85, 113, 138). There are frequent references to death. Even sex leads Mahoney to think that all life entails is "this drifting death from hole to hole" (56).[16] Father Gerald's house is next to a graveyard (69), the bell in the local Protestant church tolls for a funeral (86), and at school a visiting priest talks of last things (126). Mahoney's father breaks out in rage when he considers how he has spent "the only life I've got" (128). Mahoney himself sees the priesthood as a kind of "death" (127), while the rusting gates at Oakport and the decayed boathouse there are both reminders of transience (138). At the novel's end Mahoney wants some peace and freedom "in the face of the turmoil of your own passing" (188), passing here suggesting not only motion but also death.

In this dismal vision of life (passivity, inertia, death), motifs normally associated with life provide little solace. There is certainly a wide range of references to sex and sexual activity in the text. These are, however, almost all negative in their associations. Mahoney's sexual experiences (for the one detailed in chapter 3 is only one among several, as the first sentence of the chapter indicates) with his father produce "shame and embarrassment and loathing, the dirty rags of intimacy" (19). His sexual encounter with his cousin, the priest, produces similar anguish (67, 70–71, 75). Ryan's molestation of Joan is sordid and distressing for his victim (92), and he himself leers suggestively over his own daughters (92). All this contrasts with the sublimity of the erotic classical verse that Mahoney is reading on the bus trip to Father Gerald's (60).[17] Mahoney's escape into masturbation is also seen in fundamentally negative terms. Despite the pleasure it brings him, afterward he feels that "everything is dead as dirt" (31). The fact that he usually masturbates into his sock or onto newspaper, which he later burns, is symptomatic of the act's negative associations (75–76, 118). Even Mahoney's sexual fantasies are tainted: he masturbates over an advertisement for a depilatory torn from the *Independent* newspaper (30–31); he imagines himself as a priest interrogating and then raping a girl in the confessional (54–55); the women he imagines are no more than body parts and clothes (118, 177). Throughout all the sexual experiences in the text, there runs a strain of crude and ultimately drab physicality.

This is matched by motifs of physically unsavory experiences. These include the fleas that Mahoney and his father must kill in their bed (21–22) or the cockroaches that infest their home (109). In this respect, too, one should notice Mahoney's constant retreat into the family's malodorous lavatory, the only place where he can be alone and regain some kind of calm (10, 38, 116). This physical unpleasantness is echoed in the moment when young Mahoney, naked in front of his sisters, is about to be beaten by his father over an armchair. He loses control of his bladder and urinates over the seat. "He'd never imagined horror such as this," the narrator notes (9). Physical disgust runs throughout the text.

Ireland

For all that they relate to universal human experiences such as maturation, sexual longing, family antagonisms, and inertia, the physical horror and the psychological complexities of *The Dark* are not set in a generalized environment but in Ireland, and in an Ireland that is roughly contemporary to that of the date of the novel's publication. Place names are documented or highly verisimilar. Father Gerald tells the reader that the action is taking place "after forty years of freedom," thus in the late 1950s and early 1960s (65). The novel establishes some signposts of Irish history. Mahoney senior refers to the Great Famine of the 1840s (121). Immigration to England looms in the background of various conversations (104, 108, 115). "You can go to England if it all fails," Mahoney thinks before his exams. "You'll work in Dagenham and they'll call you Pat"

(137). *The Dark* is not a purely psychological novel but frequently has a social focus. In the children's parodies of Mahoney senior's voice the reader hears a fear of poverty and destitution (28, 105). Father Gerald talks of the bourgeoisification and materialism of contemporary Irish society (99–100). The students in Galway attend a lecture in Irish that they can not understand (173). Part of Mahoney's disorientation in Galway is because he is the first member of his family ever to attend university (173). He feels that the dean's disdain is effectively a social one. He and his father can only ever be menials for such a person (187–88).

Cahalan suggests that the choice of the *Irish Independent* as the paper over which Mahoney masturbates is deliberate because it was "then the most staid newspaper in Ireland."[18] In this act Mahoney is rejecting conservative, postindependence Ireland. In *The Barracks,* Reegan's despair passes as a comment on postindependence Ireland; so too does Mahoney's anguish and inertia. It is an Irish family, an Irish community, an Irish church, and an Irish education system that have produced him. Critics insist that the novel does not just have a psychological focus but a national and social one as well. In a comment that is relevant to the picture of the father-son relationship in *The Dark,* Declan Kiberd remarks, "A concern about fathers and the adequacy of fathers is a sign of a community that fears it may have lost its bearings."[19] Corcoran argues that the dark of the novel is that "of rural Irish hatred and self-pity, that obscuring and obscurantist darkness through which all of McGahern's characters must fumble their way."[20] *The Dark* is certainly a complex piece of psychological portraiture and a despairing vision of life; it also comments indirectly and directly on social life in Ireland in the 1950s and 1960s. In addition, the text also stands out as an intriguing narrative experiment. The promise of *The Barracks* is more than fulfilled. In his second novel McGahern demonstrates himself again to be an accomplished and powerful writer.

CHAPTER 4

Paralyses

Nightlines (1970)

Publication and Reception

After the scandal surrounding *The Dark* in 1965, McGahern did not publish another novel until *The Leavetaking* appeared ten years later. In the intervening decade, however, he published his first collection of short stories, titled *Nightlines*. The British edition appeared in 1970 and a U.S. edition the following year. Denis Sampson writes that the stories in *Nightlines* were "written at various times during the sixties."[1] They had already been published in journals such as *Encounter,* the *Atlantic,* the *Honest Ulsterman,* and the *Listener.*

Nightlines has an important place in McGahern's oeuvre. It his first collection of short stories, and McGahern's reputation is built almost as much on his short fiction as on his novels. The stories in *Nightlines* have been consistently well received and seriously discussed since their first publication. The anonymous reviewer in the *Times Literary Supplement* expresses some reservations about stories that "fade out in a complacent haze of inconsequentiality" and comments that "now and then the language falls into a too lilting adjectival rut." However, the reviewer praises the intricate and strong structure of several stories and concludes, "But at their best, these stories deepen, and extend, one's admiration for this admirable writer." In the *New York Times Book Review,* David Pryce-Jones also praises the collection, despite what he calls its occasional "moments of banality." He discusses in detail "Korea," "Hearts of Oak and Bellies of Brass," and "Peaches." "Mr. McGahern usually brings together the contrasting elements of his stories," he writes. "In an irregular but calculated prose he achieves a mood all his own, which is shabby and hurtful and lyrical."[2] Academic critics have devoted much attention to McGahern's short stories, including *Nightlines.* Antoinette Quinn's insightful discussion of several stories from *Nightlines* is representative.[3]

Settings, Narrators, and Characters

Critics are unanimous in the underlying connectedness that they perceive in McGahern's short fiction both as a whole and within individual volumes.[4] The stories in *Nightlines* certainly form a coherent unit, linked as they are by shared figures, situations, motifs, and, ultimately, vision.

The title *Nightlines* governs the whole collection. Nightlines are literally the fishing lines left out overnight and gathered in the next day by the son and his father in the story "Korea." This specific reference gives that story a privileged position within the volume. Its central character's disillusion and ambivalence is typical of the situation of many characters in other stories. Yet the title also has a metaphorical force. The texts in the collection are themselves fishing lines and lines of prose let down into an existential darkness, in the hope that the fisherman and writer will be able to draw up some insights or truths to the light of day.

Commentators write of the world of *Nightlines,* and of McGahern's short fiction in general, as a small and limited one.[5] Yet the stories in *Nightlines* are of considerable scope. Even in setting they range widely. Most are, indeed, set in a world of small farms and rural communities, but the narrator/protagonist of "Wheels" now lives in the city, as does that of "My Love, My Umbrella," while the longest story, "Peaches," is set in Spain. "Hearts of Oak and Bellies of Brass" takes place among Irish laborers in London. In addition, the world of "Korea" has crucial links with the United States and East Asia. Time settings are typical of so much of McGahern's fiction; the 1940s and the 1950s of *The Barracks, The Dark,* and the early parts of *The Leavetaking* predominate. These are left, however, consistently rather vague. There are also movements back into past history, as in the father's description of an execution he witnessed during the Irish Civil War in "Korea," and in the still living legacy of the Spanish Civil War that shapes the latter sections of "Peaches." Greenbaum, the Polish Jewish shopkeeper in "Hearts of Oaks and Bellies of Brass," evokes central European history too.

Narrators and central characters range from young children to adults. "Coming into His Kingdom," "Christmas," "Bomb Box," and "Lavin" have young or adolescent central figures. In "Korea" the narrator is a young adult on the brink of leaving home. The narrator of "Strandhill, the Sea" is probably a relatively young man, while the central characters of the remaining stories are adults and, in the case of "Why We're Here" and "The Recruiting Officer," middle aged or older. The suggestion of universality in such an array of protagonists is emphasized and augmented by the arrangement of texts in the collection. Two adult stories, "Wheels" and "Why We're Here," are followed by two stories about young children, "Coming into His Kingdom" and "Christmas." These are followed by another adult story, "Hearts of Oak and Bellies of Brass," and one in which the age of the narrator is not wholly clear, "Strandhill, the Sea." "Bomb Box," "Korea," and "Lavin" have relatively young protagonists, especially the last of this trio. "My Love, My Umbrella" and "Peaches" involve adult protagonists, and the narrator in "The Recruiting Officer" seems well into middle age. Thus the collection suggests that its vision embraces many different ages and that really there is little progression in human affairs. The motif of the wheel or the cycle, which is central to many of the stories, is embodied in the circling organization of the texts in the collection.

Universality is further emphasized by the central characters' and narrators' lack of names. Only in "Why We're Here," "Coming into His Kingdom," and "Hearts of Oak, Bellies of Brass" are these named (and in the last story, Pa and Paddy are clearly generic names for an Irish laborer in London rather than the narrator's own name). However, the texts are far from impersonal. There are only three third-person narrators in the collection, in "Coming into His Kingdom," "Peaches," and "Why We're Here," and of these the first two adopt a clear point of view, and only "Why We're Here" has an objective third-person narrator. The rest of the stories have first-person narrators, all revealing their state of mind and emotions.

The central figures, be they narrators or protagonists or, indeed, secondary characters, are deeply disaffected individuals.[6] In "Wheels" the narrator travels to his father and stepmother's farm from the city. His bitter estrangement from his father is apparent from the first and only becomes more acute as the story progresses. In "Why We're Here" Gillespie and Boles discuss and mock another man, Sinclair, who has clearly always been an outsider. "Coming into His Kingdom" depicts a young boy desperate to understand human sexuality and disturbed by what he discovers, while "Christmas" is narrated by an orphan from a children's home who is emotionally distant from his foster family and from the rest of his community. The narrators of "Hearts of Oak and Bellies of Brass" and "Strandhill, the Sea" would certainly rather not be where they are, while those of "Bomb Box" and "Korea" are alienated from their fathers. "Lavin" concerns a character who has placed himself outside all the norms of decent society. The story is narrated by an adolescent uncertain about his sexuality and clearly in love with the wrong person. "My Love, My Umbrella" is told by one of McGahern's gallery of failed, malcontent, and indecisive lovers (reminiscent of the narrators of *The Leavetaking* and *The Pornographer*). The protagonists of "Peaches" are alienated from each other and from the southern Spanish landscape and politics in which they live, while the clock-watching, whiskey-drinking schoolteacher in "The Recruiting Officer" is utterly out of sympathy with job, church, environment, colleagues, himself, and, ultimately, life.

46

Language

The linguistic features of the short stories in *Nightlines* are familiar from McGahern's first two novels. Most of the stories are recounted in relatively neutral lexis and syntax, neither excessively formal nor informal. However, there are two distinctive features of McGahern's language (observable in the earlier texts too) that carry considerable meaning within the collection. The first is the loose syntax employed by McGahern's narrators. These occur throughout the collection. For example, "Wheels" contains the following paragraph:

> They'd filled the trolley, the smile dying in the eyes as they went past, the loose wheels rattling less under the load, the story too close to the likeness of my own life for comfort but it'd do to please Lightfoot in the pub when I got back.[7]

Here the accumulation of adverbial phrases and the switch in subject in the "but" clause give the sentence a loose syntactical organization. In "Coming into His Kingdom" the narrator can produce a run-on sentence such as, "As he walked his wondering changed to what it would be like to rise on a girl or woman as the bull rose, if he could know that everything would be known" (37). One can observe the same syntax in "The Recruiting Officer."

> I had got out of the Christian Brothers, I no longer wore the black clothes and the white half-collar, and was no longer surrounded by the rules of the order in its monastery; but then after the first freedom I was afraid, it was that I was alone. (151)

As in *The Barracks* and *The Dark,* such nonstandard syntax seems appropriate for the relatively humble personages of McGahern's stories. It also suggests, perhaps, a spoken voice rather than a written and formally literary one.

The second feature of the language of the short stories in *Nightlines* has been extensively commented on by critics: namely, the frequent avoidance of finite verbs and the building up of adverbial phrases. The first paragraph of "Wheels" is a good example of this (11). Four nonfinite phrases precede the only finite clause in the paragraph. The first paragraph of "Strandhill, the Sea" goes one better and has no finite verbs at all (62). This linguistic device recurs throughout the story. For example, the second page of the story contains two such nonfinite sentences, one eleven lines long (beginning, "Conversations always the same . . . ") and the other (beginning, "Even the strand . . . "). Other prominent examples occur in "Hearts of Oak and Bellies of Brass" (52, 53) and in the first paragraph "The Recruiting Officer" (151). The function of such syntax is clear: it deprives passages of any forward movement; they become static. In this they reflect the circular, nonprogressive motion of the arrangement of stories in the volume. They also embody the utter paralysis of some of the stories' protagonists.[8]

Motifs and Vision

The above discussion has touched upon some of the recurrent, shaping motifs of *Nightlines*. These are fourfold: the wheel, stasis, coarse physicality, and disillusion and nihilism.

Critics have written extensively of the motif of the wheel in *Nightlines* and elsewhere in McGahern's fiction.[9] It is clearly present in the opening story of *Nightlines*. It is in the title, in the rattling wheels of the trolley on the station platform, and in the sound of the wheels (suggested through alliteration) of the train on which the narrator returns at the story's end. It is also present in the narrator's own reflections—that life is best understood as a wheel: fathers become children; husbands become infants; it is all a "journey to nowhere" (15); a turning wheel that never brings happiness (22). The motif is also found in "The Recruiting Officer": "for it is all a wheel," the wretched schoolteacher reflects (165).

The wheel that spins and goes nowhere echoes the second major motif from the stories in *Nightlines,* that of paralysis and stasis.[10] Neither the son nor the father (nor indeed Rose) can resolve anything in "Wheels": they are locked in a pattern of bitterness, rejection, and recrimination. Nothing has been resolved about anything at the end of "Why We're Here," especially the question implied in the title. The laborers in "Hearts of Oak and Bellies of Brass" are inextricably bound in cycles of work, rest, futile conversation, casual sex, and obscenity. "Strandhill, the Sea" presents its holiday makers' similarly pointless conversations and the drab repetitiveness of their lives. In "Lavin" the eponymous character seems unable to resist the sexual mania that has destroyed his life; the male lover in "My Love, My Umbrella" can neither love the woman he meets nor move on to another; the teacher in "The Recruiting Officer" has condemned himself to live out futile days, and, indeed, he never even had the vitality to quit the Christian Brothers of his own accord. Even such hints of an escape from stasis and paralysis are questionable. The knowledge that Stevie has acquired in "Coming into His Kingdom" terrifies him; he runs to catch up with Teresa so as not to be alone. Though the narrator in "Christmas" "felt a new life for me had already started to grow out of . . . the stupidity of human wishes," one must wonder what his real possibilities are and how he will build a future out of his sordid experience. The comics that the narrator steals in "Strandhill, the Sea" will indeed provide some relief from drab stasis, but by its very nature that can only be a temporary assuaging of boredom. The narrator of "Korea" is left poised to make some change in his life although filled with sorrow at what he has lost. It is also worth noting that the reader does not see his future.

Life is not simply paralyzed in *Nightlines* but also marked by a physical coarseness and by decay. The stinking sweatband of the father's hat in "Wheels" and his corns that must be shaved with a razor (21) embody this, as do Gillespie's fart (22) and his and Boles's fornicating dogs (24) in "Why We're Here." Apples rot on the ground (26). Stevie's newly acquired knowledge in "Coming into His Kingdom" is accompanied by a sense of the crude physicality of sex and of bodily corruption (36–37). Both "Hearts of Oak and Bellies of Brass" and "Lavin" are full of physical cruelty and explicit, and rather unsavory, sexuality, features that are only somewhat modified in "My Love, My Umbrella." The action of "Peaches" takes place against the motif of a rotting shark, and "The Recruiting Officer," besides the violence of a beating (155), has references to ringworm (161) and the tinker who comes to the school to clean out and bury the children's excrement (161).

The stories of *Nightlines* also feature motifs of disillusionment and nihilism. For the narrator of "Wheels," life is going nowhere, and one will never see "the rich whole" that one was promised (22). The railway porters' conversation at the beginning is of an attempted suicide (which even ends absurdly [11]). If he has learned anything, the narrator of "Christmas" has learned an even deeper cynicism. The son in "Korea" has learned to distrust his father; the son in "Bomb Box" just finds his father ridiculous. The diligent, skilled young man of "Lavin" has become a pervert living in a decayed house. The affair and the marriage of "My Love, My Umbrella" and "Peaches," respectively, will lead to nothing save for more bitterness, more sorrow. The teacher in "The Recruiting Officer" has nothing to do but souse himself with alcohol. Life offers nothing more.

The vision of the stories collected in *Nightlines* is bleak and hopeless to a striking degree. Characters are paralyzed in destructive situations and hopeless relationships; unhappiness and disillusion pervade their lives; decay, coarseness, degradation, and boredom shape their worlds.[11] Perhaps the only hope lies in these carefully crafted, often extremely moving stories themselves, evocations of despair and chronicles of waste though they may be.

CHAPTER 5

The City (I)

The Leavetaking (1974/1984)

Story Material

McGahern's third novel, *The Leavetaking,* presents a problem for any commentator, for it exists in two different editions. The first edition was published in 1974 by Faber and Faber in the United Kingdom, and by Little, Brown and Company in the United States. McGahern records that "several years after its first publication," while working with a translator on the French version of *The Leavetaking,* he became convinced that "it had to be changed," because one of the ideas of the text was presented in too "blatant" a fashion without sufficient "distance."[1] He accordingly revised the second part of the novel for its republication in the United Kingdom in 1984. The novel has, however, never been reissued in North America in its revised form. This chapter will, therefore, deal, primarily, with the 1974 edition; only at the end of the chapter will the differences between this edition and the revised 1984 edition be addressed.

The Leavetaking has a connection with McGahern's biography. The central character is an Irish schoolteacher who, in the course of the novel, is dismissed from the Catholic school in which he works because he has offended the educational and religious establishment by marrying a non-Catholic (and a divorcée and in a civil ceremony in England). This echoes McGahern's own situation in 1965. The novel, however, is far from being only a personal apologia or settling of accounts. *The Leavetaking* is an ambitious novel, one in which McGahern attempts to broaden the scope of his fiction beyond the restricted world of small farms to a wider one of the city and, indeed, of the foreign metropolis. He also attempts to deal with a range of personal and social experience substantially beyond that even of Elizabeth Reegan and certainly beyond that of the Mahoneys. Further, he adds an optimistic note to his world vision, a note quite absent from the earlier fictions. The technical complexity of *The Dark* (in narration) is also further developed in *The Leavetaking*'s intricate interweaving of past and present in its narrative organization and in the author's overt deployment of something akin to poetic technique, both locally and throughout the whole novel. There is, in addition, a constant impulse toward generalization of the protagonist's experience in *The Leavetaking,* on both an existential and a social-historical level (as there was in *The Barracks* and *The Dark*).

Reception

The Leavetaking is divided into two parts. The first focuses on the narrator's early life; the second part deals with his adult experience, especially his emotional and sexual development and particularly his love affair with an American woman in London. The two parts are, however, closely linked. Memories of childhood and of more recent experiences in Dublin and London are interwoven with the novel's present moment, the narrator's last day at school, the day on which he knows he will be dismissed. The novel's title is precisely relevant to his situation. This day marks the end of a long phase in the protagonist's life, the moment when he will abandon almost all that he has done and been so far for a new life outside Ireland with his American wife. (The title does not, however, only refer to this departure. The protagonist as a child has also taken leave of his dying mother. In addition, his wife, Isobel, breaks with her father in the course of the novel.)

The story material of *The Leavetaking* is relatively simple. The narrator, who is scarcely named throughout the text (although the reader can work out that his family name is Moran and that his first name may be Patrick), while getting through his last day as a teacher, recalls central childhood and adult events that have led to this moment.[2] He recounts his parents' complex marriage. His mother, Kate Moran, is a schoolteacher who leaned toward becoming a nun. Instead she married Sergeant Moran, one of McGahern's harsh policemen fathers. Their married life is one of conflict and partial estrangement. The narrator tells of his early childhood, of his devotion to his mother and of her ambitions that he become a priest, of his mother's illness and death (perhaps caused by the father), and of his father's conduct before her death (he removes the children from her as she lies dying). In the second part of the novel the narrator omits any discussion of his subsequent childhood or relationship with his father and passes on to his period of training as a teacher (which he describes as a substitute for the priesthood he cannot enter). After finishing college the narrator has relationships with various women, becomes a schoolteacher, and, after one failed affair, takes leave of absence to go to London for a year. There he meets and falls in love with Isobel, an American woman from a wealthy and colorful background. They fall in love and start to live together. Isobel, however, has long been in a difficult relationship with her crude, abusive, and shady father. Eventually matters come to a head, Isobel abandons her father, marries the narrator, and they decide to go to Ireland. The narrator and she know, however, that he will not be able to keep his job once it is known he has married a non-Catholic in a civil ceremony. This proves to be the case. Nonetheless, the novel ends optimistically. The narrator returns to his beloved, and they plan to set off for a new life outside Ireland.

The Leavetaking (like McGahern's next novel, *The Pornographer*) has always had a mixed reception. In a 1975 review in the *Times Literary Supplement,* Julian Jebb writes positively of the novel. Although he argues that the two parts of the text can be read independently he does not suggest this is a defect. He notes that McGahern has remained "true to the bleak vision" of the earlier novels but "has enlarged his view of the possibilities of life." Jebb also writes that "*The Leavetaking* represents an achievement of a very high order and substantiates the belief that its author is among the half-dozen practicing writers of English prose most worthy of attention." In the Dublin *Sunday Independent,* Seamus Heaney also praises the novel. McGahern, he writes, "has transformed situations and scenes common in experience into something rich and strange, something uncommonly beautiful." Denis Sampson comments positively on the text's "experimentation" and on the manner in which it forces readers to engage in an act of discovery on their own. However, there are many dissident voices. Writing in *The Spectator,* Peter Ackroyd expresses dislike for what he sees as a dissonance between the two parts of the novel. "I can only assume," he declares, "that there are two novels elbowing each other within the same covers. They do not complement each other." In the *New Statesman,* Peter Straub lambastes *The Leavetaking* as "naïve, emotionally immature, almost adolescent: precisely adolescent, in fact." In 1990 Jürgen Kamm writes of *The Leavetaking* that "the author, in an occasionally tiresome fashion, falls back upon a number of previously employed motifs," and Jean Brihault asserts sadly that *The Leavetaking* and *The Pornographer* "sont des romans insatisfaisants sur le plan de l'écriture et plus ou moins explicitement reconnus comme tells par leur auteur" (are unsatisfactory novels on the level of writing and are more or less explicitly recognized as such by their author).[3]

The Leavetaking contains clear echoes of McGahern's earlier fiction. Place setting in part 1—small rural communities in Ireland—is familiar from both *The Barracks* and *The Dark.* Brief sections of *The Leavetaking* are even set in an Irish police barracks, as is McGahern's first novel.[4] Characters also have their equivalents in earlier texts. Kate Moran, the educated, intelligent, sensitive, dying mother, recalls Elizabeth Reegan. Sergeant Moran is a simplified version of the harsh fathers of *The Barracks* and *The Dark.* The narrator/

protagonist—a young man navigating the dangers of Irish adolescence, family, and faith—echoes Mahoney in *The Dark*. The text's strategy of leaving his name indefinite is also that of the earlier novel. Yet on the levels of setting and character there are new elements in *The Leavetaking*. The urban settings (Dublin, presumably, and London) mark an important departure for McGahern's novels (although not entirely, for *Nightlines* contains some stories with city settings). Time setting, too, is vague by the standards of McGahern's earlier work. There are no indications of year or decade in *The Leavetaking*. It takes place sometime in postwar Ireland and London, but it would be difficult to specify exactly when. This lack of definition is part of the universalization of character and action at which the novel aims. With regard to character, there is a considerable broadening of the range of figures that McGahern uses. If the characters in the rural settings in part 1 are largely familiar from earlier texts, the teachers at Moran's school, the priest who manages it, and the English and American characters in the parts of the novel set in London are all new to McGahern's novels. They indicate, as do the urban place settings, an attempt to broaden his fictional world.

Narration and Language

On one level, narration in *The Leavetaking* is quite simple. The narrator/ protagonist gives an account of his emotional and sexual education. He appears perfectly reliable and tries to give as frank an account as possible of what has shaped his life up to the moment of his dismissal from school. In part 2 he even makes the kind of general comments associated with highly trust-worthy and knowledgeable narrators, and these comments are never under-mined. For example, of the woman in one of his failed affairs he notes: "She was, at twenty, as are most women, ripe to enter fully into her sexual life" (91). At other points he comments on the possibility of an after life (109) and on belief and the progress of human life (159).

However, there are complexities in the novel's narration. First, although strictly speaking Moran is the narrator of the entire text, in part 2 his beloved Isobel narrates substantial parts. Her stories are given within direct speech by Moran and sometimes interrupted by his questions or comments, but for long parts of the text she takes on the role of narrator within his narration. This is the case in the sixty-page section in which Moran tells of his romance with Isobel in London (108–73). Isobel's narrations make up around a quarter of this section (111–12, 118, 123, 126–28, 129–34, 136–37, 157–58). Second, in part 1, Moran occasionally moves into the consciousness of another character.

This is apparent in a minor fashion when he puts himself in the mind of one of his fellow teachers (20) and, in a more important context, when he imagines and reconstructs the thoughts and feelings of his parents. For example, he is able to give the detail and progress of his mother's feelings and dreams in a way that is not explained in the text. This can be seen in the passage concerning her desire for the tranquility of a religious vocation and her feelings for her handsome young suitor (39–40). It is also apparent in her reflections after her wedding night (42). Moran does the same with his father's thoughts, for example when he attempts to regulate his infant son's feeding (47). Moran makes the whole process of imagining another's mind clear when he speculates about his father's thoughts as he bicycles to visit his wife. "As he started to sweat under the cape he thought of trees he could sell on the farm . . . or did he dream he was young?" (57).

However, Moran goes beyond this on one occasion. While recounting his father's story of childhood poverty, he starts to use the first-person pronoun and merges his own narrative personality with that of his father (53–56). With regard to literary technique in general, this is an unusual slippage in narration. This overall narrative strategy—a first-person narration mingled with another character's narration within that narration and the principal narrator's occasional going out of himself into the minds of others—is important. It gives a clear picture of Moran's consciousness, which is the central focus of the novel. However it also permits the emergence of other points of view, although it makes clear that these are, in the case of Moran's mother and father, achieved by acts of imagination. Moran's slipping into his father's persona at one point also suggests a limited self-identification with the harsh and difficult man that the rest of the novel denies.

The language of the novel's narration is marked by a great deal of variation. There is the simple but striking movement between the present and past tenses in the sections dealing with Moran's last day at school (narrated in the present) and those dealing with his life up to that day (narrated in the past). Beyond this, however, one can observe three different kinds of language in play in *The Leavetaking:* a relatively nonstandard language (reminiscent of the linguistic configuration of *The Barracks* and *The Dark*); a much more sophisticated and educated discourse; and a style that is marked by poetic features. The examples of nonstandard language are restricted to part 1, although they do not all occur in the sections dealing with the narrator's childhood. Thus there are examples of run-on sentences on pages 9–10 and 16 that deal with the narrator's last day at school and his being hired to work at the school nine years earlier. There are occasional sentences with unusual word order. For example, on page 16 the narrator says, "Tea and biscuits and fruit cake she brought in on a tray," and on page 69 he remembers, "Crazy word came Sunday from my father" (although here the nonstandard quality of this utterance may be shaped as much by the lack of preposition before "Sunday" as by word order). The narrator's omission of articles on occasion is also striking. For example, as he looks at the nearby girls' school where a former love works, he imagines "low in the window black hair I kissed once, woman that I loved once" (10). On the same page he notes, "Glass of the swing door glitters." In both these examples the absence of articles borders on the linguistically deviant. Note also the absence of article before "sun" on page 16, and before "Last of the furze bloom" on page 43. All but one of these examples are drawn from the discourse of the adult Moran about his adult experience.

Part 1 is also full of examples of two other syntactic peculiarities that are more difficult to define in terms of standard or nonstandard use. Moran's language in this part shows a fondness for fragments and for nonfinite clauses. The first occur throughout part 1, both in the adult and the child sections. Thus, during his last day at school Moran records, "As I take the bell by the tongue, shock of the erection I got when first I beat a boy with a cane, taking pleasure in my supposed duty" (12). There is no main finite verb in this sentence. Nor is there in sentences such as those on page 30: "Cheap plywood wardrobe of that room. Sprayed gold handle, Sacred heart lamp burning before the Sacred Heart, window on the empty meadow, more present than this schoolroom where I stand and watch." Another example from the same page reads: "Bare boards of the corridor, loose brass knobs of the doors; shoes on the stairs, hand on its wooden railing, relief I had cows to tie out in the darkening evening." Part 1 contains several other examples of such fragments.[5]

Part 1 also contains several examples of nonfinite clauses, that is, phrases containing nonfinite verb forms (usually participles) unmarked for tense and used to modify a noun or a noun phrase. In the following the nonfinite clauses are italicized for emphasis:

We met at the chapel gate, the rain had stopped, *sun coming and going behind white cloud out on the bay.* (16)

The bell tinkled for a last time into the shrouded coughing, into some child's crying, and it was soon over, *the altar boys in scarlet and white leaving the altar in twos in front of the priest bearing the empty monstrance, light from candles dancing on the gold of his cloak . . . the headmaster moving nervously along on the railing, searching for the best position to effect the meeting.* (16, 17)

Maloney leaned above the conversation, *beaming approval, waiting for the right pause to interject.* (17)[6]

A related linguistic feature in part 1 is the widespread use of supplemental noun phrases, usually without verb forms, that expand the meaning of a previous phrase. Examples of these are also italicized for emphasis in the following:

A smell of urine seeps from the lavatories, *their small windows half open under the concrete eve.* (10)

"Should we have a drink to celebrate?" I asked him and his face fell: *fear that he'd just hired a drunkard.* (18)

Healing rage grew, *the unfairness of it all.* (29)

We'd been taken by car into the mountains to see my grandmother a last time before she died, *the delicate blueberries under the whitethorns on the banks of the lane too narrow for the car.* (33)

. . . and quietly climbed to her room, *strips of bicycle tyre over the lino on the edges of the steps.* (40)

In the same night my father pushed behind the tunnel the hissing carbide lamp made in the rain, *the patter of the whippet's gallop behind the swish of wheels.* (57)

I looked at her with masked hatred but walked, *cement of the floor, stairs.* (70)

The function of such linguistic features is difficult to assess. However, it is likely that the nonstandard features of Moran's language in part 1 are intended to chime with his rural background and to give that language a markedly informal shape. The use of fragments, nonfinite clauses, and supplemental noun phrases, however, is meant to give the reader a sense of Moran's immediate impressions, real (in his own case) or imagined (in the case of passages dealing with his parents). Since such fragments and clauses are unmarked for time, one might also suggest that they indicate a static quality in the life depicted in part 1. Moran is simply waiting for dismissal in this part of the novel. In other sections of part 1, he is a small child shaped by others and has not left for the city, for England, or for the love that will change everything.

The language of the novel changes radically in part 2. There are continuities. For example, there are examples of nonfinite clauses in this part, too (on pages 97, 114, and 119), but there are not as many. The major difference in language in part 2 is its high degree of formality and lexical and syntactic sophistication. There are several examples of this kind of language in part 2, but a particularly good one can be found on page 104.

> The mind—the old sentinel—counselled that in one year or two what I then felt would be totally obliterated; and she, whom I desired to the exclusion of everything else in the world, would come to mean so little that the sight of her crossing the street would give rise to little more than idle curiosity. While I was able to admit that this would all probably come true, it was not truth or philosophy I wanted, but an end to the torment, and she who could end it I could not have. In the meantime I admitted I was ill, drank and ate carefully, kept regimental hours, and even rose to the hypocrisy of writing to thank her for her note, saying that on reflection I completely agreed with her that our relationship could never come to anything more serious, and wished her every success and happiness in her marriage, getting malicious satisfaction as I read through the concoction that it gave no hint of her power. Brooding over why she and no other—even others more abstractly beautiful— should embody that power, I had begun to suspect that what I was experiencing was not the losing of her but the loss of my own life.

The lexis of this passage is formal and sophisticated: "sentinel," "counselled," "obliterated," "whom," "would give rise to little more than idle curiosity," "regimental hours," "rose to the hypocrisy of writing," "on reflection," "wished her every success," "malicious satisfaction," "concoction," "Brooding," "abstractly beautiful," and "embody." The syntax, too, is formal: the paragraph's four sentences are all complex (the third sentence is highly complex and long).[7] Such language can be found in several other places in part 2, for example in Isobel's narration (132–33), and is remarkably different from the stylistic level of part 1. McGahern clearly marks his narrator's movement from a rural to an urban world, indeed from Ireland to the foreign metropolis, through language.

However, there is a third kind of language in operation in *The Leavetaking,* one that exists in both parts and merges, also, with one of the linguistic elements noted above (nonfinite clauses). It is a language that, while undeniably prose, takes on some of the features of poetry, particularly syntactic, lexical, and phonological parallelism and repetition.[8] This is the language that the narrator uses when he talks of love. The following is an example from the early stages of the text, in which the narrator expresses his feelings about a colleague's life and contrasts that life with his passion for his beloved.

Impoverishment of their house of children, not poverty but the ugly coldness that nothing—neither chair nor plate nor child—had ever been touched with care, the runny nose of a child. O the opposite of my love in the room in Howth, the love of the Other that with constant difficulty extends its care to all the things about her so that they shine in their own loveliness back to her as the circle closes in the calmness of the completed self, the love that I'll be fired from this school for at eight. (22)

The first sentence is made up of three syntactically parallel phrases: "Impoverishment . . . ," "not poverty . . . ," and "the runny nose. . . . " "Of" is repeated three times; "neither chair nor plate nor child" is organized around both syntactic and phonological parallelism; there are further phonological echoes, for example, the /ʧ/ of "children," "chair," "child," and "touched." The second sentence contains a matching set of three parallel units: "O the opposite of my love . . . ," "the love of the Other . . . ," and "the love I'll be fired for. . . . " "Love" and a variant of the word are repeated throughout the sentence; the passage is full of assonance and alliteration: the related web of vowel sounds of "O," "opposite," "love," "Other," and "Howth," and of consonants in "constant difficulty extends its care," "shine in their own loveliness," and "circle closes in the calmness of the completed self."

This kind of language recurs throughout *The Leavetaking*. In its syntactic parallelism it overlaps with some of the examples of fragments and nonfinite clauses noted above, but it is usually distinct. It is the style that the narrator adopts when speaking about his love and sets that love off clearly from the world that surrounds it. Love becomes something transcendent (which is precisely the point the narrator wishes to make). The novel ends with this kind of language (syntactically, lexically, and phonologically parallel in organization).

The odour of our lovemaking rises, redolent of slime and fish, and our very breathing seems an echo of the rise and fall of the sea as we drift to sleep; and I would pray for the boat of our sleep to reach its morning, and see that morning lengthen to an evening of calm weather that comes through night and sleep again to morning after morning until we meet the first death. (195)

In passages such as these McGahern pushes the language of prose fiction close to that of poetry.[9] While this tactic is part of a wider strategy of conveying the narrator's feelings and setting the sphere of love somewhat apart from the mundane, it can also be understood as an aspect of the novel that foregrounds fictionality, that draws attention to the text as text and thus as a self-reflexive, metafictional device, subtly embedded in a realist text.

Narrative Organization

The narrative organization of the novel's story material is similarly complex and multifunctional. It is extensively discussed by Sampson.[10] The division of the text into two parts is one of the most striking aspects of its organization. This clearly points to the distinctness of the two parts of Moran's life with which they deal. It also, however, makes them comparable. It is also important to note that the two parts are closely linked by being framed and interwoven by the day of Moran's dismissal. They are, in addition, both elliptical, inasmuch as they omit substantial parts of Moran's life. Thus part 1 does not give any mention of the narrator's childhood after his mother's death, nor does part 2 do more than summarize his young adulthood, his time of training as a teacher, or his more than nine years as a teacher. It is also worth noting that part 2 has an open ending. There is closure in Moran's narrative (he has been dismissed), but the novel's ending is one of departure and setting off into the unknown and new.

The local organization of each part is also worthy of close attention. Part 1 is shaped round a constant interplay of present and five principal different levels of the past. The present is the day of Moran's dismissal, marked off from the other sections by being given in present tenses. Sections of varying lengths deal with this day—some are longer, such as that on pages 19–25; some are short, such as that on page 35. These sections themselves contain brief retrospects, such as that about an unnamed lost beloved (10). The five levels of the past are not presented chronologically. The first discrete retrospect moves back nine years to the time when Moran is hired to teach at his present school (13–19). The second level of the past is that of Moran's mother's illness. Here episodes deal with her asking her son to become a priest (25–28), her promising not to die (28–30), and Moran's visit to his cousin Bridget the day after his mother's promise (31–34). This last episode, however, contains a further retrospect, in which Moran recalls visiting his mother's mother just before her death (33–34). The third level of the past is that of Moran's parents' courtship and early marriage, along with Moran's early childhood, and Mrs. Moran's worsening health (35–42, 45–64). Once again one should note the degree of ellipsis in presenting the past. Most notably there is no presentation of Moran's parents' actions or discussions immediately before their marriage, nor, indeed, of the wedding itself (42). This level is returned to in the last long section of part 1 (65–82), which charts Mrs. Moran's illness and death and Sergeant Moran's harsh and self-protective behavior. Even here, however, there are movements back in time. The narrator returns to an earlier episode from his parents' married life, Moran's bicycle trip to visit his wife, the trip that possibly leads to her death through her husband's sexual incontinence (65). This episode has already been presented in an earlier section (56–59). Also the narrator gives a recollection of his mother's from her youth (68–69). A fourth level of the past is that of Moran and his American wife's excursion to Howth on "our first Sunday in Ireland," that is, long after his childhood is over, and, chronologically, after most of the action in part 2 (42). (This episode is referred to again in part 2 [167].) One final level of the past stands out by virtue of its narrative peculiarity. That is the episode, related during one of the sections presenting the Morans' married life, in which the narrator tells of his father's early experience of poverty and slips into becoming the first-person narrator of his father's story (56–59).

The narrative organization of part 2 is not as complex but is still complex enough. Once again, the day of Moran's dismissal interweaves and frames the narrator's account of his life as a student, as a teacher in Dublin, and during his year's leave in London. Apart from returns to the day of departure, the narration is ordered much more chronologically than in part 1. Long sections deal with Moran's life from his days as a student to his departure to London (85–107), and his love affair with Isobel (108–73). Shorter sections deal with his return to Ireland and the short period of his living there with Isobel before their discovery and Moran's dismissal (174–80, 180–87). The novel ends with a longer section detailing the last stages of Moran's last day as a teacher (187–95). The only other level of the past that is presented in detail in part 2 is that of Isobel's life before she meets Moran. This is given in Isobel's own words in a series of accounts she gives Moran on pages 111–58. Her accounts are largely chronological.

This complex narrative organization has several functions. First, it marks clearly the interweaving of past and present. The present emerges out of the past, deeply shaped by it, as Moran sees trees twisted by the wind from the sea (82). But the novel's open ending suggests that the past can be left behind and that a new departure, a leavetaking, is possible. Second, both parts are discrete but linked, distinct but equivalent. The bipartite division asks the reader to see and compare different kinds of leavetaking in each part: Moran's from his mother, his mother's from life itself, Isobel's from her father and her past, and Moran's from Ireland and his past. Third, the local organization of the narrative—slipping among different levels of the past—creates an image of a complex relationship of past and present and suggests a model of how past and present interweave in the narrator's consciousness, as well as just how multilayered a consciousness of the past might be.[11] Ellipses, shifts among levels of the past, and the introduction of Isobel's (another's) accounts of her past, all demonstrate this complex imbrication, this intricate web of Moran's sense of the past.

A Psychological Novel

The subjective organization of events in *The Leavetaking* indicates its psychological focus. It is a traditional psychological novel that deals with its central character's existential choices and emotional, intellectual, and sexual development. The paragraph that closes part 1 makes this clear. The first part of the text has attempted to show that a "shadow" from the past falls across Moran's life, shaping it until, at the end, he can break free from it (82). Moran tells of his childhood experiences, his difficult relationship with his father, his devotion to his mother, and his sense of loss at her death. In part 2, he charts love affairs (mostly unhappy) that lead finally to his love for Isobel. The novel also deals, in some detail, with his encounter with the (for him) alien world of Isobel's wealthy father and associates. In addition, this part presents Isobel's complex relationships with father, husband, and lovers, and her eventual emancipation from her father.

This psychological novel concentrates on certain aspects of human existence: the power of memory and imagination; the possibilities of sex and love; and the role of time, transience, and death. References to memory and imagination abound in part 1. "Two worlds," the narrator reflects, "the world of the schoolroom in this day, the world of memory becoming imagination" (35). He returns to the same formulation—"memory becoming imagination"—as he escapes the schoolroom to his parents' early marriage (45). He emphasizes the power of memory in his own life and in the life of his mother (64, 68). "If I believed in a hell or a heaven," he declares, "I would believe that God was formed from the First Memory" (69). However, memory—as some of the above quotations suggest—is partly imagination, an imaginative reconstruction of the past. The narrator is clearly guessing in his accounts of past events. He was not present during his mother and father's lovemaking (65). He makes his act of imaginative reconstruction clear when he is reconstructing his father's actions (56) or assuming what his mother thinks of (68). The focus on the nature and power of memory and imagination continues in part 2. Unhappy after a failed love affair, the narrator tries unsuccessfully to gain peace through childhood memories (102). He is struck by the force of imagination (162) and of the "flotsam of the mind" that can suddenly return unbidden to consciousness (174). Most of Isobel's narratives to Moran are memories of childhood, adolescence, or adulthood. Moran, however, argues that the memories of others become altered in the mind and imagination of the listener, even those of a lover (120–21). His emphasis here on the egocentricity of memory fits in with the highly subjective ordering of time in the novel, especially in part 1.

The Leavetaking also looks closely one of the most subjective of human experiences, that of sex and love. This explains, to some extent, the ellipses in the text's narration. McGahern is not concerned in *The Leavetaking* with providing a complex picture of a son's relationship with his father or of a young man's encounter with education. The text concentrates rather on Moran's love for his mother and later for a series of women, culminating in his relationship with Isobel. In part 1, despite an early reference to a past love affair (10) and the presentation of a walk with Isobel in Howth (42–44), Moran's mother is his "beloved." His two conversations with her as she lies sick in bed show this clearly (25–26, 28–30). He refers to her explicitly as his "beloved" when he returns alone with her to the farmhouse where she lives apart from her husband. He remembers with joy how, "my beloved was home, and I was alone with my beloved" (64). Once she dies, his emotional desolation is obvious. He expresses his resentment that she has gone "to the Lord": "but the Lord has many servants, and I had but the one beloved" (80). The mother's death casts a long shadow over her son (82). Despite this shadow, Moran's devotion to his mother is presented positively; sex, however, is seen in a negative light in this part of the novel.[12] Kate Moran is said to be "looking the picture of death" at her wedding, and the narrator imagines her after her wedding night "trying to change the sheets and blood and sexual suck of the night into a sacrificial marble on which a cross stood in the centre of tulips and white candles" (42). As the narrator imagines it, it is Sergeant Moran's sexual incontinence that destroys his wife, killing her by making her pregnant (65). For Moran himself as a child, sex is a matter of trying to see up an older woman's skirt (73).

Part 2 similarly takes love and sex as its central concerns. It is largely an account of Moran's emotional entanglements with women and his eventual entry into a lasting relationship with one of them. The women are all individualized to some degree (especially Isobel), but they are also all part of the narrator's pursuit of a transcendent "love." "How many different forms had that love by now taken, by how many different names had I called to her, and yet I was calling still," the narrator reflects toward the end of the novel (184). His love for his mother is seen as related to his involvement with other women. A girl's agreement to go to a dance with him is compared to his mother's promise not to leave him (88). The girl's eventual rejection of him casts a "shadow" on his life, as did his mother's death (91). Isobel herself, for all the individual history she is provided with, is called constantly "my love," in an almost impersonal, if ecstatic, manner, echoing Moran's calling his mother his "beloved." One of the leavetakings of the novel is Moran's from the unhappiness of the loss of his mother, a movement into a new world of love for Isobel.

Part 2 also focuses on sex in a way that part 1 does not. There is both much more sexual activity depicted in part 2, and it is not all seen negatively. In Moran's relationship with Elinor, the older woman introduces him to "the rich dark mystery of a woman's body" (93), although she herself astringently balances his rapture with her insistence that what she has craved for is simply the feeling of "skin" (93). Moran's next relationship with a woman is presented in more negative terms. The physical pleasure of lovemaking (96) becomes "wantonness of mouth and glycerine" (97); it becomes crudely physical, "cold and passionate at once" (98); and the end of the relationship provokes feelings of extreme sexual violence in Moran (101). The entanglement, in Moran's mind, of his relationship with his mother and his affairs with other women is made clear once he goes to London. He connects mother and lost lover: "She [the mother] had given me a death instead of love, but it had taken the sexual death [inflicted by the lover] to burn out the first death, and give me my life late but at last" (108). His love affair with Isobel takes a different and positive turn. She appears to be both a companion and a lover, "a friend and a beloved in one," of whom Moran has dreamed (108). Their relationship is both emotionally and physically satisfying. Isobel confides freely in Moran, and their relationship is relatively uninhibited in its sexual freedom (134–35). It is, however, striking that after their marriage Isobel becomes a relatively transparent figure: "my love," but not entirely an individual.

Despite the narrator's rapturous celebration of love and sex, there are many negative sexual motifs throughout *The Leavetaking*. Moran's sexual life in Dublin is seen as a matter of "fumbled sex in the back seats of cars or on bedsittingroom sofas or against alley walls, wet trouser legs and the grey stiff stain that had to be sent to the cleaner" (92). Isobel herself has had a checkered sexual career, including a failed marriage, affairs, a disturbing relationship with her father, and an abortion (129). Above all, Isobel's father stands in the text as an embodiment of a crude and unsavory approach to sex. According to Isobel, he has sexually abused her as a child (131), and his relationship toward her and a girl friend verges on the perverse (127). He undergoes treatment to maintain sexual potency, "to give him a fillip," as Isobel says (130). A thoroughly unattractive figure physically, a glutton given to farting in public (141, 149), his attitude toward sex is couched in the crudest of terms, so much so that Moran feels "soiled" by an evening spent in his company (150, 151). All the above is part of a context—like the Logans' loveless marriage in the last stages of the novel (171–72)—within (and against) which Moran and Isobel's successful love must be seen.[13]

Time, Transience, and Death

Time, transience, and death are also parts of that context. The entire novel's nonsequential organization foregrounds the topic of time. In addition, in part 1 Moran's mother's death is a strong motif of passing time and transience. This is especially emphasized in the section of the text where the narrator imagines the various stages of his mother's funeral in juxtaposition to the movement of the hands of a clock (78–80). Transience is also evident in "the scroll of *tempus fugit*" on the clock in the bar where Moran meets his friend Lightfoot (31). It is apparent, too, in the opening of the novel in which the insubstantial and transient shadows of gulls pass over the school playground (9).

Part 2 has many references to passing time. The sight of his girlfriend's mother makes the narrator think that one day the young woman will be like her parent (89). Another lover argues that they are wasting time by associating with each other (99). In the lodgings that Moran and Elizabeth take in Howth, there is a tall clock, and, although it has stopped working, it is still a metaphor for time's progress (170–71). The clock in the bar mentioned in part 1 recurs toward the novel's end (187). Death is also a strong presence in part 2. As he drops the photograph of an early love on the floor of a public toilet, Moran reflects on death and transience (92). His angry passion for another lost lover is compared to death (101). The narrator thinks on occasion of nonexistence and oblivion (137). In fact, he sees human life as a crawling back toward "the original darkness" of death, and this on his wedding day (159). Even while he and Isobel walk, shortly after their marriage, in Howth, he feels they are walking "in the path of the dead," that is of his dead parents (167). A moment's tension between the two lovers makes Moran think of their separation "in our future deaths" (169), and he thinks of death again as he leaves school for the last time (180). Even the moments of rapture with his beloved that conclude the novel are tinged with intimations of oblivion (193), and the novel's final word is "death" (195). The rich possibilities of love are placed against the passing of all things.

Moran's experiences are constantly seen in general terms, in relation to universal human experiences, love, death, and passing time. The vocabulary associated with his (and Isobel's) lives is a suitably generic one. The other way in which McGahern universalizes his characters' situations and development is through intertextual reference. Critics point to the dense web of allusions to other texts and authors throughout *The Leavetaking.* Sampson lists Thales of Miletus, Heraclitus, Henry James, Joyce's *Ulysses,* W. B. Yeats, T. S. Eliot, Matthew Arnold, and Marcel Proust.[14] Such echoes and references serve further to broaden the concerns of the novel.

Society

A final element in the context of love in *The Leavetaking* is the social world. Although the novel focuses on the emotional development of its protagonists and on the major and general existential issues (love, sex, death, transience, and time) that their lives touch on, those lives are lived in a specific social order, the major features of which provide a context for Moran and Isobel's relationship. The leavetaking in the novel is from Moran's personal past but also from a specifically configured Ireland. The social world against which the protagonists' love is set, and which they leave at the novel's end, is one of routine, conformity, and traditional authority. This is largely, although not entirely, embodied in the school at which Moran works. Part 1 abounds in motifs of conformity and order. The pupils' chanting of *"Cle, deas, cle"* (Left, right, left) as they march, which recurs throughout part 1, is symptomatic of the rigid conformity of the school and, by extension, of the rest of Ireland (20–21). One of Moran's fellow teachers is described as a stiff, neatly dressed martinet (21), while the headmaster enforces strict discipline in the playground (10–11, 22). Parallel to this is a drive toward social conformity that Moran finds hypocritical, such as his own refusal to criticize rural Ireland (14) and his hastily pretending to be a teetotaler when it seems advantageous (18).

Much in this social world is a matter of mechanical repetition. This is what Moran feels about his work at school (9, 21, 25) and his colleagues' actions there (19). He reflects that "once it had seemed it would go on lunchtime after lunchtime as this until I withered into a pension at sixty-five" (10). But mechanical repetition is part of Moran's family world, too. His mother catechizes him, forcing him to deny that he loves her more than God (25–26), and his offering to become a priest for her partakes of the same rote repetitiveness (27). This is a world of traditional authority. The teachers and the headmaster enforce discipline in the school. The headmaster defers to the priest who is school manager (16–18). Kate Moran yields to her husband's sexual importunity: "She turned to him: it was her duty," Moran imagines (65). Repetition and routine are seen as features of the social world in part 2 also. Moran and the headmaster have their "usual playground conversation" (106). The chanting of the schoolchildren, marching in line, is again stressed (175, 183), and

Moran mentions the "even flow of banality" round the staff room table (179). The hypocrisy seen in part 1 is repeated here. Moran's conversation with the headmaster on his return from London makes him ashamed for the "general clichés" he produces (176–78). In a later conversation with the headmaster, Moran points to the simplified version of history that the Irish state asks its teachers to purvey (186).

Moran's fault is to have broken the rules of his society by his marriage. He compounds this by refusing simply to resign, thus forcing the establishment to dismiss him (185–86). His conflict is with the two representatives of established authority that have hired him, the headmaster and the priest, but behind them stands an entire society. Father Curry tells him this directly, "If it got out that I let you go on teaching up there after what you've gone and done there'd be an uproar. The Archbishop wouldn't stand for it. The parents wouldn't stand for it. I couldn't stand for it" (190). For all that Moran's experiences are universalized in *The Leavetaking,* they are also seen in relation to Ireland, a "half-arsed modern" Ireland, Moran feels (10), one that is inward looking, conformist, and traditional. "What do you want to go away for? Isn't there everything you want in this country?" Father Curry asks Moran (107). Moran himself plays up to such a view of things in his conversation with his headmaster after he returns from London (177). Moran sees in such conformity "the slavish caution of my whole forever overmastered race" and declares that his departure at the novel's end will give him "some pleasure in shaking off some of that slavishness from my feet" (174). The power of traditional authority is seen in the swiftness and ruthlessness with which the establishment acts once Moran and Isobel's marriage becomes known (182–83). Moran's union will not support him against the church (188). The lovers are expelled from Ireland, and this expulsion is seen as a liberation (180, 192–94), just as Moran sees his year in London as an escape into freedom (108).

However, the social world is seen in a complex fashion in *The Leavetaking.* London is where Moran meets the beloved Isobel, but it is also associated with her cosmopolitan unhappiness and her father's coarse viciousness. It is also connected with the narrator's unease in a wealthy, sophisticated environment that is alien to him, one in which the Irish are the servant class or primarily associated with a brand of whiskey (125, 140, 144). Further, it is important to note that the Irish establishment, for all its evident faults, is presented in a sympathetic fashion. Neither Maloney, the headmaster, nor Father Curry is a monster. From the beginning of the novel, Moran expresses his affection for Maloney. "Old fanatical peasant I'll miss you," he thinks to himself on his last day at school (12). His depiction of the Maloney family home is affectionate (13–16). His two final interviews with headmaster and priest are marked by courtesy and frankness (184–87, 190–92). The priest even offers him a reference as well as asking him to pray for him (192). Nevertheless, the leavetaking is seen as a liberation. At the end of part 1, Moran compares himself to trees misshapen by the wind (82); at the end of part 2, his final night in Ireland is associated with the open sea and with fishing boats preparing to go out of the harbor (193, 195). At the conclusion to part 1, Moran predicts that "by evening [of his last day at school] the life would have made its last break with the shadow, and would be free to grow without warp in its own light" (82).

The Leavetaking has never enjoyed the critical success of some of McGahern's other novels; yet it is a complex psychological-social work that exhibits considerable ambition. Its highly generalized perspective on human life is grounded in psychological detail and combined with a carefully integrated social focus. The text's intricate narrative organization and its use of poetic language make it a particularly rich and complex novel, one the full sophistication of which has not yet been fully assessed by scholars and critics.

The Revised Edition

The second, revised edition of *The Leavetaking* is twenty-four pages shorter than the first edition. The names of some minor characters are changed or omitted, and some details of action and setting are also omitted (for example concerning Moran's university degree or his room in Dublin). Isobel has a second abortion in the 1984 edition.[15] Major changes involve the cutting of passages of a wide variety of length. There are extensive cuts from pages 103–5 of the 1974 edition, detailing Moran's unhappiness in Dublin. Isobel's narrations (111–21, in the 1974 edition) have some cuts, and the restaurant scene (125–29, 1974 edition) is cut entirely. Moran's thoughts on memory and the subjective transformation of others' recollections (120–21, 1974 edition) are cut, although they recur in modified form on page 143 of the 1984 edition. Moran's encounter with his father-in-law on the train and boat to Dublin (161–66, 1974 edition) is cut from the second edition. It is hard to see what the novel gains from the cuts. Isobel's father becomes slightly less crassly offensive; Moran's edgy reactions to Isobel's world in the restaurant scene are lost; the reader has fewer details of the protagonist's existential anguish in Dublin. One must respect McGahern's artistic intuition with regard to the first edition but also suggest that the "distance" he wishes to achieve in the second edition brings with it certain losses.

CHAPTER 6

Deaths

Getting Through (1978)

Story Materials

"For all its many merits *Getting Through* is a depressing work," writes Michael Irwin of McGahern's second collection of short stories.[1] One can see what he means. It is symptomatic of the volume that it begins and ends with a funeral and a coffin. The title, too, carries the somber suggestion that all one can do is get through life, bear with its sad configuration of death and attenuated hope.

A brief review of the story materials of the texts in *Getting Through* indicates its concerns and overarching vision. The protagonist of the first story, "The Beginning of an Idea," is a theater director, probably Finnish, named Eva Lindberg. After the unhappy end of a love affair, she quits the theater and her native country to travel to southern Spain, where she hopes to be able to write a play about Chekhov. She is haunted by the image of the Russian playwright and short story writer's body being transported to Moscow in a railway wagon with the word "oysters" chalked on its side. Tricked by the local guardia civil, she is forced to have sex with two policemen and at the text's ambiguous end is traveling toward Granada, her writer's block unbroken and nothing in her life resolved. "A Slip-Up" concerns two elderly Irish immigrants to London, both of whom are clearly beginning to lose control of their wits and lives. The husband especially lives in a world of memory of the farm in Ireland they abandoned years ago. In "All Sorts of Impossible Things" a young man dies, his dog does not win a competition, and his friend does not get the girl he loves. "Faith, Hope and Charity" deals with the death, through his own carelessness, of an Irish laborer in London and his home community's attempt to help his family pay the cost of his funeral. In "The Stoat" a young man cynically observes his widowed father's attempts to find a wife, the most promising of which ends when the lady has a mild heart attack and the father takes flight in fear. "Doorways" is another of McGahern's reprises on the theme of a failed love affair. In "The Wine Breath" an elderly priest recalls moments of transcendence in his life but is rooted in a lonely present. His mother has died and he himself is moving toward death. "Along the Edges" details the death of one love affair but, unusually for this collection, shows the start of a new one (although its ultimate development is far from clear). In "Gold Watch," too, the protagonist meets a woman he loves and with whom he hopes to have a future, but his relationship with his father is marked by unrelenting antagonism and cruelty. The father deliberately destroys an expensive watch the protagonist has bought for him to replace the gold watch he (the father) received from his father and that he now reluctantly passes on to his son. "Swallows" is a study of disappointment. It starts with a young government surveyor and an older police sergeant documenting the scene of an accident in which a young man has died. The surveyor has chosen the security of a civil service job over a life in music. The sergeant, clearly an intelligent man of some potential, has wasted life and talents in his humdrum work and environment. The fiddle he played in his youth is long disused and his only companion is a deaf housekeeper. In "Sierra Leone," another love affair ends without a lasting relationship being established. The story ends, as "The Beginning of an Idea" began, with a funeral, in this case that of the narrator's step mother.

Timor mortis conturbat me (the fear of death disturbs me)—the medieval motto might serve as an epigraph to *Getting Through*. Literal deaths and deaths of the soul, deaths of the intelligence and the emotions, intimations of mortality, the withering of dreams and prospects pervade the stories. All one can do is get through. There is little hope—only perhaps in "Gold Watch" and, more ambiguously, in "Along the Edges."

Writing and Reception

McGahern wrote the stories in *Getting Through* in the 1970s.[2] The U.S. edition, which was published in 1980, contains one more story—"Gold Watch"—than the 1978 British one. As can be seen from the discussion above, however, this addition in no way disrupts the overall tenor of the volume. As with *Nightlines, Getting Through* has always had the respect of critics and academics. Although Irwin in the *Times Literary Supplement* calls the collection "depressing work," he also writes of "these graceful, melancholy tales," of McGahern's "unobtrusive concision" and "economy," and calls the text "this accomplished collection." Tom Paulin in *Encounter* praises *Getting Through* as a "new and very distinguished collection of stories," calling it "a fine and interesting development from *Nightlines*," although he, too, has reservations, in his case concerning the short stories' being "too distanced from the contingencies of social reality" (he means by this that they are too focused on general existential issues). A discussion of *Getting Through* is an important part of Shaun O'Connell's early appreciation of McGahern's work in 1984, and individual stories have elicited subtle (and sometimes ambitious) analyses from Denis Sampson, Wolfgang Schmitz, Claude Maisonnat, and Antoinette Quinn.[3] If the stories in *Nightlines* are compared to those of Joyce, *Getting Through* is usually discussed as echoing Anton Chekhov's short fiction. Clearly McGahern's work is seen as part of the central European tradition of the short story.[4]

Narration, Language, Ordering, and Setting

As in *Nightlines,* the stories in *Getting Through* focus on single individuals and their experiences. Narration varies from third person with a predominant character point of view (as in "The Beginning of an Idea," "A Slip-Up," and "The Wine Breath") to first-person narrations (as in "Along the Edges" or "Sierra Leone"). Once again, as in *Nightlines,* these narrators and protagonists are deeply alienated from, or at least at odds with, the world and people around them. Eva is a blond female stranger in Francoist Spain ("The Beginning of an Idea"); Michael is an Irish farmer standing outside a London supermarket, an economic exile from a poor country ("A Slip-Up"); the young student in "The Stoat" is disdainful of his father's folly, and the father himself has little time for all the women who propose marriage to him; the narrator in "Doorways" identifies himself with the Beckettian tramps he can see from his flat; the sergeant in "Swallows" hates those he must socialize with and is driven to fury by his deaf and eccentric housekeeper; and the narrator in "Sierra Leone" seems isolated from the city in which he lives and from his family in the country. Even Sharkey, the hat-wearing schoolteacher at the center of "All Sorts of Impossible Things" and "Faith, Hope and Charity," has never married and sets himself off from social norms by the hat he never removes from his head. The priest in "The Wine Breath" continually slips out of the present into moments from the past. In "Along the Edges" and "Gold Watch," alienation is overcome but only partially. The social world has a positive role only in "Faith, Hope and Charity," in which the rural community does try to assist Cunningham's family after his death (although one wonders if this motif is strong enough to outweigh the destructive folly associated with the laborer's death and the self-interest of the young people who use the dance as an opportunity to pursue their own lusts). Isolation is general in these texts, and although there are no children in *Getting Through* (unlike in *Nightlines*), the age range of narrators and protagonists is considerable, reinforcing the implication of almost universal disaffection.

Linguistically some of McGahern's narrators in *Getting Through* show some difference from those of *Nightlines.* Some features remain from the earlier volume: an occasional loose and informal syntax (for example in "The Stoat")[5] and a piling up of adverbial phrases in psychologically important moments (for example, in "A Slip-Up" [29], "Gold Watch" [123], and "Swallows" [143, 151–52]). What is linguistically distinctive in *Getting Through* is some narrators' use of a formal and sophisticated lexis. For example, in "Doorways" the narrator's vocabulary is rather elevated at times.

> There are times when we see the small events we look forward to—a visit, a wedding, a new day—as having no existence but in the expectation. They are to be, they will happen, and before they do they almost are not: minute replicas of the expectation that we call the rest of our life. (71)

Here the phrases "as having no existence but in the expectation," "they almost are not" (in an existential sense), and "minute replicas of the expectation" give the story a much more linguistically sophisticated flavor than stories in *Nightlines* have. One can note something similar in the latter stages of "Along the Edges" ("She was not garlanded by farms or orchards . . ." [121–22]). This linguistic movement upward in style (which also occurs in "The Wine Breath," for example), with its increase in abstraction and intellectual dignity, both reflects the universality of McGahern's scope in *Getting Through* and also embodies it. All styles, informal and formal, are appropriate to the collection's concerns.

As in *Nightlines,* the arrangement of stories in *Getting Through* is also part of the text's vision. The U.S. and British editions have the same order, apart from the insertion of "Gold Watch" between "Along the Edges" and "Swallows" in the former. The overarching movement from coffin to coffin, from "The Beginning of an Idea" to "Sierra Leone," has already been noted. These stories can be further paired by the foreign settings in both. In "The Beginning of an Idea" the protagonist goes to Spain to resolve problems in her life (and fails to do so). In "Sierra Leone," the narrator's lover is about to depart for that African country to join another lover, also in an attempt to resolve a difficult situation. The pairing with "The Beginning of an Idea" suggests that little will come of this departure.

Further groupings of stories in the collection are suggestive. Some stories are set in urban environments: "The Beginning of an Idea," "A Slip-Up," parts of "Doorways," "Along the Edges," parts of "Gold Watch," and most of "Sierra Leone." Some are set almost exclusively in the country: "All Sorts of Impossible Things," "Faith, Hope and Charity," "The Stoat," "The Wine Breath," and "Swallows." But even some of these have urban settings intermixed with the rural (such as "Faith, Hope and Charity"), just as urban stories have rural elements

71

in them too (such as "Gold Watch"). This mingling and juxtaposition of settings suggests a generality to the vision of life in the collection. Hope withers equally in Spain, Sierra Leone, Dublin, London, Strandhill, and the country.

Stories can also be grouped according to their orientation toward past or future. Some stories remain firmly rooted in the past: "A Slip-Up," "All Sorts of Impossible Things," "Doorways," "The Wine Breath," "Gold Watch," and "Swallows." Characters look back at lost places, people and past events, or, as in "Doorways," there seems no way out of the stasis of a present that has emerged out of past events. Even when a character looks forward to future events, as in "Swallows," the sergeant does so with despair and with a sense that the evening's socializing will just be a repetition of previous banalities. Where there is some orientation toward the future, texts are inconclusive or ambiguous. What will Eva do at the end of "The Beginning of an Idea?" Where will she go? Are the young lovers at the end of "Faith, Hope and Charity" only going to breed another generation of Cunninghams? What will become of poor Miss McCabe, or, indeed, the narrator's father, rabbits, as they are, pursued by the stoat of death? Will the second romance bring happiness in "Along the Edges?" Where does the narrator go from here at the conclusion of "Sierra Leone"? Only at the end of "Gold Watch," and then only for the narrator and his love, does the future hold promise.

The sequence of stories, too, is suggestive. The young exile with her writer's block in "The Beginning of an Idea" is echoed in the elderly Irish farmer in exile in London and lost, too, in an obsessive dream ("A Slip-Up"). Tom Lennon's death in "All Sorts of Impossible Things" chimes dismally with that of the laborer Cunningham in "Faith, Hope and Charity." The middle-aged father's pursuit of a wife in "The Stoat" parallels the younger narrator/protagonist's unsuccessful pursuit of his American friend in "Doorways." Both end in rather tawdry and ludicrous partings. The picture of isolation and doubt in "The Wine Breath" is not immediately paired with another story but rather echoes that in "Swallows" two stories later, in which a younger and a middle-aged protagonist weigh up their choices and failures. These two stories envelope the only two substantially hopeful texts in the volume, "Along the Edges" (which is only hopeful because of the order in which its two parts are recounted) and "Gold Watch." Such an ordering undermines any escape from desolation that the middle stories contain, and the volume finishes with the dismal resolution of "Sierra Leone" (lovers parted, stepmother dead, father and son unwilling to discuss past or future). Once again, the volume's organization suggests universality. The young, the old, the middle aged, Scandinavian and

Irish, educated and uneducated, urban sophisticate and country priest, teacher and policeman, all face unhappiness, disappointment, and death.

Transcendence?

In this almost unremittingly unhappy world in *Getting Through,* McGahern does offer moments of transcendence, although some of these are sad in themselves. Eva's obsessive interest in Chekhov's funeral and her desire to write about it give her something beyond the everyday ("The Beginning of an Idea"), just as Michael is temporarily happy working his farm in his imagination ("A Slip-Up"). The sight of Tom Lennon preparing himself for his exam the next day moves Sharkey deeply—"he felt for the first time ever a mad desire to remove his hat and stand bareheaded in the room, as if for the first time in years he felt himself in the presence of something sacred" (46). The priest in "The Wine Breath" passes occasionally beyond the mundane present to moments of transfigured beauty in the past (100, 105), moments that the lovers draw near to at the end of the "Morning" section in "Along the Edges" (121–22). The narrator/protagonist in "Gold Watch" has his grandfather's and father's gold watch and, repaired, it is a thing of beauty, emerging from the petty bitterness and unhappiness of his family life. He also has a good relationship with his wife; perhaps he has been able to "outstare the one eye of nature" (125) and achieve something beyond the mundane misery of others (although the story ends not with the restored watch but with the petulant and gratuitous destruction of a new one by the protagonist's father). The protagonists of "Swallows" and "Sierra Leone," however, certainly do not achieve much, but at least there are dreams or moments of transcendence: memories of Avignon (143), the example of the great musician Paganini ("Swallows," 147, 153), and the transient, heightened awareness of life in the shadow of the Cuban missile crisis of 1962 ("Sierra Leone").

It is not much, but it is something. However, the motif of simply getting through, making do with what disappointments and cruelties one encounters, predominates in the collection. Eva keeps on traveling at the end of "The Beginning of an Idea;" Sharkey behaves as best he can although he knows dreams are for impossible things; Tom Lennon keeps going in the face of his own physical weakness ("All Sorts of Impossible Things"); and the surveyor and the sergeant at least know themselves as they continue their half lives ("Swallows"). In "Doorways," most striking of all, the two homeless men, Barnaby and Bartleby, survive and live somehow in a world of failure and emotional impoverishment.[6] They are emblematic of an unillusioned stoicism that several stories recommend.

"The Wine Breath"

This story is one of the strongest expressions of the vision that permeates *Getting Through*. The title has an ambiguity typical of the stories in this collection. The only reference to wine in the story comes at its end, as the priest remembers or imagines a young man, "not unlike he had been once" (108), waiting outside a girl's door with a bottle of wine. In the story the wine is never drunk; therefore how can it be on anyone's breath?[7] The organization of the story material is striking and, ultimately, suggests an answer.

"The Wine Breath" starts in the evening in autumn (it is October), as the nameless priest goes to visit a parishioner to inform him that a place has been found in the hospital for his wife to have her piles treated. The dying year and the mundane and unglamorous purpose of the priest's visit are suddenly transfigured when the sight of chips of beech wood flying from the chain saw that the parishioner is using transports the priest back to another day "nearly thirty years before" (97). He travels back in his mind and, indeed, almost entirely to a day in February 1947, a day of deep snow in which a farmer called Michael Bruen was buried. From the first page of the story, the priest constantly shifts back in time, staying in the present only briefly. After his memory (which is more than that and is much more like a physical return to the past) of the funeral in the snow (97–99), the priest returns to the present, only to revert to a past day with his mother that the smell of crushed mint has brought back (99). On going back to the presbytery in the darkness, the priest recalls a visit to Bruen's farm when he was young (100–102), and then, once more, the time of his death and funeral (102). The priest then imagines himself as a doddering old man being both helped and mocked by young boys (102–3). He recalls his childhood, his choice of the priesthood, and, above all, his mother, her role in his life, her illness, and her death (103–5). After a brief return to the present, he passes again into the past, to his mother's life in the priest's house, to the legend associated with it, and then to a conversation he had with a friend of his who has become a bishop (105–7). The final two paragraphs of the story gather memories connected with Bruen's funeral and the snow that surrounded it, and then, finally, present the image of the young man waiting with his bottle of wine outside a girl's door.[8]

As one can see, the story barely stays in the present at all but constantly shifts back to other times and places. The present is mundane, a matter of "dead days" (99, 102). What is alive for the priest is the past: the light of Bruen's funeral, the vitality and warmth of the man himself and his home (with his pretty daughters), his mother's care for him (and her illness and death), and a dispute in which he argues for the beauty of the commonplace. In this respect, the concluding paragraph in which the young man waits with his wine is either an actual memory or an imagined possibility, in either case a richer moment than any the drab present can afford. The priest's memories, the moments when he seems to fall through time, are the wine breath, more intense than anything in the present and, thus, carrying all the transfigured and transfiguring associations of the wine in the Eucharist. He sees them as "the Mystery" (98), as "all timeless," seeming "at least a promise of the eternal" (105).

Narration in "The Wine Breath" is typical of the stories in *Getting Through* and quite typically subtle. McGahern employs a third-person narrator, but the point of view is entirely that of the priest, and his subjective experiences form the central concern of the text. Yet at times the narrator comes close to the priest's own voice. For example, on page 99 the narrator remarks, "The most difficult things seem always to lie closest to us, to lie always around our feet." These could easily be the priest's own words. Another example occurs on the next page: "Always when about to give birth or die cattle sought out a clean place in some corner of the field, away from the herd" (100). Here free indirect speech brings the reader close to the priest. Language, too, is typical of the collection, moving from a neutral and even informal style to a more sophisticated one, for example in the priest's reflections on aging (102–3). As in other stories, shifts in language move the story between the quotidian and the universal.

The motifs, too, in *Getting Through* are given memorable embodiment in "The Wine Breath." The power of memory and of the past (so marked in other stories such as "A Slip-Up" or "Swallows"), the drab mundane of the present (echoed in "The Stoat" and "Doorways"), the power of death over the good and the vital ("All Sorts of Impossible Things")—all these motifs are strongly realized in "The Wine Breath." This story also provides, particularly clearly, a sense of the transcendent moments that can illuminate the humdrum and the dead days that must be got through, although here, too, it is the ultimate failure of hope, the disappointment of life that is emphasized in the conclusion. The young man never stood on the doorstep with the bottle of wine and never went in to the woman inside to enjoy "a pleasant and uncomplicated evening, feeling himself immersed in time without end" (108). And now he is a ghost, one of those dead before his time (107).

CHAPTER 7

The City (II)

The Pornographer (1979)

Reception

The Pornographer has never been popular with critics. Gerd Kampen argues that it has largely met with incomprehension, and Denis Sampson states baldly that reviewers "were almost unanimously puzzled." Tom Paulin, writing in *Encounter,* declares that the novel shows evidence of "a fundamental sense of failure within his [McGahern's] own imagination." Jürgen Kamm, too, sees the text in negative terms: he argues that there is a lack of tension in it and that there is no connection between the novel's separate parts. In the *New York Times Book Review,* Alice Adams sees it as a waste of McGahern's abilities: "one is inclined . . . to wish that the highly talented Mr. McGahern had chosen to write about a more interesting and appealing subject," she opines. But *The Pornographer* has its advocates. In the *Times Literary Supplement,* Patricia Craig, after expressing reservations about the parts of the novel set in London, concludes: "But this is the only notable weakness in a novel that succeeds beautifully in doing what it sets out to do: to record, and illuminate, varieties of disenchantment." Seamus Deane sees *The Pornographer* as a brave examination of "the forces which have been dominating his [McGahern's] work" to date, and he argues that in it the author "enriches without softening his vision of the lives of quiet desperation." Most notably, the eminent U.S. novelist John Updike wrote a positive review in the *New Yorker* in 1979. Although he calls *The Pornographer* "an old-fashioned novel," largely on the basis of McGahern's suggestion that adultery can produce guilt in those involved, he describes it as "this vivid and involving novel," praises the author as "a shrewd psychologist" and ends by insisting: "But let it be admitted—nay proclaimed—that by and large Mr. McGahern writes entrancingly, with a lively pace and constant melody."[1]

Story Material

The lurid title gives the profession of the novel's protagonist and narrator. A former teacher, he is now a writer living in Dublin sometime in the late 1960s or early 1970s who makes his living by writing pornography for a flamboyant magazine proprietor named Maloney. The narrator/protagonist is never named. The story material of the novel is relatively simple. It has two main strands that remain quite separate throughout the text, apart from the figure of the protagonist. The first concerns his affair with a slightly older woman named Josephine. He is recovering from a failed love affair and meets her in a dance hall. Although he does not love her and tells her so clearly, she professes to love him deeply and clearly wants a long-term relationship with him. At Josephine's insistence, they make love without using condoms. The narrator determines to end the affair after a brief boat trip on the Shannon River. He has started to detest his lover, a feeling that blossoms in the course of subsequent events, as Josephine becomes pregnant. After much consideration, the protagonist refuses to marry her. Josephine leaves for London, where she has the baby, convinced, despite his refusals, that her lover will relent and marry her. On a brief visit to London, the narrator is beaten up by an outraged, conservative Irishman with whose family Josephine now lodges. This cathartic moment makes the protagonist feel free, and he returns to Dublin.

Interwoven with this strand of action is material concerning the narrator's aunt and uncle. The novel, in fact, begins with the uncle's trip to Dublin to visit his sister who is seriously ill in the hospital. The narrator visits his aunt (who brought him up after his parents' death) frequently in the course of the novel, bringing her brandy and companionship. He also travels down to the country to visit her on two occasions. He greatly admires her and her brother. Both are shrewd businesspeople who live in a small rural town and are also clearly attached to the narrator. He also starts a relationship with one of the nurses attending his aunt. She is once called Nurse Brady but apart from that remains, like the narrator, his uncle, and his aunt, unnamed. The narrator falls in love with her. He is quite frank and tells her of his unhappy relationship with Josephine. She nonetheless enters into a sexual relationship with him, a relationship that the narrator clearly sees as having much more potential than his affair with Josephine. The health of the narrator's aunt declines radically, and she dies immediately after he returns from London. Despite his disfigured face— for he has been badly beaten by Josephine's outraged protector—he attends her funeral, a funeral to which Maloney also, surprisingly, comes. His uncle makes it clear he thinks his nephew will come back to the country some day. Indeed the narrator starts to consider returning to his parents' farm and announces to Maloney at the novel's end that he intends to marry his dark-haired nurse and do so. The novel's ending is, however, open. It concludes with Maloney's derisive crowing sounds as they travel back to Dublin.

Narration and Narrative

The Pornographer has none of the complexities of narration and narrative organization present in *The Dark* and *The Leavetaking.* The narration is given in the first person by an ultimately reliable narrator. No other point of view is given in the text, but the reader has no reason substantially to distrust the narrator. He is not necessarily a morally upright figure by many standards, but he is an honest narrator, at times disturbingly so, particularly about himself. For example, after Josephine has told him about her being pregnant, his comments about himself are unsparing (102). He is, however, a figure with pronounced opinions of a general and particular nature, which he expresses frequently in the course of the text. For example, early in the novel he says of his and his uncle's visit to his aunt in the hospital, "Now that it was taking place it amounted to the nothing that was the rest of our life when it too was taking place."[2] Two pages later he notes of his uncle, "There are many who grow so swollen with the importance of their function that they can hardly stoop to do it, but there was no such danger with my uncle. In him all was one" (15). Shortly afterward he remarks of his own writing (and he repeats this later), "Nothing ever holds together unless it is mixed with some of one's own blood" (24). He immediately also expresses his view of the soul and its relation to the body (24). This habit of passing judgment and giving his reflections on life is apparent in the narrator's discourse throughout the text. His observations are almost always gloomy and express a deep existential pessimism. "What had I learned from that clandestine night?" he asks after Nurse Brady smuggles him into his aunt's ward at night. His answer is, "The nothing that we always learn when we sink to learn something of ourselves or life from a poor other—our own shameful shallowness" (203). However, not all is gloom. The narrator's reflections on love, for example, can suggest hope (219), and at times his observations are neither pessimistic nor optimistic, as, for example, those on destiny or age (32, 33). But generally his view of the world is somber, stressing the unhappiness of human life (53, 88) and the "darkness" and emptiness that surrounds it and that can only be kept temporarily at bay (238). There is no God, "no one to turn to," he stresses (62); prayers can not be answered (252). The best one can do is to endure and to get through life (97), an opinion that he also gives in direct speech to other characters (13, 67, 81). Life is a matter of "the womb and the grave. . . . The christening party becomes the funeral, the shudder that makes us flesh becomes the shudder that makes us meat" (30).[3]

However, the narrator does not always reveal his thoughts and feelings. At times he is reticent about these. For example, he simply notes that children throw stones at the car in which he and Josephine are driving (82). He also only hints at the depth of emotion he feels as his aunt speaks to him in the hospital (143–44). "I'd to turn away," he simply says at one point, merely implying his grief (223). In addition, it is noteworthy how much of the novel is given in direct speech, in dialogue that is without any extensive narrative input. This narrative technique is established early in the novel, for example during the uncle's visit to Dublin (16–19), and it recurs throughout the text. A great deal of the narrator's first evening with Josephine is given in dialogue (32–44), a pattern that is repeated elsewhere (for example, 52–59). The collapse of their affair, their unhappiness over Josephine's pregnancy, and their working out what to do—these are also presented predominantly through dialogue, with limited narrative intervention (for example, 114–21). The narrator's relationships with other characters are also frequently embodied in playlike dialogue. Good examples are his conversations with Maloney (for example, 122–29) and with his uncle when the narrator arrives for his aunt's funeral (231–37). Thus, although the narrator remains the narrator throughout the text and therefore filters all utterances, his subjectivity is partially balanced by dialogue, in which other characters become prominent and express their views of things.

On two occasions, the narrator provides the reader with extracts from the pornographic stories he writes (22–24, 153–61). These are relatively brief and are clearly contained within the narrator's discourse. They resemble the extracts from letters or from diaries that have been part of the narrative repertoire of the English-language novel for nearly three centuries. Their main interest lies in what they reveal about the narrator's state of mind and how he transforms his experience into something different. They are also part of the novel's scrutiny of what pornography is. However, they do not disrupt the narrator's discourse in any substantial way. The only way in which they might be so interpreted is if they are considered as showing that all narratives are false and contaminated, inasmuch as the narrator's second pornographic tale of the trip on the Shannon is clearly a distortion of what actually occurred in the world of the novel. However, there is little else in the text to suggest this. Certainly the narrator makes it clear that he sees the world in a specific way and that Josephine, for example, sees it differently, as do, in a different fashion, his uncle and aunt. But there is nothing in the novel to suggest that the narrator is wrong in his sense of things or is in any way misleading the readers about what takes place. Quite the reverse—the novel as a whole endorses his vision throughout. No other version of things is set up to contradict it.

The story material of *The Pornographer* is presented in a logical, chronological fashion. It is chapterless but divided into shorter or longer sections set off from each other by spacing. There are a few retrospects (for example, on page 21, on pages 25–28, and on pages 39–41), but these are clearly marked and limited in number. The sections largely present one completed episode, although this is not always the case, and some have several strands of action (for example, 60–68 and 215–44). The sections largely keep different areas of the narrator's life apart—his relationship with his aunt and uncle, his affair with Josephine, his relations with Maloney, and his attachment to Nurse Brady. The novel also interweaves them, although not in any mechanical way. The separate sections allow for clear differentiations within the text—between the country and the city, above all, and between two ways of life, the anonymous metropolis of transient relationships and the closeness and relative stability of human contacts in the small town. They also allow for a clear distinction between Josephine and the narrator's dark-haired nurse. Yet the largely discrete sections also permit comparison between different areas of the narrator's world. The rural world is not all warmth and charm. The city is not all cold anonymity. The narrator's aunt has made an unfortunate marriage to the self-indulgent and unreliable Cyril. His uncle is calculating about where to live when his sister dies. Cyril is sentimental, hypocritical, and self-promoting, all at once, in his choice of gravestone for his dead wife. In the city the narrator is able to find help and support from his doctor friend. Maloney, the arch representative of urban life, is morally perceptive and unsparing in his judgment of the narrator. One does want to ask, too, in what way Nurse Brady is so different from Josephine, apart from being younger and lacking in Josephine's annoying verbal quirks.

Setting

Setting in *The Pornographer* is clearly divided into the urban and the rural. The novel starts with the narrator's uncle's visit to Dublin and his out-of-placeness in the city (9–19). The novel's different sections keep the two settings largely apart. There is the small rural town with its small businesses and farms, on one hand, and the Irish capital with bars, dance halls, and bedsit flats, on the other. Beyond Dublin there is London, the metropolis, where one can escape one's family and friends, as Josephine does, and be almost wholly isolated apart from chance acquaintances. The novel's shifting between the urban and the rural is part of its vision of the world. That is how the world is constructed. But the movement to and fro also suggests the narrator's indecision, his lack of firm grounding in one or the other. A man of the city, he still maintains intense emotional ties to a rural world.

Characters clearly distinguish between these two settings. The narrator recalls Mass in his rural home and contrasts it with his present empty life (21). His aunt says she prefers vegetables to the flowers city people give (61), while the narrator himself loves the anonymity of city crowds (62). Cyril nastily refers to him on one occasion as "our friend from the city" (92). His aunt wants him to come "home" (120), and the narrator clearly sees the small rural town as a distinct place (141–42)—although it should be noted that he does not necessarily love what he observes about it. His uncle, too, wants him to return to his own house (221), suggesting that he should by now have had enough of rootless city life. It is noteworthy that the hospital where the narrator's aunt is treated stands outside the city (45), and when the narrator visits it with Nurse Brady, he is struck by the "old sweet scent" of hay that recalls the country (172–73, 176). This is an element in his increasing infatuation with the nurse.

As was suggested above, the country and the city are not as clearly differentiated morally as they are in terms of space. However, the country is associated with the narrator's aunt and uncle, figures who, despite their flaws, embody real strengths and intelligence. Indeed, at the novel's end the narrator is on the brink of asking his dark-haired nurse to marry him and to come back to the country with him (250). It must be stressed that this is not atavism or the abandonment of the modern world—only a contemplated abandonment of the city. The country maintains old ways, certainly, as is evident during the aunt's funeral, but the town has changed with the times (141), the aunt and uncle are successful businesspeople, and the local farms seem perfectly viable economically (233–34). It must be noted, nonetheless, that this intention provokes Maloney's derision (250–52). The novel looks at the two spheres of its setting in a complex manner and avoids any easy or sentimental response to them.

Both geographic settings are rendered with a considerable amount of detail. The reader knows the names of the pubs where the narrator and Josephine meet up. The dance hall, the hospital, the city park, and the narrator's apartment are all presented in concrete particularities, as are London bars, streets, and squares. The small country town's appearance and that of the uncle's sawmill and his new house are also all described fully. But these are generic places. London is named, but, in fact, Dublin never is (although the city can only be Dublin). Nor does the reader know exactly where the narrator's aunt and uncle live. The novel suggests a generality of perspective here. The action takes place in Ireland but perhaps could run a similar course elsewhere in the world.

Time setting is also both precise and vague (and ultimately generic) in *The Pornographer*. It is vague in terms of its historical setting. There is a reference to the "Troubles" (54), which indicates that the action takes place after 1968, but this is the only such marker. It is part of the generalizing strategy of the novel. The text is set mostly in Ireland in the late twentieth century, but the lack of clear dating suggests that its action could take place in other times and, perhaps, in other places, too. The novel is precise, however, in terms of seasonal setting. It begins in spring (60, 62, 81, 100, 105) and then moves through "early summer" (119, 136) to summer (195) and then to the end of summer (215). The narrator starts his relationship with Nurse Brady at harvest time (172–73, 176). Josephine and the narrator's baby is born just after Christmas (224), and the narrator travels to London, rejects Josephine finally, and is beaten up a few days later (225). His aunt dies and is buried at the beginning of a new year, in seasonably rainy weather (233, 241, 251). In this organization of time, the novel follows a traditional literary pattern (and one that McGahern uses in modified fashion *The Barracks*), moving from the beginning of one year to the start of another. Again there is a suggestion of time-lessness and the generic in this. The narrator's, Josephine's, the nurse's, and the aunt's experiences are all linked to the passage of the seasons. It has happened once; it can happen again. The passage of time brings disaster and death but also renewal.

A Psychological Novel

In terms of genre, *The Pornographer* can be most readily understood as a psychological novel. There are echoes of other genres in the text. It can also be read as a piece of social satire, above all in its cruel mockery of Josephine, the respectable Irish lady moving toward old-maidenhood whose mental world is bedeviled by verbal quirks and platitudes. One can also treat *The Pornographer* as a kind of moral tale, one in which the narrator/protagonist, after causing much suffering, realizes the wrong he has done and how to amend his ways. But these are genre echoes only, and the novel is a study, above all, of the narrator, his emotions, his impulses, and his attitude toward life. It is also, to a lesser degree, a study of the five characters who play major roles in his life: his aunt, his uncle, Josephine, Maloney, and Nurse Brady. These are all (except Nurse Brady) more or less complex figures in their own right, although they are seen entirely from the narrator's point of view. To a large extent, *The Pornographer* is a study of the interaction of these characters and what emerges from that interaction.

Nurse Brady is the least substantial of all. She is first seen by the narrator as a symbol of life in the midst of her dying patients (49). She is provided with a perfunctory background (one should note that it is rural, like the narrator's and, indeed, Josephine's [91, 95–96, 170]), but her appeal for the narrator is that she is young, strong, vital, decisive, and lacking in hypocrisy (171, 176, 209). The only moments when she is allowed to be more than that are when she brings the narrator by night into his aunt's ward and is thus seen as somehow an initiator into mysteries of life and death (175–76) and, later, when she acutely analyzes Maloney's character (219).

Maloney is a much more substantial and complex figure. He is a successful businessman (28–29), a disappointed poet (25–28), a bohemian (76), a cynic (124), and a man who sees what he is doing as liberating his country's culture—although there is a degree of irony in what he says about this (25). He can be astute about the narrator's character ("exile" is the mark of his life and writing, he declares [125]), has a wildly grotesque imagination (for example, his ambition to wheel a baby carriage/coffin through a Paris park [126–27]), and is utterly unsparing in his judgment of the narrator's conduct (133, 151, 163, 205). Toward the end of the novel, he refuses to spare the narrator his criticism (244, 250). "And don't think you've been washed clean by the beating. Don't imagine you've been washed in the blood of the lamb by any of those cathartic theories. Don't try to slip out in any of those ways," he insists (243). It is also striking that he turns up for the funeral of the narrator's aunt, an urban bohemian paying his respects to a quite different character with a different way of life (230–31, 240). He is aware, as is the narrator, that his flamboyant cynicism is a role that he works at (134), but his cruel mockery of the narrator at the novel's end provides an astringent balance to the happy ending that the pornographer aspires to (250–52). Despite his unsavory profession, he is a figure whom the narrator likes and one whom the reader is invited to respect.

The narrator's aunt and uncle are centrally important figures in the text, despite the fact that they take up a much smaller part of it than do Josephine and the narrator himself. The aunt is important for four reasons in the text. Her illness and death frame the whole novel and provide a counter balance to the narrator's sex life and hope for happiness at the end. Her ultimately unsuccessful struggle with disease embodies the narrator's view of the best that one can do in life (it is a matter of getting through and enduring). The narrator's devotion to her adds an extra dimension to his otherwise often chilly persona. Finally, the ways in which her life is not so different from that in the city make the novel's view of the contrast between country and city more complex. Above all, however, it is what she means to the narrator that is most important in her character.

The narrator's visits to his aunt in the hospital are interlaced with the other strands of the novel's story material. They constantly recall the ultimate end of all things, illness, pain, and death. This is particularly apparent during the episode where Nurse Brady takes the narrator to his aunt's ward at night. Placed between a moment of lovemaking and one of liberating fun in a hayfield, the encounter with the sleeping women in the dark ward becomes a memento mori (173–76). The narrator greatly respects his aunt's courage and strength in combating her disease. "She was tough," he notes, "There was nothing but to salute that proud hardness with a perfect silence" (144). She has "this fierce will to live," he tells his nurse (215). The aunt, however, eventually acknowledges defeat (223), but even at this point she has the narrator's complete respect. "Her coldness shook me," he says, "her perfect mastery" (224). When she does die, he celebrates her independence, her lack of illusion, her kindliness, her anger, and simply her life. It is at this moment that the narrator finally breaks down in grief for his relative (230). However, the aunt is a more complex figure than is suggested by the above. She is a shrewd businesswoman (120) and someone who has made an unfortunate, and late, marriage to the ne'er-do-well Cyril. In the end, she leaves him all her money but on condition that he never see her again (235). Life in the country is not idealized. Here, too, there are unhappy and mistaken relationships. Indeed, the aunt is twice compared to Josephine, once when she waves from her brother's car (76; cf. 44) and once when the narrator aligns his visits to her with those he has with Josephine (135).

The narrator's uncle plays a similar role in the novel to that of his sister. Like her, he is a resilient figure and someone the narrator admires. His appearance and behavior both contrast with and parallel life in the city. The novel begins with his arrival in Dublin, "childishly looking around" on the station platform (9), seemingly out of place in the large city. But he is not really so, for, although he does not like the place, he takes the narrator to the warehouse where he wants to go and is quite able to deal with the personnel there (15–16). Indeed, the narrator makes it clear that his uncle's business (he owns a sawmill) is successful and that he has plenty of money (19, 236–37). The narrator describes him as "small and indestructible" (19), and he embodies a "rude health" that contrasts with his sister's illness (13) and a dynamic self-confidence that contrasts with the narrator's drifting (222). He is also seen quite complexly. He is moved by his sister's illness (14), but in the final stages of that illness and at her death he is filled with self-importance and self-pity (220, 231). In addition, he is a shrewd and calculating figure. He looks after his nephew's farmhouse in order, according to the narrator, to have a place to go if he has to leave his sister's (95). When he finally breaks with Cyril, he is able to buy another home and move in with relative ease (233–34). He starts work again the day after his sister's funeral (236–37). The aunt sharply compares uncle and nephew (and thus rural and urban, sawyer and pornographer). "If you were to strip off those city manners you'd find that both of you are the exact same breed. What passes for quiet is stubbornness and you're both thick as ditches" (73).

Josephine is dealt with in much greater detail than any of the other central characters, except the narrator himself. However, it must be noted that she is only seen from the narrator's point of view and, like the other characters, has no independent existence in the text. Nonetheless, the narrator does present her in a complex, if largely negative, manner. Eight years older than the narrator, she has led a relatively blameless and conservative life until she meets him (33, 39, 79). However, she decides to have sex with the narrator and enters into an affair with him (38). The narrator detects an element of calculation in her actions (52–53). She claims to love him although he is frank about the fact that he does not love her, and she seems to be maneuvering him toward marriage (56, 67, 70). It is she who insists that they make love without condoms (56). It is interesting to note that she has a more reductive view of sex than the narrator. "O boy," she says after making love the first time with the narrator, "That is what I seem to have been needing for ages" (57). Is it her voice that calls out, "This is what I needed. This-is-what-I-need-ed" (39)? When she finds she is pregnant, she immediately starts to plan her wedding (99). The narrator begins to detest her (for example, 53, 135, 211) but, even so, acknowledges an attractive side to her character when he sees her working (88). In addition, she shows a degree of resilience in going off to London on her own, although it appears that she always retains hopes of winning the narrator (134, 225–26). When he visits her in London, she has undergone considerable change: her self-confidence is gone, and she is desperate and jealous (180, 187–89, 193). However, she remains certain to her last appearance in the text that "angels" are looking after her and her child (216–17).

Josephine's language is marked by certain repeated phrases. She keeps saying "O boy" (for example, 40, 52) and, after making love, insists that she does not "feel guilty at all or anything" (42, 43, 52, 57, 79). Throughout the novel, when she is vexed by the narrator's obduracy or coldness, she intones "O boy, o boy, I sure picked a winner" (101; see also 97, 116, 136). She also insists that all will turn out well for her and her lover "because both of us are good people" (106, 118, 124, 148, 183, 216). These verbal quirks and other platitudes (122, 216) irritate the narrator deeply. "If she said O boy once more," he thinks, "I wasn't sure I'd be able to hold myself in check" (101). The novel also implies that she is a fantasist and a liar. Her story about the wealthy English publisher who looks after her when she first goes to London (129–30, 130–32, 147–49, 150–51, 164–65) is described by critics as "unconvincing" and "novelletish."[4] Although the narrator seems not to see this, because he is desperate to believe that he is free of his responsibilities toward Josephine, there are hints in the text that she is lying and that there is a different version of events (181–82). Maloney is certainly a little skeptical (151–52).

Josephine is a complex figure. However, it has to be noted that she is a largely negative one and that she is presented entirely from the narrator's perspective. Indeed, she seems at times to conform to a traditional male stereotype of the conniving, entrapping female who uses sex and a pregnancy to beguile a man into a respectable and boring marriage. The portrait of Josephine in *The Pornographer* could not be further from the highly complex and sympathetic portrayal of a female character that McGahern draws in Elizabeth Reegan in *The Barracks*.

The center of the psychological element in *The Pornographer* is the nameless narrator himself. It can be argued that all the other principal characters are only seen in a fragmentary and limited way by the narrator and thus reveal the narrator's character rather than having any independent existence. This is, however, only partly true. The aunt, uncle, Maloney, and Josephine are complex enough to seem at least somewhat independent of the narrator's subjectivity. Not only that, but it must be stressed that McGahern nowhere suggests that his narrator is unreliable. If Josephine is seen negatively in the text, that is because—the novel as a whole indicates—she deserves to be. However, the real psychological richness and complexity of the novel lies in the narrator's self-portrait and confession.

There is a temptation to discuss the narrator in terms of development, almost of an *éducation sentimentale*. It is striking, however, how static and consistent he is, although he does undeniably change slightly in the course of the novel. The major features of his character are laid down at the start of the text and are much the same at the end. He is conscious that he is living in the aftermath of an unhappy love affair in which he has been rejected (17, 80). This has led, it appears, to an emotional deadness in him. He calls himself "dead of heart" (13) and expresses boredom on two occasions (20, 136). The second time is a response to the staleness of his affair with Josephine, but ennui was there earlier in his makeup, too. When Josephine agrees to have sex with him, he feels "only an odd sadness" (38). Josephine's intense emotions at the start of their affair alienate him (52). The world is a "farce" for him (66); he begins to feel no more than "perfunctory desire" for Josephine (123); and life seems "horrible," empty, pointless (190). This void is powerfully captured in the time-killing desolation of his first visit to London (180–201). He is emotionally stirred by little: by his failed love in the past (103–4); by sexual desire, for sure (he has sex with Josephine in London even though he feels nothing but pity for her [188–89]); by affection for his uncle (19); by grief over his aunt's illness and death (62, 230); and by admiration at her courage and self-control (224). But little else seems to touch him. Josephine is convinced that his profession as pornographer has made him "twisted and awkward," with a diseased and false view of life (64, 81, 96, 136). She also loathes what she calls his having "it all worked out" (96), by which she means his emotional reserve toward her.

His character is further marked by a lack of belief in any God. He makes this clear from the beginning to the end of the novel. When he prays that his uncle live forever, he says "the prayer with a force all the greater because I knew it could not be answered" (19). "There was the need, to, to give thanks and praise," he reflects, "and no one to turn to" (62). "The womb and the grave. . . . The christening party becomes the funeral, the shudder that makes us flesh becomes the shudder that makes us meat," he observes (30). His prayers at the novel's end—"for myself, Maloney, my uncle, the girl, the whole shoot" (but not specifically for Josephine, one should note)—must be made but "cannot be answered" (252). He also has little time for most fellow human beings. As he sits in the dance hall and looks out on O'Connell Street below him, the passers by seem "comic" to him (31). He likes the anonymity of his city block of flats (59, 139) and wandering the crowded city streets, unconnected to those around him (62). He loathes and fears the life of suburban respectability that many lead (103), although he rather admires it when he visits his successful doctor friend (111). The narrator's contempt for other people is apparent when he meets Josephine's protector, Kavanagh, in London (226). Once Josephine leaves for London, he feels a release into freedom (139–40). He reveals at one point that he has had a horror of being the center of Josephine's affections and, indeed, the center of anyone's (201).

But there are other aspects of the narrator's character besides those of an emotionally dead atheist who has little time for other human beings. His love of and admiration for his aunt and uncle are prominent. It is notable that he will not sell his family farm (17), and he pronounces himself "happy" when he stays with aunt and uncle for five days (147). He falls deeply in love with the young nurse and treats her in a different way from how he treats Josephine. He becomes fascinated by her ("I had so fallen under the influence of her charm") and takes her with him to see Maloney, his friend and mentor (213, 214, 218).

Even if he suggests that this relationship is somehow a lesser love than the one he felt for his unnamed lost love, it is still a strong emotion in him (219).

The narrator is also an extremely honest figure, almost disturbingly so. He is frank about his feelings for Josephine from the start, both to himself (she is "a wonderfully healthy animal" [34], and what he craves is her "flesh" [36]), and to her (he never tells her he loves her, quite the reverse [42, 56, 67, 112]). He is conscious of the implications of his own words and deeds. When he speaks to Josephine, he accuses himself of sounding "like an advertisement" (39). When he visits his doctor friend and his wife, he knows he is looking for "allies" to give him support and the advice he wants to hear (105, 114). He is clear about his own responsibility for the shabby turn that his affair with Josephine takes (70). He notes that when a friend tells him he should not marry her, he is so happy that he is "careless that my rich prize was won from her [Josephine's] ruin" (108). Maloney's criticism can still disturb him (205), but he says that any good behavior he engaged in during his affair was the result of "cowardice" (218).

The narrator does alter to some extent in the course of the novel. His feelings toward Josephine are not simple and do develop. He can feel disgust toward her (44), lust (77, 78), and indifference (227). He can find her attractive (88) and nearly changes his mind about not marrying her on two occasions (115–16, 198). But mostly he comes to feel a hatred for her (101, 102–3, 135, 180, 182, 185, 211). Toward the novel's end, the narrator experiences three moments of revelation and change. One is after he has been beaten up in London. He feels "happy . . . in an amazing clarity that was yet completely calm," separated from the rest of the world (229). Although he does not say that he feels liberated from Josephine and their dead relationship, she falls out of the novel at this point. Maloney, however, certainly indicates that the beating has solved nothing and absolved the narrator of nothing (243).

Maloney similarly calls into question the narrator's two other moments of revelation. One is his decision to ask his nurse to marry him and come to the country with him (250). Maloney's response is derision. The second moment occurs shortly afterward, when the narrator accuses himself of moral inattention. "I had not attended properly," he says to himself and thus caused pain to another. He had been without imagination and had not looked for "the true" but had drifted into a casual indifference that had led to suffering (251–52). It is notable that he says none of this to Maloney but merely makes a remark about watching the road. It is as if, however, Maloney has overheard his thoughts. He (Maloney) has been "watching the bloody road all his life, and it tells me nothing," he mocks. He has been paying attention and nothing much has come of it. Maloney's dark raillery closes the novel (252).

Certain elements in the narrator's character and behavior are motivated in the text. His emotional deadness can be seen to stem from his earlier failure in love. Josephine's platitudes and calculation would try the patience of a saint. However, some aspects of his character are obscure. Why is he a pornographer? His choice of profession is not clearly motivated. What role does his parents' death play in the formation of his character (68)? The reader encounters something similar with regard to the narrator's dead mother. Why did she cross out all those dates for seven years in the calendars the narrator finds after her death (200–201)? *The Pornographer* often leaves the reader with questions.

Nevertheless, *The Pornographer* is, in a large measure, a character study. The figure of the narrator/protagonist that emerges from the text is both static and complex—an emotionally cauterized unbeliever, hesitant of human attachment, who falls into a tawdry and disastrous affair with a woman he dislikes, but who also possesses a redeeming honesty and a deep attachment to four other characters (his aunt, his uncle, his young nurse, and Maloney). McGahern scrutinizes the possibilities in life for such a figure and suggests that something of lasting value may emerge even from such a sorry life. However, Maloney's mockery remains as a cautionary astringent to any sentimentality.

Pornography, Sex, and Death

Besides being a complex psychological portrait, *The Pornographer* focuses on three topics that emerge from the protagonist's life: the relationship between writing and life, the nature of sex and love, and the omnipresence of death and transience.

The narrator/protagonist of *The Pornographer* is a writer and a pornographer. One might, accordingly, expect a detailed consideration of the relationship of art to life, of the trials of being a writer, or of the role of pornography in a person's or a society's life. However, it is striking just how unimportant writing and, in the literal sense, pornography are in the novel. The narrator, in fact, spends little time writing. The reader only encounters extracts from two of his productions (22–24, 153–61), and the composition of several of them is passed over quickly (50, 60, 161–63, 201–4). Nothing that the narrator or, indeed, Maloney says about pornography is complex. The narrator is explicit in his contempt for what he is doing (21). "It's heartless and it's mindless and it's a lie," he tells his doctor friend (109). Maloney proclaims a liberating social function for pornography, but it is not clear with what degree of seriousness he does so (25). There are observations about art and life throughout the text: for example, the narrator's insistence that he must put something of himself, his own "blood," into his writing, even into such shoddy work (24, 50, 202). The reader can also observe the transformations of life into art in the narrator's pornographic version of his trip on the Shannon (83–91, 153–61). All this is fairly straightforward, however, if not to say crude. In addition, Maloney is recorded as making remarks about art in the narrator's retrospect about his friend's time as a small-town journalist (27). He makes further similar observations on the subject later in the novel to the narrator (163). These are generalities, however—true, but near platitudes—about the ordered nature of art as opposed to the contingent makeup of reality and about the vicarious thrill that readers get from the lives of imagined characters. A further section of the text that touches on the relation of life and fiction is that which presents Josephine's account of her friendship with the English publisher and what takes place between them in London (129–32, 147–51, 164–65). This reads much like a modern romance-based fantasy drawn from women's magazine fiction, an equivalent of the narrator's pornography. However, this aspect of Josephine's character is not developed, and the topic of the role of popular romance in human behavior is not explored.

In fact, neither art nor pornography (in the literal sense) is a major theme in the text. The narrator is a pornographer, but his work is marginal in his life. Almost any dull, repetitive, unsatisfying urban employment would have a similar function in the novel—to emphasize the narrator's emotional aridity and discontent with himself and life.[5]

It does not, in fact, seem different from Josephine's work in a bank ("this boring bank job" [54]). The motif of pornography, however, is vitally important in relation to another of the novel's concerns, that is the nature of love and its connection with sex. The novel is full of motifs that present sexual activity in a negative light. In the dance hall where the narrator meets Josephine (and, later, the dark-haired Nurse Brady), he perceives the atmosphere as being that of a hunt for prey (31). He talks of the light in the hall as "this cattle light" (32, 34). The couples dancing already seem to be linked in "coitus" (35). They are in pursuit of an anchorage "in the ideal greasy warm wetness of the human fork" (33). Later the narrator feels that sex with Josephine has been just "grappling" (44). He thinks of sex with her at times in crude physical terms: "bollock to bollock naked" (56) and "raw meat" (57). Sex is presented mechanically and crudely in the narrator's pornographic writing. The Shannon trip story is representative of this (159–61), and the narrator talks of "the shaft and clutch, the oiled walls opening to take the fat white spunk" of his Colonel and Mavis tales (202). Indeed, the narrator argues (against Josephine's insistence that his writing has harmed him) that its very crudity gives a perspective on life and suggests that sex is not everything and that "love or living" is more important (81).

Sex is certainly sometimes deeply disappointing for the narrator. There is an oscillation in his feelings between ecstasy and despair. For example, when he and Josephine make love for the first time, "there was this instant of rest, the glory and the awe, that one was as close as ever man could be to the presence of the mystery," a moment that almost immediately is corrupted by the body's "clamouring" and leaves the narrator wretched and separate from his lover (39). However, the narrator's language becomes impassioned, with biblical parallelisms and repetitions, when he evokes the glory of their next lovemaking (42). This has been preceded, however, by the ominous, "We played, cumbersomely" (41). The same pattern is followed on pages 56–57 but, this time, leaving a few pages later only "dank bodies" (59). The pattern of ecstasy and disappointment is echoed when the narrator and Josephine make love after a meal and "all the grossness of the food and wine seemed drained away" so that the narrator can achieve "a peace that was almost purity" (80). But as the novel progresses, sex between Josephine and the narrator becomes a matter of "perfunctory desire" (123) or even, later in London, drunkenness, pity, and desperation (189). Indeed, one of the most powerful and psychologically acute sections of the novel deals with the narrator's first visit to London (180–201). It is a memorable evocation of deep psychological distress, sexual disgust and debasement, ennui, antagonism, and time killing—a horror-filled emblem of an affair gone sour.

The narrator presents his sexual relations with Nurse Brady in a somewhat different way. The striking thing is that they are always seen as positive. But what is even more striking is his relative reticence about them. He barely goes into any details, whereas he is quite lavish in his descriptions of sex with Josephine. Indeed, sex with the young nurse is presented elliptically (173, 177, 215, 219).

What is McGahern doing here? There are several possibilities. First, there is a suggestion that no matter how rapturous sex is with someone, if that person annoys the living daylights out of you with her verbal quirks and platitudes and her rather reductive ("O boy, I needed that") view of sex, then there is no hope for the relationship. Nurse Brady is younger, more dynamic, more self-assured, more fun, and considerably less annoying than Josephine. There is still "glory" in sex with her (177), but she has other qualities that endure beyond coitus. As the narrator tells Josephine, "love or living" is perhaps more important than sex (81). Second, the text may here really be calling the narrator's moral character into question. How does Josephine differ so much from Nurse Brady, except in being older and in having evident marital designs on the narrator? Is he just an exploitative male who will inevitably go for the pretty young nurse, rather than the slightly older woman, after he has had his fun with her? Third, does the novel suggest that the narrator has matured or changed somehow and that a delicacy and reserve is necessary in his accounts of sex? Fourth, is this part of the novel a weak part, not fully worked out? Is there, finally, a kind of sentimentality in the narrator's, or the author's, view of the possibility of good sex combined with love? These questions are not easy to answer, and they are part of the unsettling quality of *The Pornographer.*[6]

The novel asks a direct question through the motif of pornography. The title of the text is always taken to refer to the narrator/protagonist. This is clearly so, but one can ask whether Josephine, too, in her way is a pornographer, a respectable woman who looks for sex to satisfy physical needs and who then is foolish or calculating enough to get pregnant in order to achieve the suburban idyll she has long desired. She is also prepared to try to manipulate her estranged lover into maintaining a relationship that has gone dead. Are her dreams of traditional, socially sanctioned, romantic love ultimately pornographic? Are she and her conservative London-Irish protector the real pornographers, purveyors of a debased and travestied view of human relations? Compared to Josephine, the narrator—the true professional pornographer—seems strangely honest and idealistic in his approach to sex and love.

Finally, one should notice that *The Pornographer,* like much of McGahern's fiction, is full of motifs of death and transience. The narrator's aunt's dying frames the novel and is interwoven throughout the text. The small town in which she has lived her life becomes a metaphor for change, despite the continuities that the narrator recognizes (141). He is well aware that his aunt's garden is the last she will see grow before her death (143). The novel ends with memento mori after memento mori: the aunt's funeral, with all its attendant ceremonies (232, 237–41), the coffins in the hardware and carpentry store (246), the names on the narrator's family gravestone that are being erased by the rain (248). The narrator, in an echo of a medieval and Renaissance topos, thinks of life as a wheel when he approaches the hospital where his aunt lies dying (172). He is driving there in a taxi fondling the breast of a young woman. One day he will lie there while another couple live intensely outside. All will pass; we will all touch death. All the to-do about sex and love in the novel will come to that in the end. The novel's generic setting is reflected here, and the narrator's bleak vision of things clearly expressed.

The Pornographer is a difficult text. After several readings, the reader is still left with questions. Is the text really contrasting city and country? How is one meant to judge the narrator—in terms of moral quality and reliability? How is one meant to judge Josephine? The ambiguous conclusion of the novel, in which the narrator seems to have gained some kind of moral, personal, and emotional insight but in which Maloney's astringent and derisory laughter is also heard, is emblematic of the entire text. Often sordid, bleak, and unsettlingly enigmatic, *The Pornographer* will perhaps never be popular among McGahern's novels, but its very difficulty and ambiguity, and its powerful evocation of desolation, are its strength.

Changes

High Ground (1985)

Writing and Reception

In an essay published in 1984 on the Irish short story, Robert Hogan writes that "the issue is in doubt" as to whether McGahern can broaden his technique and subject. After the publication of *High Ground* in 1985, there was a critical consensus that McGahern had been able to do just that. In the *London Review of Books,* Pat Rogers writes that McGahern's "strikingly good collection of short stories" demonstrates "a subtler sense of the interaction of character and environment" than is the case in earlier works. Denis Sampson also notes a broadening of concern in his chapter on *High Ground* in *Outstaring Nature's Eye.* He writes, "These short stories of the early eighties extend the drama of opposites that shaped *Getting Through,* although even more than the earlier collection the book seems to be designed to reflect a coherence of preoccupation and style. Studies of personal vision and communal life are given a new emphasis by the introduction of longer perspectives, and a more overt concern with moral issues is joined to a sense of change that is social as well as metaphysical." Sampson also argues that the collection shows a more overt and sympathetic interest in the position of women within Irish culture and society than had hitherto been the case in McGahern's work.[1]

Patricia Craig in the *Times Literary Supplement* sees no opening out toward women's experience in *High Ground* and emphasizes continuities in McGahern's work; however, she also points to certain departures: the "flourishing" relationship of the concluding story ("Bank Holiday") and an interest in the details of social change. She concludes that McGahern "writes, as always, with authority and gravity, and with an instinct for the most appropriate detail." The collection has always met with praise. Rogers compares McGahern's short stories to the fictions of William Faulkner and William Trevor, and in the *New York Times Book Review,* Joel Conarroe describes it as "a fine new book" that places McGahern in "a charmed circle of contemporary Irish writers that includes Edna O'Brien, Seamus Heaney and Thomas Kinsella." The whole collection is analyzed in a serious (if rather general) fashion by Nicola Bradbury in an essay published in 1989.[2]

The stories in *High Ground* were written in the 1980s and appeared in a British edition in 1985. A U.S. edition was published in 1987 and is identical to the British one. Some slight confusion is caused by the inclusion, in both the British and American editions of *High Ground,* of "Gold Watch" from the U.S. edition of *Getting Through.* Not only is this messy bibliographically, but more important the context of the stories in *High Ground* gives this story a different coloration from the one it has in *Getting Through.* A further complexity with regard to *High Ground* is that this was not McGahern's original choice as a title. He wished to have "Oldfashioned" as the title story, and the decision to change the title affects interpretation of the volume.[3] Had it been titled *Oldfashioned,* the stories about the former Protestant ruling class in southern Ireland would have been even more foregrounded in the collection than they are. Further, the original title would have suggested a nostalgia for past states, which is part of, but not the only element in, the collection's overall vision. *High Ground,* with its implication of a point of vantage from which one can observe things, is perhaps more appropriate to the volume. In addition, the story of that name is unresolved in its ending, and this is something that fits in with other texts in the collection and, indeed, with the volume's complex vision of history and change.

Narrators and Narrative

Half the stories in *High Ground* are first-person narrations; the other half employ third-person narrators. The first-person narrators are unnamed in four of the relevant stories; in one, "High Ground," the narrator is referred to simply as "young Moran."[4] The third-person narrators either have a restricted point of view, that of a single character (in "Like All Other Men" and "Bank Holiday"), or are fundamentally omniscient narrators able to move freely in time and space and from character to character ("Oldfashioned," "Eddie Mac," and "The Conversion of William Kirkwood"). The collection begins with two first-person narrations; three third-person ones follow; then come three first-person narrations; and the collection closes with two third-person ones. The effect of this mixture of narrators is to combine an individual perspective with a wider social panorama. The reader moves from the personal, domestic world of the narrator in "Parachutes" to the broad sweep of social change in "Oldfashioned." Several stories combine an individual focus with a social one: for example, the anonymous first-person narrator in "A Ballad" describes provincial ennui in postwar Ireland and combines that with a concomitant perception of historical forces in his brief excursus on Irish-speaking farmers transported by the de

Valera government from coast to inland areas, as part of a policy of social engineering (29–30). The third-person omniscient narrator of "Eddie Mac" is able to do something similar; in this text there is a strong sense of historical and social change and the way in which individual lives are caught up in it.

Most stories in *High Ground* are linear in their narrative organization. The only exception is "Parachutes," which has extensive retrospects (13–14, 19–20, 23–24). The last of these is important, as it returns the narrator to a time of hope and possibility, a time that the present has destroyed. However, despite its difference from the other stories in this respect, "Parachutes" echoes seven of the remaining texts in its openendedness. In "Parachutes," this is of course a false openendedness, as the reader knows that the narrator's romance will come to nothing but bitterness. The other stories, apart from "A Ballad" and "Oldfashioned," are genuinely inconclusive in their endings. In "Like All Other Men," the male protagonist must make his way through an empty life, while the future life of the female protagonist is completely unknown. "Eddie Mac" finishes with the eponymous protagonist setting off to disappear into the cities of mainland Britain, with Annie May's fate unresolved. The narrators' futures in both "Crossing the Line" and "High Ground" are completely open. Will the young teacher stay to have the chains of provincial life laid on him? What will young Moran do: betray his old teacher or reject Reegan's offer of advancement? In "Gold Watch," the narrator seems to have achieved happiness, but the text ends with his father's vicious destruction of the watch he has given him. What will happen next, one wonders. The same question arises at the end of "The Conversion of William Kirkwood." If Kirkwood marries Mary Kennedy, Annie May and Lucy will be driven out of their home. The story ends with Kirkwood's realization of this and leaves him in indecision. The whole story material of "Bank Holiday" moves toward such a positive conclusion that it is easy to forget the hypothetical nature of its ending—"it was as if they were already in possession of endless quantities of time and money" (156). Bank holidays always come to an end.

The overall ordering of stories in *High Ground* is, as is always the case with McGahern's work, crucial to analysis and interpretation. The collection moves from a failed love affair ("Parachutes") to one ("Bank Holiday") that seems, at least provisionally, to be successful. However, each story balances the other, with "Parachutes" casting a malign light on "Bank Holiday" and "Bank Holiday" suggesting that even out of the despair and drifting of "Parachutes" something good may come. Stories with resilient and probably successful female characters—"A Ballad," "Like All Other Men," "Gold Watch," "The Conversion of William Kirkwood" (in Mary Kennedy), "Gold Watch," and "Bank

Holiday"—both echo and qualify each other but also interweave with much more male-centered stories, such as "Parachutes" and "High Ground," and with stories in which women characters get a distinctly raw deal, such as "Eddie Mac." Similarly, stories with a personal focus interweave with ones with a much more social purview. The volume, taken as a whole, offers a wide and complex look at human affairs, as different stories both chime with each other and also set each other off.

Settings and Subject Matter

Many of the settings and subjects of stories in *High Ground* are familiar from McGahern's other collections, although even when McGahern turns to familiar places, times, and topics, he does so with a new twist. Several stories are set in small towns and cities, in approximately contemporary times, although with a lack of specificity that is typical of McGahern's work. The disaffected men, younger and older and slightly at odds with their environments, are familiar in "Parachutes," "A Ballad," "Like All Other Men," "Crossing the Line," "High Ground," "Gold Watch," and "Bank Holiday." However, the bohemian netherworld of "Parachutes" gives the city setting in that story a new dimension, and the at least partial integration and social success of the protagonists in "Gold Watch" and "Bank Holiday" are also something new. In these stories, too, it is evident that McGahern is writing of a new Ireland, urban, relatively prosperous, cosmopolitan, and socially and morally much more relaxed than in any of his previous fiction. "We live in a lucky time," declares the female protagonist in "Gold Watch" (110), and her and the narrator's relatively stress-free and socially liberated liaison and marriage, the good flat, the wine and pleasant food, all belong to a different world from the sexual guilt and social and moral furtiveness of *The Dark* or *The Pornographer.* It is notable that "Gold Watch" and "Bank Holiday" largely conclude the collection, and, despite their ambiguities, the setting of these stories, in a relatively modern and cosmopolitan Dublin, helps to give the collection its optimistic coloration.

However, the major departure in *High Ground* is in the remarkable trio of stories, "Oldfashioned," "Eddie Mac," and "The Conversion of William Kirkwood." These are extraordinary both because of the milieu that they depict, that of the descendants of the pre-1922 Protestant ruling class in southern Ireland, and because of the broad sweep of history that they encompass. "Oldfashioned," for example, summarizes twenty years of independent Ireland's history in its first one and one-half pages. The last three pages bring the story up to contemporary times. In between there is a sad—but not entirely sad—

tale of Catholic-Protestant / Irish-English relations and misunderstandings. Colonel Sinclair and his wife can return to the southern Ireland their kind once ruled and can even play a role in and be integrated, in part, into the new system. However, when they try to make a young boy a substitute for their dead son and turn him into a British officer (in the army of the country his Garda father fought against), they meet with virulent and implacable resistance. The encounter with the Sinclairs, nevertheless, shapes the young boy's life, not to make him happier but to help to open his horizons beyond his father's life.

Among its several focuses, "Eddie Mac" depicts life in a Protestant landowner's house after the British have left southern Ireland. The Kirkwoods are presented with great sympathy by McGahern and are seen as decent, honest, cultured and well mannered, if somewhat feckless and incompetent. In this story, they largely provide a background, if a thoroughly substantial one, for the story of Eddie Mac, a local hero and lady-killer who, once his power and charm begin to wane, must opt for the unglamorous Annie May and, once she becomes pregnant, must rob his employers and escape to England. The transitoriness of all the things that the Kirkwoods and their home embody is reflected in Eddie Mac's fall from glory. The Kirkwoods and Annie May return in "The Conversion of William Kirkwood." This story takes up the lives of the protagonists and Annie May's daughter by Eddie Mac, Lucy, some thirteen years after Eddie Mac's departure. Unlike most McGahern short stories, this text shows a process of integration into society, for William Kirkwood gradually joins the world of his Catholic neighbors, serving in the Irish army during "The Emergency" (World War II) and eventually even converting to Catholicism. His integration and his marriage to Mary Kennedy, however, will destroy Annie May's and Lucy's lives, for the new wife will not tolerate them in the house.

These three texts read like mini novels, with their large cast of characters, their broad historical scope, and their focus on social details and intricacies (such as Kirkwood's complex relationship with his social peers in the new Ireland, the schoolmaster and the policeman [127–29, 131–35]). They read almost like sketches for a historical novel that McGahern never wrote. However, they stand on their own as fascinating and rich short works of short fiction.

Changes

Nicola Bradbury and Paul Gueguen in separate essays on *High Ground* both suggest that these are stories about disappointment and loss.[5] This is undeniably true. "Parachutes" depicts the aftermath of a failed love affair in a milieu of shabby disillusion. The Sinclairs are lonely and disappointed in "Old-fashioned"; the ex-seminarian loses a chance for love in "Like All Other Men." The young teacher in "Crossing the Line" sees the fetters of provincial, middle-class life falling on him, and the narrator of "High Ground" clearly sees his old teacher with a certain distance at the story's end. In "Gold Watch," nothing has been resolved or bettered between father and son, while Annie May is abandoned at the end of "Eddie Mac," and the same is about to happen at the end of "The Conversion of William Kirkwood."

But the events depicted in the short stories in *High Ground* do not only have negative aspects. Some of the thistledown that floats through the air in "Parachutes" will find earth to grow in (23). The ending of "A Ballad" is positive; the outcome of the story's events is a marriage, a family, and a successful career. The young woman in "Like All Other Men" has chosen her path and will follow it, while the headmaster in "Crossing the Line" has achieved a better life for himself and his family by his choices and his diligence. In "Gold Watch," the narrator and his love do have a more civilized and better existence in a new urban, bourgeois Ireland, as do the protagonists of "Bank Holiday." Change, which is everywhere in this collection, is far from negative in all its consequences. Kirkwood's integration into independent Ireland is seen as largely positive. Even the Sinclairs in "Oldfashioned" can adapt and become part of an altered world. The protagonist of this last story (probably a partial self-portrait on McGahern's part) may have a jaundiced view of his country and change (he is interested in "the darker aspects of Irish life" [55]), but the text does not wholly endorse his vision.

McGahern returns to the topic of change and adaptation in a major short story, "The Country Funeral," which he places at the end of his *Collected Stories* (1992) as almost a summation of his work in short fiction. In this text he shows characters coming to terms with the past and uniting it with a changed present. However, in the novel that follows *High Ground, Amongst Women,* perhaps McGahern's most successful and best-known piece of work, the author focuses on a figure, the ex-guerrilla Moran, who cannot easily adapt or accommodate himself to change.

CHAPTER 9

The Father

Amongst Women (1990)

Reception

Amongst Women is McGahern's most successful and popular novel. Eamon
Maher recounts the "almost universal" positive responses to it and points out
that it achieved third place (after Joyce's *Ulysses* and *A Portrait of the Artist as
a Young Man*) in an *Irish Times* poll in which readers were invited to name the
greatest Irish novels written in English.[1] In the *Times Literary Supplement,*
Lindsay Duguid admires McGahern's "fastidiousness of style" and says of
Amongst Women, "Rich yet spare, it is at once a portrait of a particular era and
a survey of a nation's past and future." However, she notes that "for all its Irish-
ness . . . *Amongst Women* addresses universal themes." John Banville's review
is, as usual, unstinting in its praise. "Rarely nowadays," he writes in the *New
York Review of Books,* "does one come upon a novel that one senses will out-
last one's own time. *Amongst Women,* despite the quietness of its tone and the
limits deliberately imposed upon it by the author, is an example of the novelist's art at its finest, a work the heart of which beats to the rhythm of the world
and of life itself. It will endure."[2]

However there have been more hesitant responses to *Amongst Women.* In
the *London Review of Books,* John Lanchester calls it "a risky book" because
of its traditional technique and because "it commits itself so resolutely to its
ordinary story" (which is surely another way of saying its traditionality). The
word "risky" is also used by Rand Richards Cooper in the *New York Times
Book Review.* "To place this prose," he suggests, "one begins with Hardy and
moves backward. It's risky for a contemporary writer to express himself in
bygone cadences. The reader may feel artificially enclosed by them." Fintan
O'Toole in the *Irish Times* comments on the old-fashioned nature of McGahern's
technique in *Amongst Women* and finds it inappropriate to contemporary Ireland. This view is echoed in Robert F. Garratt's essay of 2005 on *Amongst
Women,* published in the *Irish University Review.* He points to McGahern's
"signature conservative style" but also suggests that some readers have been
uneasy about the "reluctance" of the novel "to engage with contemporary Irish

culture."[3] Nonetheless, the novel remains the text of McGahern's that most educated readers have heard of, and it has won major literary prizes and been filmed jointly by the Irish and British state television companies.

Story Material, Narrator, and Narration

The story material of *Amongst Women* is deceptively simple. At the book's center is the figure of Michael Moran, ex–IRA guerrilla, now a farmer who, after the British have been expelled from southern Ireland, feels himself an outsider and undervalued in the new independent Irish state. His first wife dies, and he brings up his three daughters and two sons on his farm, bought with money he receives for his service in the IRA, called Great Meadow, in the northwest of Ireland.[4] He quarrels bitterly with his elder son, Luke, who leaves for London and refuses to have anything to do with his father for the rest of the older man's life. Moran's relationship with his daughters, Maggie, Mona, and Sheila, is one of patriarchal exploitation and cruelty; they both fear and love him, as children and as adult women in their lives in Dublin and London. Moran's relationship with his younger son, Michael, is similarly complex, but he, too, leaves for London, although he makes no definite break with the older man. When Maggie is eighteen, Moran decides to remarry.[5] He chooses Rose Brady, a woman in her late thirties (24) who has returned home after working for twelve years in Glasgow. The novel charts the complexities of their courtship and the conflicts and compromises of their marriage. Moran is much older than she is (27) and is as difficult, moody, and cruel with her as he is with his daughters and sons. By tact, good humor, and judicious threats, she, however, is able to make life bearable both for herself and, largely, for Moran's children (although his relationship with Michael, when his son is fifteen [102], is bitter and violent). The family disperses. Maggie leaves home to work as a nurse in London. Mona and Sheila are successful at school and take jobs in the civil service in Dublin. Maggie marries an Irishman from London, Michael an English Catholic, and Mona a fellow civil servant. These events are interwoven with accounts of work on Great Meadow. The daughters and Michael return regularly to their home to be with Moran and Rose and to help with farmwork. Luke never returns, however, and he and his father remain unreconciled. Moran grows older and increasingly in the power of his wife and daughters. An attempt to revive his spirits and health fails. At the novel's conclusion Moran dies, a disappointed, harsh, and embittered man to the end. His womenfolk, however, use his funeral to reaffirm their love for him and his centrality to their lives.

This story material, itself deeply traditional, of the passions and tensions of rural family life, is narrated by a traditional omniscient narrator. Denis Sampson calls the narration objective and close to "invisible." He relates it to McGahern's admiration for the work of Tomás Ó Criomhthain and for Joyce's *Dubliners*.[6] However, the narrator is, in fact, far from invisible and is only objective in that narration is not restricted to one character's point of view but, rather, moves among several. The narrator in *Amongst Women* performs the tasks of a traditional nineteenth-century narrator (such as one in a novel by Dickens, George Eliot, or Hardy). He moves freely in time and place and from character to character; he provides necessary information at crucial points; and he comments on character and action, often in general terms. The unrestricted nature of the narration is made clear throughout the novel: at an early stage, when it shifts from Moran's old age and decline to the last day, many years previously, on which he met his friend and fellow IRA veteran McQuaid (8); later, when the narration follows Michael and Nell to Strandhill (104–6); later still, when it can slip easily from Great Meadow to London and back again (140–47). These are only three examples among many. The narrator is also continually able to switch viewpoint from character to character. Again examples abound. The novel begins with Moran's thoughts about his daughters (1); it rapidly moves to the daughters' minds and feelings (2). Rose's point of view is given in detail on pages 22–25, and again on page 30. But one also encounters Moran's thoughts about her (27), and those of the village postmistresses and of a neighbor (25). This strategy runs throughout the whole novel. Moran's mind is given to the reader (108, 130) but so is Nell Morahan's (110) and that of Sean Flynn's mother (154). After Rose and Moran's wedding, the point of view moves to that of Rose's family and presents their unease (44–45). The novel ends with the collective consciousness of Rose and her stepdaughters after Moran's funeral (183).

In addition, the narrator provides necessary information for the reader throughout the text. For example, on page 1, he explains what Monahan Day has been for the Morans. During the account of the Christmas dance, he offers information (unknown to Rose) about Moran's earlier success with women at such events (36–37). The narrator can explain reactions to Maggie's boyfriend Mark in Great Meadow (135). He also presents brief but detailed pictures of characters' lives at particular stages in their development: for example, Michael's (91–92). In addition, he attempts at times to explain characters' conduct: for example, Moran's distaste for Rose's visits to her family (68) and his opposition to Sheila's going to university (88–89). The narrator predicts, too. For example, after the failed attempt to revive Monahan Day, he notes, "The house was to be as full again only once more"—that is, at Moran's death and funeral (168).

Frequently, the narrator passes comment (in a manner reminiscent of a nineteenth-century narrator) on character, action, and situation. Often these comments generalize their particular focus. For example, the daughters' plan to restore Moran's spirits by organizing another Monahan Day is dismissed by the narrator as "a gesture as weak as a couple who marry in order to try to retrieve a lost relationship" (8). Narrative remarks need not always be general; they can be fixed on the particular too. For example, the narrator sums up Rose's and her stepdaughters' approach to Moran on the wedding day. "They were already conspirators. They were mastered and yet they were controlling together what they were mastered by" (46). The "attempt to revive Moran with the [Monaghan] day had been futile," he concludes toward the end of the novel (177). However, the narrator does frequently generalize situations. Thus, of Nell and Michael's visit to Strandhill, he comments that "they had the whole day," but "there is nothing more difficult to seize than the day" (106). Of the behavior of the civil servants in Mona's and Sheila's offices in Dublin, the narrator comments, "Such is the primacy of the idea of family that everyone was able to leave work at once without incurring displeasure" (123). Michael's attitude to Great Meadow is summed up by the narrator thus: "In the frail way that people assemble themselves he, like the girls, looked to Great Meadow for recognition, for a mark of his continuing existence" (147). The narrator combines the general and the particular at Moran's death. "There are some who struggle and rave on the edge of dying, others who make a great labour of it like a difficult birth, but Moran slipped evenly out of life" (179–80).

The function of such a traditional narrative strategy, echoing past literary achievements, is quite straightforward. It dovetails with the traditional subject matter of the rural family, its conflicts and its passions. It is also appropriate to the central figure of Moran, a character whose stature is based on the past and who is out of sympathy with the world that has emerged out of Irish independence, including the modern world of cities and relative prosperity. In the 1990s such a narration is powerfully out of step with current trends in Irish and British novel writing.[7] Readers must decide for themselves whether it is retrograde and ossified or provocative and appropriate to the novel's subject matter.

McGahern, however, is never simple, either in his approach to his topics or in his technique. If narration is traditional, narrative (that is, the organization of the novel's story material) is far from being so and shows a striking complexity. Unlike the great nineteenth-century novels that it echoes in its narration, *Amongst Women* has a decidedly nonlinear narrative. The novel's present (that is, its latest moment) is the time of Moran's increasing frailty and death. This is when *Amongst Women* begins (1–4). This time level, however, is quickly disrupted by Moran's reminiscence about the Anglo-Irish War of the 1920s (5–6). The novel returns to its present over the next two pages (6–8) but thereafter enters a long section (8–22) that presents McQuaid's last visit to the Morans.' This time level, too, is disrupted by McQuaid's and Moran's recollections of their guerrilla war against the British army (14–18).

Thereafter the novel maintains a logical and chronological direction until near the end, when it returns to the present of the text's start. However, even here there are complexities, for the novel returns on page 176 to a point somewhat before the beginning of the novel and provides another brief account of the revived Monahan Day (177) before moving to recount Moran's death and funeral (177–84). There are also narrative complexities in the long central section of the novel (22–176). These lie in its ellipses and summaries.[8] Certain parts of the story material are omitted: for example, Moran's first wife is mentioned only twice (27, 48) and then only briefly. Luke's quarrel with his father is alluded to almost equally sparingly (176–77). The reader knows next to nothing about Moran's life between the end of the Anglo-Irish War and the last Monahan Day and his decision to court Rose. Why has Moran not taken the IRA pension he is entitled to (15)? What did he do in the Irish Civil War, so succinctly alluded to by McQuaid (18).[9] Relatively long periods of time are summarized: for example, Rose's first weeks or months in the Moran household (48–51) are given less space than her and Moran's trip to Strandhill (56–61). The same summarizing method is used with regard to the daughters' visits, over a long period, to Great Meadow (93–94, 130–33, 142, 168–70). It comes as a shock when the reader is told that Moran has become old and frail (148–49) and a person of little importance in the community (174–75). The relevant years have been radically summarized.

The counterbalance to elision is narrative expansion. The novel highlights, by the amount of space it gives over to them, specific elements in the story material: for example, Rose and Moran's courtship and marriage (22–45), their trip to the sea (56–61), and Moran and Rose's two bitter quarrels (52–56, 69–72). Weight and space are also given to Maggie's departure and first return (61–63, 77–82), Mona's and Sheila's examinations (74–77, 85–91), Michael's relationship with Nell and his rebellion and departure (104–30), Maggie's bringing Mark to Great Meadow (133–41), and Sheila's wedding in Dublin (150–57). In addition, certain events are not simply given prominence but are provided with enhanced status through repetition. Moran and Rose's quarrels are examples (52–56, 69–72). The trip to Strandhill is also repeated—by Rose and Moran (56–61, 173–74) and by Nell and Michael (104–6). There are two accounts of Christmas dances, again with a generational change of characters

(36–37, 94–104) and of cutting hay (83–84, 157–68). In addition, two weddings are recounted in detail: Rose and Moran's (38–45) and Sheila and Sean's (150–57). Other weddings are alluded to more briefly: Maggie's (141–42) and Michael's (171).

Such a narrative organization carries a great deal of meaning. The novel's end is present at its beginning. Moran's frailty is already known to the reader from the first few pages. His death is inevitable from the start and stands in ironic contrast to his days of military success and the vigor of his later years. This sense of inevitable decline is further enhanced by the fact that Moran is a relatively old man for almost the entire novel. The reader never encounters a young Moran, except in his and McQuaid's stories of the war or in Moran's own brief account of his time at school before 1919 (74). In addition, the unstoppable passage of time is marked by the summaries of long periods, which matches a set of motifs central to the text (see, for example, Moran's moment of realization of transience [130]). Time passes almost without one's noticing it. Further, the novel makes clear what are the key moments and aspects of its author's vision of the world. These are to do either with family (quarrels, weddings) or with collective work on the family farm. They are also to do with recurrence: for example, cutting hay, Christmas dances, trips to the seaside. In contrast, however, these key moments also suggest change. Moran and Rose are replaced by their children at a dance; Michael and Nell replace Rose and Moran at Strandhill. The children's departures for London and Dublin and the exams that allow Mona and Sheila to live in the city also embody change. The narrative organization of the text makes substantial the text's key concerns: family, continuity, and mutability.

Setting

Critics have written of the restricted space of much of McGahern's fiction.[10] This observation is substantially true of *Amongst Women*. Most of the action is concentrated on Moran's farm, Great Meadow, largely within the farmhouse itself, although also in the fields surrounding it. There are, indeed, excursions beyond the farm—to the settlement of which it is part, with a church, a post office, a hall for concerts, and other houses; to a dance in a neighboring farm's barn; to Rose's family's farm. In addition, the text moves at certain points beyond the rural community to which Great Meadow, however loosely, belongs: to the seaside (most notably to Strandhill), to various provincial towns that are the goal of Michael's and Nell's excursions and of Rose and Moran's in later life. Beyond those places there is Dublin, where Mona and Sheila go to live and, beyond that still, London, where Luke, Maggie, and Michael make their lives. Rose, too, has lived abroad: for twelve years in Glasgow (22). (Even further away is New York where Nell Morahan wins money and independence [102], and Colorado where Moran's school fellow Joe Brady becomes a bishop [74].) Space is organized in bands that radiate out from the center that is the Moran farmhouse, but, although substantial parts of the action may take place outside the home, that is where the novel's dead center lies, the heart of Moran's patriarchy.[11]

As is typical of much of McGahern's fiction, time setting is left deliberately vague in *Amongst Women.* Sampson places the novel's principal action in a period from the 1940s through the 1960s.[12] In the bulk of the text it is difficult to place events, even within a single decade. An exception is when Maggie returns to Ireland with her London-Irish boyfriend (133). Mark is a Teddy Boy, as Sheila registers with shock, and thus this moment must be set in the mid- to late 1950s.[13] However, such a clear marker is unusual. It is nevertheless wrong to say, as Lanchester does in the *London Review of Books,* that no "events in the larger world impinge on family life" in *Amongst Women.*[14] The great wave of post–World War II emigration from the Ireland to mainland Britain is the background to the departure of three of the Moran children to London. Its psychological consequences are made vivid in the text. "More than half of my own family in England. What was it all for?" Moran mutters when he reflects on the struggle for Irish independence and the subsequent history of independent Ireland (5). When Michael marries an English (albeit Catholic) woman, "that day all the Morans, in their different ways, were made to feel what they were—immigrants," the narrator notes succinctly (171). Clearly, too, McGahern is pointing to the emergence of a new Ireland, more urban and quite distant, materially and emotionally, from the past of the Troubles and the 1940s and 1950s, in the episodes when the Morans visit Sheila's new suburban home in Dublin (151) and when they go to their bank and are ignored by the bank manager (174–75).

There are references to a more distant past that is still operative in the present when the narrator suggests that Moran's behavior is driven by traditional fears of famine and the poorhouse (68, 89). However, one set of historical events is of crucial importance in the novel. That is the war against the British army fought by the IRA between 1919 and 1922. This is presented in striking, if partial, detail in the opening pages of the novel, when Moran reminisces by himself and with McQuaid about incidents in their guerrilla war (5–6, 15–20). Pages 15 to 17 are given over to their account of the assassination of a British colonel and the killing of a detachment of British troops sometime toward the end of the war. The whole novel must be seen in the light of this one set of historical events. They reveal much about Moran: his intelligence and his ruthlessness. They also show those moments as "the best part of our lives," as Moran says of himself and McQuaid (6). After such glory (which is not glamorized), everything pales in vividness and importance. It is striking in the novel that only the incidents from the Anglo-Irish War can be accurately dated. All other events in the novel are placed in a vague temporal continuum that stretches from somewhere in the 1940s to somewhere in the 1960s. The lack of clear historical markers in the bulk of the novel, however, has another function, namely, to suggest a universal aspect to Moran's and his family's experiences. These are certainly born out of a specific time and place but not limited to those circumstances. The lack of historical compass points elevates the Morans and Great Meadow to a highly general level.[15]

The Family

Maher describes *Amongst Women* as "one of the great novels of family life in Irish literature."[16] Sampson calls it "less a novel of character . . . than a study of the bonds that form individuals into a 'whole,' represented by the 'house.'"[17] The novel's story material concentrates on family experiences and events; its central setting is the Morans' farmhouse and home. Family is at the heart of the novel's concerns, and the novel explores the intricate relationships and tensions among family members. These members are divided into three groups: Moran's daughters and Rose, his sons, and Moran himself.

Morans' daughters (Maggie, Sheila, and Mona) dominate the first three pages of the novel, just as they (along with Rose) dominate the text's last six paragraphs. In these passages they form a powerful unit, attempting to revive Moran's health and mourning him once he is dead. Moran is even afraid of them in the novel's opening pages and is certainly in their power. This motif is picked up later in the novel (178). The parts of the novel, however, that lie between the opening pages and Moran's funeral show a complex picture of an evolving relationship between daughters and father. It is striking to note that there is little difference among the daughters in their attitude to their father, despite their other varied choices in life. When they are together, the narrator describes them as "something very close to a single presence" (2).

Once the novel moves back into the past (from page 8 onward), the reader sees the daughters' developing and complex relationship with their father. Maggie and Mona are shown cowering in their father's presence yet also able to mock him behind his back (8–9). Maggie bows to his will (27) but can also find him comic (40). Rose observes the utterly oppressive force of Moran's presence on his daughters (53). When Maggie leaves for London, however, she feels deep love for him as "her first man" (62). Sheila and Mona find escape from Moran and their home in their schoolwork and also in the promise it offers of a life away from Great Meadow (64, 67). Although the oppressive discipline of Moran's presence does not wane until the novel's end (80–81), the girls can still express love for their domestic tyrant (81) and, once they have left home, continue to return to Great Meadow. The narrator points out that they accept treatment from Moran they would tolerate from no other and cherish the times when he deals with them gently and charmingly (129). He remains the center of their lives (131), providing them with a sense of belonging, of being someone (2, 145). They are utterly devoted to him in his old age and frailty in a way Moran himself finds intimidating (178). There is little defiance of the old man, although Sheila does take issue with his contempt for her future husband (158). The novel's end shows them grieving Moran but powerful in their sense of their commitment to him. The narrator even suggests that they have become their father in some fashion (183).

Rose's relationship to her husband is equally complex. She is attracted to him during their courtship by his intelligence, his attentiveness, his separateness from the rest of the community, and his "outlaw" quality (23, 25). She understands equally well, however, the motives of self-preservation that lie behind her decision to marry him (24–25). She is also well aware of his awkwardness from the start of their relationship (24). Rose's relationship with her husband is a mixture of deference, manipulation, and defiance. It is striking that she hardly ever refers to her husband as Michael but almost always as Daddy (see 47–48). She certainly gives into his moods and his distaste for the outside world. "She felt inordinately grateful when he behaved normally," the narrator notes (58). "She seemed willing to go to almost any length to appease, lull his irritation to rest, contain all the exasperation by taking it within herself" (69). Moran's presence, even late in the novel, can make her fall silent (142). But throughout the novel, Rose is able to modify Moran's behavior, to make life easier for the children and herself (for example, 48–49). The narrator sees the complexity of her position in the house as being, like the girls, "mastered" by Moran yet also "controlling together what they were mastered by" (46). In the end, she has even some measure of power. She secretly orders Moran's clothes for his death (8); she drives the car (173). She is also able on two crucial occasions to resist Moran and bend him to her will. These occasions are when he insults and attacks her (52–56, 69–72), and both times she emerges victorious from the conflict. Her relationship to Moran remains complex to the end. In the face of her stepdaughters' rapture at their father's funeral, she, although part of the group of powerful, grieving women, is more ambiguous than they, immersed in her own thoughts and saying only "Poor Daddy" (183–84).

Many readers may feel disturbed by the depiction of male-female relationships in *Amongst Women*. The nature of Moran's daughters' relationship with their father and Rose's relationship with her husband is certainly traditional. The women are in thrall to the patriarchal father and husband. They exercise power by indirection, appeasement, and manipulation. They remain devoted to the domestic tyrant and, indeed, find self-realization in glorifying their oppressor. Because there is an attempt to universalize the world of Great Meadow, these relationships are similarly generalized. There is certainly no other model of male-female relations indicated substantially in the text, and, in fact, the only other detailed presentation of marriage is that of McQuaid's, which seems even crueler and more exploitative than anything in the Moran household (12–13). Readers must come to their own terms with McGahern's picture of family life in mid-twentieth-century rural Ireland. There is certainly plenty of literary evidence to suggest that it is a highly probable one, and it should be stressed that McGahern is objective to the extent that he never endorses Moran's or his womenfolk's behavior. Indeed, as the analysis set out below of Moran's character and conduct suggests, he comes much closer to seeing his protagonist as a monstrous figure.

The relationship between father and sons is presented as much more simple in *Amongst Women*. The novel does not indicate the cause of Luke and Moran's quarrel, which certainly leaves Luke embittered and unreconciled to his father, refusing all attempts to bring them together again, including Moran's own (176). He does not reply to the telegram informing him of his father's death (181). Luke is responsible for the acute and damning remark that only women can live with Moran (133). A similar pattern of estrangement is repeated in the case of Moran's youngest child, Michael. Like his sisters, Michael can mock his father and find him deeply oppressive (104). The father's intolerance and desire to dominate poisons his life with his son (107–8). Between father and son violence erupts once Michael makes it clear that he wishes to escape from Great Meadow (119–21). Yet Michael, unlike Luke and like his sisters, continues to see Great Meadow and his father as what give his life a center and shape (147). He, like the girls, returns frequently over the years (170).

James M. Cahalan describes Moran as dominating *Amongst Women*, and, although Sampson questions whether the novel is strictly a character study, the complexities of Moran's psychology lie at the novel's heart, shaping (or perhaps twisting) the intricate web of family relations it depicts.[18] Banville suggests that the reader's response to Moran is central to a reading of the novel and that this response can not be simple. "It is a mark of this writer's [McGahern's] extraordinary skill as a novelist that we can understand the women's [his daughters'] regard for such a man—indeed, that we can at times share it. Moran may be a monster, but he is a monster with principles."[19]

The best way to discuss the character of Moran is to look at the major features of his makeup. These are resentment, isolation, violence, willfulness, weakness, and fragmentary realization. Resentment marks Moran's character throughout the novel. His resentment is directed from the start against Ireland (in this echoing Reegan in *The Barracks*). "What did we get for it?" he asks about the war of independence.

> A country, if you'd believe them. Some of our own johnnies in the top jobs instead of a few Englishmen. More than half of my own family work in England. What was it all for? The whole thing was a cod. (5)

He refuses to stay in the army after the end of the war because he is not prepared "to arse-lick" and because he does not "know the right people" (6). He will not take his IRA pension (15), at least not at first; he does later (172). His disdain for the Irish state is unrelenting for much of the novel. "Sometimes I get sick when I see what I fought for," he grumbles to McQuaid (15). "Look where it brought us," he goes on. "Look at the country now. Run by a crowd of small-minded gangsters out for their own good. It was better if it never had happened" (18). It is important to note that McQuaid does not concur in all Moran says, but McQuaid's voice comes through strongly, and he does feel that Moran has been "wasted" in postindependence Ireland (15).

Moran's resentment is based on his own relative failure in independent Ireland. Part of his unease with McQuaid stems from the fact that his former lieutenant has surpassed him in power and wealth (4, 14). McQuaid sums Moran up acutely: "Some people just cannot bear to come in second" (22). The novel's protagonist, indeed, can not tolerate not being the center of things. For example, he will not go to dances once his youth and fame are gone; he "would not take a lesser place" (37). But Moran's social resentments do have their reasons within the world of the novel. His education has been disrupted by poverty and political turmoil (74). He has fought for a country to give power to priest and doctor but not to himself (88). So emotionally alienated is he from the Irish state that he identifies himself with his Protestant neighbors rather than with his Catholic ones (163).

However, Moran's dissatisfaction is existential and not only political. He feels a "frustration against the inadequacy of life," the narrator informs the reader (39). He must always be the center of attention in his home and hates it when he is not (45). His son Luke has let him down utterly, he feels (82). He sees himself as abandoned by family at various points (108, 124–25). Toward the end of the novel his refrain is, "Who cares? Who cares anyhow?" (109, 175, 178, 179). His last words are a peremptory "*Shut up!*" to his praying daughters, who are praying because he instructed them to, and as he has instructed them all their lives (180). Resentment and dissatisfaction mark his character to the end.

These character traits have pushed Moran into isolation, a self-willed estrangement from others. He separates himself and his family from the surrounding world and, even within his own family, is himself separate from the other family members. "I was never any good at getting on with people," he reminds his daughters "half humorously" at the beginning of the novel (6). Moran's isolation is first evident in the novel in his daughters. "On the tides of Dublin or London," the narrator informs, "they were hardly more than specks of froth but together they were the aristocratic Morans of Great Meadow, a completed world, Moran's daughters" (2). Moran makes a sharp distinction between the family and the outside, between Great Meadow and the rest of the world. Throughout the novel he is reluctant to have dealings with that outside world. For example, in his last conversation with McQuaid he is reluctant to give information about family (12). He even insists on an "inviolate secrecy" around himself (19).

Indeed, within the family Moran maintains his own separateness: before his marriage to Rose, he eats alone (35); he is often seen sitting self-absorbed, brooding, turning his thumbs (45). At the end of McQuaid's last visit, he feels he has lost his old friend but has done so by sticking with his family (22). Moran constantly sets himself apart from his surroundings. Rose notes this about him from the first (23, 30). His children do not mix with others (33, 34). At the railway station when Maggie departs, Rose greets those who are waiting with them on the platform. Moran stays aloof (62–63). Marriage to Moran means that Rose is increasingly divorced from her family and the wider community (45, 68). Moran continually insists on his and his family's superiority vis-à-vis the rest of the world (93, 106, 128). For him, family is "the basis of all society and every civilization" (117, 153), and all else is intrusive and polluting, a sentiment that his daughters concur with emotionally and in their behavior (85, 94, 96, 145, 162, 171). The world outside the farmhouse is a threat. Moran is conscious of this once all his daughters have left home. As he, Rose, and Michael say the rosary, there is a high wind outside. "For the first time the house seemed a frail defence against all that beat round it," the narrator notes (90).

Family is not just a matter of exclusiveness, however. It is given a positive coloration in the two episodes of hay cutting (83–84, 157–68). Here the reader sees the family working together (despite tensions) and achieving a momentary unity of purpose and emotion. However, the motif of separation is marked in Moran's character. Toward the end of his life he withdraws from everything and everyone, retreating to his bed in a move symptomatic of his attitude toward the world (149). At the very end he even attempts to escape from the house (178). His actions continually reveal a deep estrangement from others. On two occasions he observes others from hiding: once when McQuaid arrives for the last Monaghan Day (10) and once when Maggie arrives from London with her boyfriend (135). He is a gunman to the marrow of his bones.

Moran is certainly a violent man, both physically and emotionally. The narrator says of him that he seems unable to return love (6), and, indeed, one of his earliest utterances is the chilling statement, "The closest I ever got to any man was when I had him in the sights of the rifle and I never missed" (7). Great Meadow is a place of repressive tensions, where his daughters fear their father's rages (33). His two verbal attacks against Rose are brutal (52–56, 69–72); it is a measure of her toughness that she resists Moran at these points and defeats him. His relationship with Michael degenerates into crude physical violence, with Michael almost fearing for his life (120). One of Moran's first acts in the novel is to shoot a jackdaw (7). When he does talk of the war against the British, he does not gloss over the intense violence of his acts. "Don't let anybody fool you. It was a bad business. We didn't shoot at women and children like the Tans but we were a bunch of killers" (5). He and McQuaid retell the story of their attack on a British general and detachment of soldiers, an attack that, depending on one's point of view, could easily be classed as a terrorist outrage (15–17).

Moran's character is also one of willful moodiness, mostly demanding and difficult, at times charming. The narrator writes of his "high-strung nervousness" (51), and it is clear that his wife and daughters spend much of their time with him watching for his sudden changes of humor. One sees an example of this during the seemingly happy and successful day with Rose at Strandhill. Rose watches him "carefully." "He was changing less predictably than the tide" (60). He can utterly charm his daughters at one point in the day and then by evening be mired in a dark despondency that oppresses those around him (81).

He is also, finally, a weak man, insecure, mistrustful, driven by a need to control and dominate others. For all his sense of his own superiority and his willingness to breach social norms (32, 41), he has not the courage to expose himself in wooing Rose Brady of his own volition (26–27). He can not expose himself to the possibility of failure in looking for a place to eat in a strange town (59). He must be the center of attention in whatever circle he finds himself (45, 79). He is also capable of disingenuousness, for example, concerning the possibility of Sheila's studying at university (89), while his attitude toward the women who surround him is a mixture of contempt and complete dependence (91). He ends up afraid of his own daughters (178). One can see the repeated telling of the rosary in the light of Moran's need to dominate others. He seems to have no religious belief himself, yet insists on the ritual, for he decides when the beads are to be told, and he controls the whole event. His patriarchal power is never more evident.

For all his violence, blindness to others, and deep egocentricity, Moran is not a wholly contemptible figure. He is clearly a man of intelligence and courage of a specific kind; his strictures against independent Ireland are both self-serving and acute; he does not glamorize his actions as a guerrilla. Yet he is also a deeply flawed, damaged, and damaging man. However, the reader is certainly invited to sympathize with him, out of place in a state that he fought for, partially deserted by his children. He also has moments of dark and honest insight. For example, when he feels time passing once his children have left home, "he set out to walk his land, field by blind field" (129). Here the narrator offers Moran's point of view, and one is being asked to sympathize with the monster.

> It was like grasping water to think how quickly the years had passed here. They were nearly gone. It was in the nature of things and yet it brought a sense of betrayal and anger, of never having understood anything much. Instead of using the fields, he sometimes felt as if the fields had used him. Soon they would be using someone else in his place. It was unlikely to be either of his sons. He tried to imagine someone running the place after he was gone and could not. He continued walking in the fields like a man trying to see. (130)

Another moment of realization comes when he knows he is dying. He begins to look closely at the land around the house.

> To die was never to look on all this again. It would live in others' eyes but not in his. He had never realized when he was in the midst of confident

life what an amazing glory he was part of. He heard his name being called frantically. Then he was scolded and led back to the house. He stopped stubbornly before the door. "I never knew how hard it is to die," he said simply. (179)

The same is true of this passage as of the previous one. One feels sorry for the egocentric, insecure patriarch, for all his sins.

The Past, Change, and Death

A novel about two generations of a family almost inevitably touches upon the past, change, and death, and such motifs are prominent in *Amongst Women*. The novel begins with an attempt to revive the past (1), and its organization is shaped by a return to the past to illuminate the present of Moran's weakness and dying. In addition, the entire novel must be seen in the light of Moran's and McQuaid's reminiscences about war against the British (14–18). "Things were never so simple and clear again," Moran insists (6).

One can notice two recurring ways of seeing the past throughout the text. On one hand, there is Moran's unglamorized and unglamorizing view of it. "Don't let them pull wool over your eyes," he tells his daughters. "The war was the cold, the wet, standing up to your neck in a drain for a whole night with bloodhounds on your trail, not knowing how you could manage the next step toward the end of a long march" (5). "We were a bunch of killers," he says bleakly (5). In fact, Moran is reluctant to speak of the past (3, 58) and, when he does, is sober and austere in his version of it. He is reluctant even to recall his courtship with Rose (173). His estranged son Luke similarly refuses to forget or to prettify the past (143–47). He is quite unwilling to be reconciled with his father. "I hold no grudge," he declares. "But I have a good memory" (143). The depiction of Moran's funeral strikes a delicate balance between suggesting the grandeur and importance of Moran's war and yet its distance from and irrelevance to the present (182–83). The Irish tricolor over the coffin is "faded"; the veteran in attendance shows "deep respect" but is small and seems from an impossibly distant world; there is no firing party; and the local politicians attend to present business immediately after the funeral.

In opposition to this is a glamorization of the past. Moran's warnings about sanitized versions of his war are relevant here. His own daughters and one son constantly reshape the past to make it more attractive. For example, they suppress the tensions and difficulties of Monaghan Days—"with distance it had become large, heroic, blood-mystical" (2). For the family the shared work of haymaking becomes a source of "healing" in their urban lives, something that gives them relief and meaning (85). Michael, too, is revealed as talking of Great Meadow as paradisial, although his own experiences there have been fraught with conflict and unhappiness (132). Moran's cruelties and selfishness are all forgotten by the daughters at his funeral (183).

Change and differing attitudes to change haunt *Amongst Women*. Change is presented frequently as something positive. Moran's decision to marry Rose excites him (28), just as her decision excites Rose herself (25, 30). Their marriage evokes "all the wonder and fear and awe of change" among Moran's children (38–39). Even after their marriage, Rose feels "a strange excitement" around Moran "of something about to happen" (58). Mona and Sheila view their studies as a way out into a new life (67, 80), while Michael, too, opts for something new and exciting in his relationship with Nell (101, 110). All the children liberate themselves in some way from Moran. Their marriages and new lives are complicated but finally positive, even Luke's unforgiving distancing of himself from his father. At the same time, the novel notes unchanging elements in its characters' lives. The wren boys' visit to the Moran home on page 100 is a repetition of an earlier visit (36). Hay cutting is repeated, too (83–84, 157–68). Moran's daughters see him as unchangeable (131). "Nothing but the years changed in Great Meadow," the narrator declares toward the novel's end (168).

It is not entirely true, however, that Moran is unchangeable. Moran has earlier noted how, now that Great Meadow only has to support him and Rose, the fields and walls are falling into disuse and disrepair (130). There is a one negative picture of change in the novel too. When Moran visits Dublin to see Sheila's new home, he is clearly at a loss (151). This is not a world he recognizes or likes. He himself suffers the change of aging (149) and almost complete irrelevance in the community, evidenced by his and Rose's visit to the local bank (174–75). Alone in the fields, Moran has a sense of passing time and the transience of all human life (130).

Indeed, the motif of death is prominent in *Amongst Women*. The novel starts with Moran's increasing weakness and his clear movement toward death; it ends with his funeral. Early passages describe violent death in war. Within the first few pages Moran shoots a jackdaw (7), and his wife smuggles his death clothes into the house (8). "There is nothing more difficult to seize than the day," the narrator comments on Nell and Michael's excursion to Strandhill (106), while Nell herself is aware of the passing of Michael's youth in her arms (114). The repeated haymaking is a positive event but also inevitably conjures up associations of transience. These associations are reinforced in the second haymaking episode by the discovery of the mutilated mother pheasant among the cut grass (160). Maher describes the whole novel as a "swansong" of a disappearing rural Ireland of the mid–twentieth century.[20] Certainly it is partly shaped around transience and complex attitudes to change and the vanished past.

Ireland

Critics and commentators stress both the particularity and universality of the created world of *Amongst Women*. Corcoran describes it as "a fine study of how love and power are both collusive and antagonistic in the traditional patterns of Irish domestic life." On the other hand, James Whyte notes the "mythic" quality of much of McGahern's work (including *Amongst Women*). While writing of its Irish specificity, Maher also remarks on its "timeless, universal quality." Sampson captures this double perspective of the novel when he calls Moran "the Lear of Oakport, the Cronos of Cootehall."[21]

Clearly much is specifically Irish in *Amongst Women*—the settings, the history, the institutions, and the characters. Yet much is generalized too—the patriarch, the children, and the experience of time, change, and death. Moran's death is that of all human beings; his glorious past and his final irrelevance are experiences that many readers (of both genders and of various nationalities) can identify themselves with. McGahern further generalizes the story material of his novel by a subtle intertextuality. The echoes of D. H. Lawrence's novels of family life, such as *Sons and Lovers,* are unobtrusively present throughout, and Moran surely has similarities with the elder Morel in that novel. The haymaking in *Amongst Women* suggests the haymaking of Lawrence's *The Rainbow.* Further echoes of Wordsworth's rural antiepic "Michael" are persistent: in characters' names (Michael, Luke), in events (Luke's estrangement in the city, Moran's working with Michael [107–8]), and in attitudes to familiar landscapes (80, 128). Mutatis mutandis, Great Meadow could be as easily in Lawrence's Midlands or Wordsworth's Lake District as northwest Ireland.

Amongst Women is a complex and ambitious novel, threading Irish history, landscapes, and characters with universalized concerns and experiences. It will be remembered for its ambivalent portrait of a domestic tyrant who is also a national hero and a human being for whom the reader is asked to have sympathy, as well as for its depiction of the painful intricacies of family life and change. Its combination of the personal and the national, the individual and the historical is luminous and moving. One feels that Banville is right in saying simply, "It will endure."[22]

CHAPTER 10

The Community

That They May Face the Rising Sun (2002)

The Power of Darkness (1991) and "The Country Funeral" (1992)

Between the publication of *Amongst Women* and that of *That They May Face the Rising Sun,* McGahern published two major texts, a play, *The Power of Darkness,* and a short story, "The Country Funeral." The latter appeared in McGahern's *The Collected Stories,* first published in Britain in 1992 and in the United States in 1994. Both are interesting additions to his output and demonstrate different attitudes toward rural Ireland and its communities.

The Power of Darkness was first performed at the Abbey Theatre in Dublin on October 16, 1991. It is based on a play by Lev Tolstoy of the same title from 1895 and tells a grisly and melodramatic tale of adultery, murder, profligacy, illegitimacy, and hypocrisy. The play, which proved controversial, is set in a rural Irish community, loosely at the time of McGahern's childhood in the 1940s.[1] As Nicholas Greene notes, Irish reviewers were hostile, while British reviewers were positive in their responses. The play, however, also received respectful commentary from the eminent contemporary Irish writer Colm Tóibín.[2] The play certainly paints a savagely critical picture (even by McGahern's standards) of the mendacity and cruelty of rural Irish communities. In the introduction to the Faber edition, McGahern writes of "the moral climate in which I grew up" and which he tries to render in *The Power of Darkness.* "The old fear of famine was confused with terror of damnation. The confusion and guilt and plain ignorance that surrounded sex turned men and women into exploiters and adversaries."[3] With regard to the discussion below of *That They May Face the Rising Sun,* it is striking to note how viciously corrupt McGahern depicts rural Ireland as being and how the dramatic technique of the play is transferred to the later novel.

"The Country Funeral" is one of the two new short stories added to *The Collected Stories* (the other, "The Creamery Manager," is a minor piece that echoes an incident in *The Barracks*). This long short story (over thirty pages in both the British and American editions), while indicating the weaknesses and cruelties of a contemporary Irish rural community, nevertheless concludes with a positive picture of its strengths and possibilities. Three brothers, Philly,

Fonsie, and John Ryan, travel from Dublin to attend to the funeral of their Uncle Peter. Philly works in Saudia Arabia as a well-paid laborer; Fonsie is confined to a wheelchair; John is a Dublin schoolteacher. All have ambivalent feelings about their dead uncle. In the course of the funeral preparations, they become drawn into, and partly drawn to, the rural community that they knew as children. At the story's end, Philly is determined to return to the country and take his uncle's farm. This story clearly points toward the complex vision of a country community that is central to *That They May Face the Rising Sun.* Michael L. Storey calls it "McGahern's finest story."[4]

Faber published McGahern's sixth novel in the United Kingdom in 2002. The U.S. edition was published in the same year but under a different, and no less appropriate, title, *By the Lake.* The change in title, however, does shift the reader's attention in the text. The British and Irish title clearly points to death and last things. The U.S. title obscures this and highlights the text's focus on the rural community and on nature.

Reception and Story Material

That They May Face the Rising Sun enjoyed a thoroughly positive reception on its appearance. In the *Independent on Sunday,* Paul Binding calls it a "superb novel" and praises the text's careful, detailed, and yet economical, picture of rural life and the natural world, with its complex portrayal of the community that lives within its bounds. Binding concludes his review by declaring the novel an "extraordinary and original achievement." The distinguished novelist Hilary Mantel writes a long and laudatory review of *That They May Face the Rising Sun* in the *New York Review of Books.* She concentrates on the complex relations among the characters in what she calls "this simply constructed and gently paced book," its delayed but powerful introduction of historical matter into the text and the respect that McGahern shows for the unglamorous lives of his characters. Mantel writes of the "grave integrity" of the text and insists that "by virtue of its simplicity the novel accretes power." In the *Guardian,* Seamus Deane writes with approval of McGahern's "capacious style" in *That They May Face the Rising Sun,* a style that is marked, as always, by "lucidity and intensity" but also "inflected by a tone of forgiveness and acceptance that adds an amplitude and serenity rarely achieved in fiction." Scholarly responses to the novel have come quickly. The special edition of the *Irish University Review* in 2005 devoted to McGahern contains three substantial essays on *That They May Face the Rising Sun:* essays by Denis Sampson, Eamonn Hughes, and Declan Kiberd.[5]

Such universally positive responses are striking, for *That They May Face the Rising Sun* is a peculiar text. It lacks many of the elements of story material that traditionally mark novels: a story line, more or less intricate, that runs throughout the text, intense conflicts, climaxes, moments of denouement, and complex character development. Maher writes that some readers have been "somewhat bemused by the lack of plot or of character development" in McGahern's sixth novel. In fact, Maher argues, *That They May Face the Rising Sun* is "not a novel in the conventional sense, more a lyrical evocation of a particular place and its inhabitants."[6] This is certainly true, although the text is not quite as devoid of incident as might seem at first glance.

The novel's central characters are Joe and Kate Ruttledge, a married couple who have decided to leave London and live in a small farm (twenty acres) by a lake in the northwest of Ireland. They both worked in advertising in London, and Joe Ruttledge still does freelance work. Ruttledge (he is almost never referred to by his first name) comes originally from the vicinity of their farm, although he has lived away for many years; Kate Ruttledge is part American and spent at least some of her childhood in the United States. It is not clear how many years the Ruttledges have been settled in the farm, but clearly it is a considerable number.[7]

The novel presents episodes (in the form of recollections) of the Ruttledges' early days by the lake. It also follows the couple through approximately a year, charting seasonal change and the work associated with life on a small farm (lambing, calving, harvesting, taking beasts to be sold or slaughtered). In addition it presents the lives of a group of characters from the local community, largely neighbors of the Ruttledges, who live on farms around the lake or in the nearby small town. Certain simple story lines interweave throughout the text. These are usually connected with characters who visit the Ruttledges. Patrick Ryan has promised to help Ruttledge build a shed. While they are working together, Ryan is attacked by bees. At the novel's end the building is still not complete. Bill Evans, a former charity boy and now an elderly man, visits the Ruttledges regularly for cigarettes and food; through the agency of the local priest, he first is provided with transport into town one day a week and then is placed in a small flat of his own, thus finally escaping a life of miserable toil and exploitation. Jamesie and Mary Murphy, the Ruttledges' closest friends and neighbors, visit regularly, too (although the Ruttledges also visit them). At Christmas, the Murphys go to their son and his family in Dublin. Later in the novel, the son and family visit them. Jamesie's brother, Johnny, who has left the community "twenty years before" (6) to go to England, where he has worked most of those years for the Ford automobile company in Dagenham outside London, comes home, as he does each summer, on two occasions; on the second he dies. Ruttledge's uncle, known as "the Shah" (because of his girth or wealth—it is not clear), goes on a brief holiday with his widowed niece and also decides to give up control of his successful scrap business, leaving it to his longtime employee, Frank Dolan. Parts of the novel involve Ruttledge's attempts to negotiate a loan for Dolan from the local bank (an attempt that ends in comedy when Dolan refuses to prevaricate about his future plans for the business).

There are marriages. The Shah's niece Monica remarries. John Quinn, a lecherous local farmer much given to exploiting women, gets married again (he has outlived two wives already [27]); his new wife abandons him a few days after the wedding; he pursues her. Not all the story material directly concerns characters other than the Ruttledges. An old business friend, Robert Booth, visits the couple and offers Kate her old job in London. The Ruttledges are tempted but decline. When Johnny Murphy dies, Ruttledge must help to lay out his body; it is he, also, who, at the funeral, is delegated to talk to Jimmy Joe McKiernan, the local head of the Provisional IRA, auctioneer, undertaker, former prisoner in Long Kesh, and paramilitary man of violence, although Ruttledge himself has no time for the cause McKiernan represents.

The countryside of the novel is not entirely devoid of incident. Certainly the past offers action that is traditionally the stuff of novels. The account of John Quinn's first wedding day, during which he forces sexual intercourse in public on his new wife, is one such. So, too, is Jamesie's recollection of an incident in the Anglo-Irish War in the 1920s in which British irregulars ambush and massacre a unit of Irish guerrillas. Johnny Murphy's departure to England many years previously has been for love, and the unhappy affair has destroyed his life.

But despite this the overriding emphasis in the novel is one the unglamorous and the quotidian: the visits of friends and relatives, work, trips to market, shopping in town, a meal in a hotel, discussing a loan in a bank, building a shed, watching a TV program, drinking in a local bar. *That They May Face the Rising Sun* does indeed have conflicts (and some of these are the traditional stuff of novels), but also, and to a large extent, it avoids the glamorous, the colorful, and the conventionally exciting for the mundane and the seemingly trivial. This makes its popularity and success remarkable.

Narration and Narrative

The narrator of *That They May Face the Rising Sun* is an omniscient third-person one. The narrator fulfills all the traditional roles of such a narrator. He is able to explain characters' thoughts and feelings, set out the contexts for present occurrences and situations, and comment on what is going on at specific moments in the text. This narrative strategy is set out early in the novel, within the first few paragraphs, when, for example, the narrator sums up salient features of Jamesie's appearance and character (4). Within the same opening scene, the narrator explains who Johnny is and that he returns every summer (6). At almost the same moment the narrator also explains who Jim, Jamesie's son, is and what his life has been up to now (6). Immediately after this, the narrator sets out what preparations have been made by Jamesie and Mary for Johnny's return (6–7). The strategy continues through this opening sequence of the novel. Bill Evans arrives. His reticence is explained by the narrator (11), and the narrator goes on to generalize Jamesie's experience of being put down by the former charity boy (11). On the next page Bill Evans's past is given in summary by the narrator (12–13). Like all omniscient narrators, this one can also move freely in time and space. Thus, immediately after setting out Bill Evans's past, the narrator can move back in time to a meeting between him and Rutledge (12–13). As this particular sequence ends, he can pass from the Rutledges' bidding farewell to Bill Evans, to Jamesie's resting at the top of a hill, and to Cecil Pierce, the local Protestant small farmer, fishing in the lake from his tractor (19).

McGahern follows this narrative strategy throughout *That They May Face the Rising Sun*. However, although the narrator is a classic omniscient one, he does adopt Ruttledge's point of view consistently throughout the text. This is clear when the text gives Ruttledge's recollection of his time in a seminary and his experience of charity boys like Bill Evans (13–15). It is also evident at other moments: for example, when Ruttledge reflects on Patrick Ryan's work habits (79); when he visits Frank Dolan (162–65); when he thinks about Robert Booth (172); and when he considers the possibility of Johnny Murphy's coming back to the lake (213). There are many such passages in the text, and also many where the omniscient narrator and Ruttledge indeed come so close to each other that it is difficult to distinguish them, as, for example, in the general reflection on Bill Evans's mental make up (189). Ruttledge even speaks directly to the reader on one occasion, in a peculiar mixture of indirect speech and free direct speech ("What do we have without life? What does love become but care? Ruttledge thought in opposition but did not speak" [231]). But Ruttledge is not the sole consciousness that the narrator works through. Jamesie's point of view is given on the first page (3) and again later on page 126. As he and the Ruttledges are walking toward the lake, it is not clear whose point of view, if any, is being used by the narrator (18–19). Kate Ruttledge's point of view is clearly used at times (200–201, 240–41). At other times, the reader is aware of both the Ruttledges' perspectives on events (21, 295). In addition, two brief episodes at which Ruttledge is not present are narrated (86–88, 195–98). Although Ruttledge's point of view is most prominently employed in the novel (even in descriptions of nature [for example, 148, 216–17]), it is not the only one. At times, the omniscient narrator adopts a point of view that belongs to no particular character, for example in the first paragraph of the novel (3), or in some of the general reflections on life that are scattered through the text (for example, "But how can time be gathered in and kissed? There is only flesh" [141]). Even here, however, it is hard to demarcate clearly Ruttledge from the omniscient narrator; their views of life and appreciation of nature are so similar.

One of the most striking features of narration in *That They May Face the Rising Sun* is its near absence on occasion. A great deal of the novel is embodied in passages in which dialogue predominates over narration. At times, *That They May Face the Rising Sun* comes close to being a dramatic text. Almost the whole first fifty pages of the novel are done in this way, with minimal narrative intervention. This strategy runs throughout the text, although there are extensive passages in which narration predominates (for example, 77–84, 99–103, 117–22, 200–205, 292–302). Nevertheless, McGahern's reliance on dialogue is one of the novel's most distinctive features. The last pages of the text (324–36) return firmly to this configuration. *That They May Face the Rising Sun* is not just marked by an extensive use of dialogue but also of monologue. Throughout, characters speak for extended periods, usually giving accounts of past events. This can be observed with Jamesie on several occasions (7–8, 29–34, 35–39, 271–75, 332). Other characters provide monologues or near-monologues (with minimal interruptions from others): for example, Ruttledge (23–24), Quinn (26–27), Johnny (91–93, 294–95), Monica (114–16), and the clockmaker (328–29). There is even a monologue by what, it must be assumed, is a communal voice (305–6).[8]

The functions of this narrative strategy are complex. On one hand, the novel possesses a classic omniscient narration, traditional, flexible, and accessible to a wide range of readers. This reflects the estimation of tradition, community, and accepted mores that marks the novel. In addition, however, that omniscient narrator frequently adopts one character's point of view throughout the text but without committing himself entirely to it. Ruttledge is central to the novel as an observer, but his is not the only pair of eyes watching people and things. The narrator combines an individual with a collective perspective, as well as an even more general, nonpersonalized one. In the extensive use of dialogue, the text demonstrates forcibly the importance of community, for dialogue involves characters' talking to each other. At the same time, the frequent occurrence of monologues suggests the importance of the individual and the individual's story within that community.

The organization of the novel's story material seems utterly relaxed, episodic, and unshaped (but is, of course, far from being so, at least at a certain level). Pages 3–64 form one long sequence covering one day. However, in the course of that day the narrative moves back continually into the past: through Ruttledge's memory of his time in the seminary (13–14), through Jamesie's reminiscence of Bill Evans (16–17), via Kate's and Ruttledge's memories of finding the house they now live in and their early years there (20–41), and through an account of the Shah and his past (42–47). Interwoven with these retrospects are Jamesie's and Bill Evans's visits, the Ruttledges' walk in their fields, and Patrick Ryan's arrival to announce that he will come to restart work on the unfinished shed. He and Ruttledge also make a trip to Carrick to visit Ryan's dying brother. The sequence (and the day) ends with the Ruttledges and Jamesie delivering a calf from an elderly cow.

This long sequence is typical of the manner in which the story material is organized. There is a leisurely forward movement and many digressions into the past. Events recounted have little in common, except for some of the participants. The rest of the novel is shaped in the same episodic way. Progression in time is often marked by introductory statements concerning the weather or the seasons (for example, 65, 99, 117, 147, 152, 166, 205, 232). It is also marked by casual indications of time such as "next morning" (126, 143), "on a showery Sunday" (147), "Not many days later" (150), "At that same time" (170), "the day after" (195), "one evening" (263), "another Saturday evening" (207), or "A few days after the funeral" (324). There are also some more specific markers of progression, such as the names of months (205, 209), Monaghan Day (245), and religious festivals (263, 269). The impression is of a leisurely progress through a period of just over a year, without any plot providing cohesion. One has a sense of a chronicle (a listing of events) rather than a highly integrated narrative.

Indeed, *That They May Face the Rising Sun* is a collection of short narratives, episodes joined together, in large measure, only by the chronological progression of the text. These include the building of the shed, various visits to the Murphys' by the Ruttledges and vice versa, the Ruttledges' cat bringing in a dead leveret, harvesting, the Shah's giving up the scrap business, the trip to Roscommon slaughterhouse, Quinn's marriage, Jamesie and Mary's visit to

Dublin, and so on. In addition, as in the novel's long opening sequence, there are numerous digressions into the past within this relaxed movement forward (for example, 69–70, 76–77, 100–103, 113–16, 123–25, 129–30, 156, 173, 235–38, 271–74). However, at the novel's end there is a clearly integrated and extended sequence: that involving Johnny's return to the lake, his death, and funeral (292–335). This matches the long sequence (3–64) at the start of the text.

The partial balancing of opening and closing sequences indicates that the narrative of *That They May Face the Rising Sun* is far from unorganized. The loosely connected mini narratives, the interwoven retrospects, offer a specific vision of life. A certain kind of life is not susceptible to the artful cohesions of literature. It is plotless in the long run. The past is omnipresent. In addition, the two longer sequences, at start and finish, suggest a vision too. The long rich day and the memories of welcome and friendship are balanced by the death of the returned emigrant and the community's response to it. Further, with regard to the text's organization, the separate items of the narrative are, in fact, linked by shared motifs. This will be discussed below.

One of the most striking aspects of the story material of *That They May Face the Rising Sun* concerns absences. Ruttledge's work is referred to on a few occasions (166, 171, 211, 217, 322), but it is pushed to one side by the events and personalities of the community. This in itself carries considerable meaning in the text. The metropolitan world is sidelined. However, another omission is less easy to understand. Ruttledge's past is almost completely elided in the novel. Jamesie reveals that he was born nearby (5). Ruttledge recalls his studies in a seminary (13–14). He has abandoned the priesthood long ago, despite family disapproval, with the Shah alone supporting his decision (46). The reader is provided with little more information about the character who is, ultimately, the central consciousness of large parts of the novel. Kate's past, too, is scarcely more than alluded to (5, 226). The functions of such an omission are complex. Does it serve further to separate the world of the lake from the city and metropolitan centers beyond it? Does it suggest that the local here-and-now-and-then, the community and its present and its past, are much more important than the life of the consciousness that, in part, observes them? It certainly emphasizes that the focus of the novel is not on Ruttledge and his problems of belief or his relations with his family, for example, but on the lives and experiences of the farmers, tradesmen, businesspeople, and laborers of the lakeside community. A figure like Ruttledge was the center of earlier McGahern novels—*The Dark, The Leavetaking,* and *The Pornographer.* This is not the case in *That They May Face the Rising Sun,* and the novel's elisions mark that clearly.

Language

The language of *That They May Face the Rising Sun* is distinctive. Above all, it is varied. Dialogue, in which so much of the novel is set, is informal and at times contains obscenities (see, for example, Jamesie on "the boggy hollow" [female genitalia] [10] or Ryan's "What the fuck is this?" [229].) This makes the dialogue verisimilar and marks the social humbleness of most of the novel's characters. The narrator's language, however, is complex. In its lexis, it runs a gamut from informal through neutral to formal vocabulary. In syntax, it is varied, moving from complex sentences and complex-compound sentences to simple ones. The novel's opening paragraph illustrates this reasonably well.

> The morning was clear. There was no wind on the lake. There was also a great stillness. When the bells rang out for Mass, the strokes trembling on the water, they had the entire world to themselves. (3)

In four sentences, much of the lexis is neutral to informal, but words like "a great stillness," "the strokes trembling on the water," and "the entire world" move the paragraph in a more formal direction. Further three simple sentences are balanced by a complex final one, which also contains a parenthetical adverbial phrase (virtually unknown in spoken English), thus making it even more formal. Many other passages might be chosen to illustrate this subtle shifting through levels of formality and sophistication, a movement that is entirely appropriate to the novel's concern with a restricted and relatively uneducated community that, nevertheless, is connected with and illustrates great and universal concerns.

One feature of the language of *That They May Face the Rising Sun* echoes that of earlier novels, especially *The Barracks;* namely the widespread occurrence of the passive voice throughout the text. There are many examples of this. Two must suffice here. The narrator (or Ruttledge) imagines the preparations that Jamesie and Mary have made to receive Johnny back from England.

> The house and the outhouses would be freshly whitewashed for the homecoming, the street swept, the green gates painted, old stakes replaced in the netting wire that held Mary's brown hens in the space around the hayshed. Mary would have scrubbed and freshened all the rooms. Together they would have taken the mattress from the bed in the lower room, Johnny's old room, and left it outside to air in the sun. The holy pictures and the wedding photographs would be taken down, the glass wiped and polished. His bed would be made with crisp linen and draped with the red blanket. An enormous vase of flowers from the garden and the fields

. . . would be placed on the sill under the open window to sweeten the air and take away the staleness and smell of damp from the unused room. The order for the best sirloin would already have been placed at Carroll's in the town. The house couldn't have been prepared any better for a god coming home to his old place on earth. (6–7)

The passive voice predominates in the entire paragraph. In only two sentences is there active voice (those beginning "Mary would have scrubbed . . ." and "Together they would have taken . . ."). Another later example of the use of the passive occurs during the laying out of Johnny's body. The narrator reports, "A row of chairs was arranged around the walls of the room. A bedside table was draped with a white cloth and two candles were placed in brass candlesticks and lit. A huge vase of flowers was set in the windowsill" (311). In between there are many examples. The use of the passive has a similar function in *That They May Face the Rising Sun* to the one it has in *The Barracks*. Actions are depersonalized; they become communal or actions prescribed by a culture, not entirely a matter of personal choice. The fact that here they are directed toward an individual (Johnny) and are performed by people makes their depersonalized, communal nature even more striking.

With regard to language, it is also noticeable that the narrator of *That They May Face the Rising Sun* often presents nonhuman occurrences. The novel's opening paragraph is typical in this respect. Not people, but the morning, wind, stillness, and the sound of bells are the agents. There are many other such examples. The frequent descriptions of natural phenomena are depersonalized (205, 281, 334). In addition, even human actions are frequently presented in ways that downplay human agency. For example, when the Ruttledges move into the house above the lake, the narrator presents the process thus:

The addition of rooms to the house, the new roof, the drilling of a well for water—with the lake a stone's throw away—the coming and going of the large Mercedes, were all carefully observed, and resentment fuelled an innate intolerance of anything strange or foreign. (25–26)

This paragraph is remarkable for its avoidance of human subjects, even though it relates actions performed by human beings. As with the use of the passive, such language deindividualizes actions. Things happen, they are done, emotions are felt. The communal, the general, the nonindividual aspects of life are emphasized. This is clearly embodied in the action of the novel. "The time came when the lambs had to be sold," the narrator informs the reader (152). "I'm certain. It's time," the Shah declares of his decision to sell the scrap yard

(169). In *That They May Face the Rising Sun* the aspects of life over which individual humans have little control are made prominent.[9]

Setting

Where and when is *That They May Face the Rising Sun* set? The question of where is easier to answer. McGahern places his lakeside community in relation to documented places. It is approximately two hours from Dublin by car and by train (143, 222). One can drive with ease to places such as Carrick (53–59) and Roscommon (152–62). Enniskillen in Northern Ireland is close (171–73). The topography of the local community in which the novel is set is clear. Ruttledge travels on foot and by car among the farms and dwellings and to the small town near them. It is striking that the novel rarely moves physically beyond the community and the nearby towns. Jamesie and Mary's visit to Dublin is reported on after their return (235–38). London is present only in Johnny's stories of his life there (90–93, 294–95). It is, however, important to note that the community is not an isolated one. Boston and England are there as places where people go to better their lot (102, 187). Patrick Ryan takes work all over the country (304). Telephone lines are only being installed at the text's end (324), but the use of farming machinery is widespread and characters watch television (81, 88, 164–65, 213). At Christmas time the nearby town is a bustle of commercial activity and sights and sounds recognizable in any provincial center in most of Europe (221).

The when of the novel's setting is more complex. On one hand, it is easy to establish time setting. As has been noted above, the novel marks its forward progression by noting the passing of days and the months and seasons of the year, as well as religious festivals. The movement of the seasons is particularly clear. The novel begins in summer (18, 65) and moves through to another summer, seasonal changes and seasonal labor being duly noted and described as the text progresses. The changes in the natural world are particularly presented (54, 64, 148, 200, 207).

But other aspects of time setting are vaguer. It is not obvious when the novel's present is, although it is clear that violence in Northern Ireland is still current and memories of terrorist actions fresh (173, 255, 321, 323). However, if Jamesie can vividly remember an incident in the Anglo-Irish War from around 1921 (the Black and Tans, British irregular forces that he refers to, were only deployed in Ireland from March 1920) that he observed as a child (271–77), he must be an extremely old man indeed, if the novel's time of setting is anywhere near that of its publication. In fact, in contradistinction to his carefulness with regard to place and to seasonal time, McGahern is consistently vague about the dating of the novel and its action. Johnny left England twenty years before (6) when the "whole country was leaving for England" (7, 43). Does the author mean the reader to understand the 1940s and 1950s here? That makes the novel's present sometime in the 1970s, which seems wrong given the details of the references to the troubles in Northern Ireland. The Ruttledges moved into their present home "years before" (150). Their visitors from London have dwindled in numbers "over the years" (170). Jamesie and Mary's last trip to Dublin took place seventeen years previously (222), although it is not clear when that was. Ruttledge reflects that he saw Patrick Ryan's house for the first time "ten or fifteen years before" (228). McGahern has never been particularly scrupulous about precisely dating his novels (compare the discussion of setting in *The Barracks* in chapter 2). However, in *That They May Face the Rising Sun* he is quite cavalier with dates and quite evasive in the matter of dating. One can only assume that this is quite deliberate. Indeed, one can suggest that such vagueness suggests that, actually, historical dates are not centrally important in the vision that the novel holds. Seasons are important, changes in plant life are worthy of note, recurrent festivals and periods of work are significant, but although the past is everywhere the particular year or even decade in which something takes place is not the most important aspect of it. McGahern is suggesting a view of time that somehow, at least partly, transcends history. How convincing such a suggestion is, is something readers must decide for themselves.[10]

Characters

The characters that inhabit the world of the lakeside, its small farms, and town, have provoked some discussion among critics. Part of the strangeness of *That They May Face the Rising Sun* that commentators note has to do with what they see as the kind of characters that McGahern creates. Sampson describes them as belonging to "a closed, rural community" and writes that "they are almost medieval humours" (in that they manifest specific, unchanging moral, social, or psychological characteristics). Maher points to their advanced age.[11] Given that so much of the novel is done through dialogue and concerns the interactions of its characters and their pasts, the lakeside's population is clearly central to the whole text.

It is true that most of the characters seem middle aged and older: the Ruttledges, Jamesie and Mary, Bill Evans, Partick Ryan, Johnny Murphy, the Shah, John Quinn, Robert Booth, and others. Most of them are also from the lakeside area. Jamesie, indeed, has hardly ever left that world (11, 333). However, the range of characters is not quite as restricted as it might seem. Jimmy Joe McKiernan is clearly younger than the characters mentioned above and has also moved beyond the lakeside community. The Murphys' son, Jim, and his young wife and children make two major appearances in the text; they also now come from the outside. Robert Booth is an incomer, too, from Northern Ireland and from London. Partick Ryan travels all over Ireland to work. The Ruttledges themselves hail from a metropolitan, English world, even though Ruttledge, it is hinted, is returning to his point of origin by coming to the lake. The community of the lakeside is not quite as geriatric and closed as some commentators suggest.

Further, the characters of the novel, although they can be seen (as Sampson sees them) as quasi-medieval humors, in fact show much of the complexity of traditional novel characterization. The novel consistently points out psychological intricacies and surprising emotional features of its characters. Johnny's throwing everything up for love and his ambivalent coming to terms with emigration are examples (8, 292–303). Jamesie's relationship with his brother is similarly complex—loyal to him, delighted at his annual returns, angry and disappointed at his past conduct (8), avoiding him once he does return (215), terrified by the thought that he might come home for good, yet unwilling to give a refusal (209–10). Jamesie by himself is a peculiar figure—sneaking round the Ruttledges' house and land, to help, certainly, but also out of curiosity (61, 177). His relations with others in the community can be surprisingly conflict ridden, too (279). The celibacy of both the Shah and Ryan also points to psychological depths that the novel hints at but does not explore (44–47, 229). Ryan himself is a complex figure—kind to the Ruttledges, even friendly toward Ruttledge, but also capable of sudden, unprovoked aggression toward him (75, 227–32, 95).

The novel frequently depicts unexpected forms of behavior among its characters. The amateur dramatics that Johnny and Ryan have engaged in in the past (performing a high literary text such as Synge's *The Playboy of the Western World*) are at odds with the factory and construction work that they are now engaged in (7–8). When the two men meet, they act together and dance in a way that many readers may find remarkable (86–88). This episode is echoed later when two truck drivers defuse their animosity toward each other by singing a romantic song and dancing together (158–59). Irish farming and working-class life is presented as capable of surprising turns.

While Kate Ruttledge is a somewhat transparent figure, Ruttledge himself is a figure not without complexities. His attitude to the Catholic Church forms one such element of this complexity (4–5, 39, 93, 324). So, too, does his tendency to watch and to detach himself from things. This is evident at several moments in the text: when he watches Jamesie creep round his house (177), when he observes Frank Dolan (201), when he is reluctant to become engaged in Bill Evans's problems (241), and when he slips away from Jamesie (256). The most striking of such moments, however, is when he watches the household cat drag a dead leveret over the bed to his wife (118). Connected with such complexity is the reticence of some characters in *That They May Face the Rising Sun.* Reserve is peculiarly coupled with garrulousness. Characters speak a great deal—but not about certain things and not to certain other characters. The Shah and Frank Dolan, who have long worked together, never speak to each other, something that dumbfounds even Ruttledge (148–49, 239). Ruttledge notes of Jamesie and Mary that their lives are shaped round not speaking of certain things (210). Robert Booth, Ruttledge feels, conceals feelings that he will not acknowledge (172). Johnny's brave version of the emptiness and disappointment of his life also fits in here (91–93).

Despite the novel's pointing to individuality and complexity among its characters, its perspective on them is, finally, to see them as a community. No one character dominates the text (as Moran does, for example, in *Amongst Women*). The novel presents a range of important characters (Jamesie, the Shah, Partick Ryan, Johnny, Ruttledge, Quinn, McKiernan) whose interrelations form the central substance of the text. In this set of interrelations, it is striking that women characters, while present (Kate, Mary, Monica, Lucy), are not at center stage. The novel focuses on male relationships above all, both in the present and the past. Ruttledge's greatest moments of happiness and tenderness are linked more with Jamesie than with Kate (207, 291, 333). The novel not only displaces the individual from the center of its concerns but also, in part, the human. There are numerous descriptions of natural, nonhuman phenomena—landscapes, plants, birds, and animals—and these assume an equivalent weight and stature within the text. The individual and complexly human is present in *That They May Face the Rising Sun,* but the novel places this within a group and, indeed, a nonhuman context.

Place, Time, Change, Death, and History

Certain motifs are found in *That They May Face the Rising Sun,* forming one of the principal means (besides setting and character) by which the novel's episodic organization is held firmly together. One of the most prominent of these is the relation of the local to the wider world. For all that it is open to outsiders and not nearly as closed and isolated as some readers suggest, the lakeside is a specific, provincial world, separate from the wider world outside its limits. Jamesie particularly embodies this separation. "I've never, never moved from here," he declares, "and I know the whole world" (10). In a sense, he does not. Mary mocks him because he is unclear on geography outside the limits of his provincial community (105). However, he insists that he knows "the whole world," and Ruttledge, the metropolitan traveler, acknowledges that this is so (333).[12]

McGahern goes to great pains to universalize the world of the lakeside. He does this by pointing to highly general experiences and phenomena that play out in the small, provincial community. These can be seen in the novel's focus on the passage of time and the movement of the seasons, which have been discussed above. "Everything that had flowered had now come to fruit," the narrator remarks of lakeside nature, emphasizing the generality of his perspective (200). The universal can also be observed in the recurrent motifs of death, change, and loss in the novel. The novel's first day contains a trip by Ruttledge and Ryan to visit Ryan's dying brother (56). Mary later recounts a story about Jamesie's father's death (129–30). Death is never far away from Ruttledge's consciousness. "The bad go with the good, in and out the same revolving doors," he muses (262). "And all we have is the day," he notes grimly to Kate at Christmas (226). This is echoed in Ryan's observation in a bar that "all we are on is a day out of our lives. We'll never be round again" (258). One of the conventional climaxes of the novel is Johnny's death, funeral, and burial, which takes up more than thirty pages at the end of the novel (303–36). The digging of his grave is an episode especially full of mementos mori (315–18).[13]

Change, besides seasonal change, runs through the novel. Johnny has lost his skill with a gun (89); the house in which Mary grew up is now a ruin (100); she stares at her son and his wife, wondering at the passage of time (141); Ryan's house both has not changed since Ruttledge first saw it, yet is also falling into ruin (227–28); Johnny has turned in on himself on his second visit in the novel (296). Other kinds of change occur. Characters show a strong sense of transience. This is the case with Ryan and Johnny on Johnny's first visit in the novel (90, 94). "We're no more than a puff of wind out on the lake," Mary reflects (130). When he hears the story of the final days of Jamesie's father, Ruttledge observes that they may all be in that situation some day (139). One can also perceive social changes in the novel. Ruttledge thinks that fewer people recognize Ash Wednesday in the traditional way (263), while Jamesie reckons that there are many fewer at the Easter march to commemorate the incident in the Anglo-Irish War (276). Telephone poles appear in the landscape at the novel's end (324). Such changes must be seen in the context of continuity and changelessness. The seasonal changes and the recurrent kinds of work (lambing, calving, harvesting) about the farms are kinds of continuity. So, too, is Jamesie's and Ruttledge's watching the all-Ireland football finals on television (207). Johnny visits the same friend every Christmas; Ryan does something similar (93, 231). Johnny's summer visits are repeated (6). The Shah comes to the Ruttledges every Sunday (41). Ruttledge knows that the heron he observes flying over the lake cannot be the same one as he saw when they first moved there, but he thinks of it in that way (213). When Easter morning comes, it repeats the sounds and the sights of an earlier Sunday (3, 269).

One of the most marked aspects of change in *That They May Face the Rising Sun* is exile. This is most clearly embodied in the figure of Johnny, who is seen as representative of many Irish people who have sought better (or different) lives away from their rural origins. The omniscient narrator or Ruttledge feels that Johnny is "speaking for multitudes" at one point when he talks of his exile in London (293). Jamesie relays Father Conroy's words that echo this observation (332). (McGahern complicates the matter by having Johnny choose his exile. In this way he avoids sentimentality and cliché and makes the whole business of Irish emigration not just a matter of victimization but also of choice.) There are other emigrants in the novel. Ruttledge is one, although his time out of Ireland is scarcely touched upon (46). The Ruttledges' friend Robert Booth is also an emigrant, from humble Protestant Northern Irish origins to the English metropolis (170–71). In the novel's present Jamesie and Mary's son Jim, too, is an emigrant, from the provinces to the capital (42, 290).

Social change and emigration point to another aspect of change that maintains a subtle presence in *That They May Face the Rising Sun,* namely, history. The kind of change in religious and patriotic observance that Ruttledge and Jamesie note is part of history, as is emigration. The troubles in Northern Ireland remain a motif in the novel, coming to prominence in Ruttledge's dialogue with McKiernan before Johnny's funeral (320–23). Ireland's bloody twentieth-century history comes vividly to the fore (and all the more vividly for the complexity and restraint with which it is presented) in Jamesie's story about the incident in the Anglo-Irish War (271–75). The incident is presented in an antiheroic fashion (worthy of Moran in *Amongst Women*) and is shown as something complex by Jamesie: the brutality of the British irregulars, the nationalist reprisal against an innocent local Protestant farmer, Jamesie's and his father's own standing by while the violence takes place, the ingratitude of the guerrilla whom they help survive. Throughout the rest of the novel, too, the realia of the late-twentieth-century conflict are present: Irish police detectives outside McKiernan's bar (153), road blocks and British soldiers on the border between the Republic of Ireland and Northern Ireland (172–73), and memories of recent IRA violence (255).

In a world of change, transience, and death, McGahern looks for some kind of balancing force. Traditional institutional religion does not offer this in the novel. Ruttledge has little time for the church, although he appreciates the efforts and integrity of Father Conroy (93, 243–44, 287–88, 333). There are two sources of balance in the novel. These are the rituals of the community. Johnny's wake, the community's digging of his grave, the funeral—these are presented as dignified and worthy ways of dealing with loss. Ruttledge may not believe in the resurrection of the dead, but Ryan's words and Johnny's interment facing east are seen as appropriate and humane (318). In addition, the texture of everyday life—the conversations, the mutual aid, the shared visits, trivial kindnesses—is also seen as redemptive. Jamesie and Mary are frequently seen as secular religious figures. Kate calls Jamesie one of the "lay angels" (285). Ruttledge sees him and his wife as "communicants" on their trip to Dublin and Jamesie's recitation of the names of the houses on the road to the station as like a "prayer" (222). When Ruttledge brings them back, he sees the light in the window of their house as "the light of a vigil" (261). Such religious references only make more obvious a central element of the novel: it is in the humane interactions of the community that there is some kind of counterweight to the transience of the world and the brutality of history. But this is not a sentimental evasion on McGahern's part: the community is complex and often far from charming (Quinn is a particularly good example); death comes for Johnny, as it presumably will for all the elderly denizens of the lakeside; exile and emigration have not come to an end; and the forces of history will continue to show themselves in the future.

That They May Face the Rising Sun is a remarkable novel—at once seemingly loosely organized and yet carefully crafted, deeply traditional yet subtly playing with tradition—a novel about a community that also gives weight to individual human complexities; a text that focuses on the local and yet one that has a highly generalized purview. It is a powerful continuation of McGahern's varied and yet coherent oeuvre.

Conclusion

When John McGahern died after a long illness on March 30, 2006, the obituaries in newspapers in Ireland, the United Kingdom, and the United States were full of praise for his writing, and many contained moving tributes to the writer as a human being, emphasizing his resilience in the face of the ostracism that he met after the banning of *The Dark,* his modesty, his honesty, and his sense of humor. The major British daily newspapers, the *Guardian,* the *Independent,* and the *Daily Telegraph,* contained particularly full and insightful discussions of McGahern's work and career. All emphasize his stature at his death. In the *Guardian,* Richard Pine calls him "arguably the most important Irish novelist since Samuel Beckett."[1] The anonymous writer in the *Daily Telegraph* points out that the "honesty and unsentimental candor" of his work "earned comparisons with Chekhov."[2] All the obituaries set out the arc of McGahern's life as a writer: early success followed by official hostility, years of wandering, and finally, for the last three decades, a return to Ireland and increasing recognition by the establishment of his native land. W. J. McCormack in the *Independent* even writes of Ireland as a "guilty country" that tried to make amends for its earlier ill treatment of the writer.[3]

The obituaries place McGahern squarely in a tradition of Irish realist fiction about rural life. McCormack puts it most clearly: "Neither in formal nor thematic terms did he break from the tradition of modern Irish fiction established by George Moore in *The Untilled Field.*" Later he writes of *The Barracks* and *The Dark,* "Manifestly these were not innovatory novels. No comparisons with Joyce or Beckett were warranted on that score. Through his short stories McGahern kept in touch with the well-established tradition of Frank O'Connor and Sean O'Faolain."[4] The power and resonance of McGahern's writing, however, is celebrated by the obituarists. Joseph O'Connor writes that "like Heaney, or Patrick Kavanagh, or Raymond Carver, or Joyce, he was able to take the stuff of ordinary lives and create of it the highest art. This is why his books were so frequently bestsellers in his native Ireland. His work spoke to readers about their own lives; its silences were also ours. It crackled with a kind of hopefulness, though it offered no tricks." O'Connor concludes by declaring that "John McGahern's work brings a fierce kind of pleasure" even "on such a sad day" as that of the author's death.[5]

That death will permit a critical discussion of McGahern's output as a whole and an assessment of its place in Irish and European literary history. Certain aspects of this discussion and assessment are evident already, although time will inevitably alter these and make them more complex and better. McGahern is one of the major Irish novelists (and one of the major English-language novelists) of the second half of the twentieth century. His oeuvre is rich and complex. In his early novels, *The Barracks* and *The Dark,* he provides bleak and moving pictures of family life (especially of women and children) in rural Ireland in the mid–twentieth century. These are notable for the detail with which they present unglamorous and failed yet—especially in *The Barracks*—somehow luminous lives. His middle-period texts, *The Leavetaking* and *The Pornographer,* move into urban settings and approach the complexities of metropolitan existence. In these novels, too, McGahern offers his recurrent dark themes of death and failure (this is particularly true in the pictures of emotional desolation in the critically underrated *The Pornographer*) but shows, too, even in their midst, possibilities of survival, goodness, and joy. McGahern's last two novels, *Amongst Women* and *That They May Face the Rising Sun,* return to a rural world and are searching examinations of family and community. In both, as in his two first novels, he weaves a dense fabric of personal experience, social change, and historical events, so that *Amongst Women,* above all, has been seen by many Irish readers as embodying and making vivid at least two generations' lives in an independent Ireland.

The complexities of McGahern's work have not always been fully recognized by critics and scholars. The author's relation to literary convention and history still remains to be thoroughly explored. Throughout his life, McGahern worked within the conventions of nineteenth- and twentieth-century realism, writing complex psychological-social novels. This affiliation is widely recognized by commentators. Yet there is a constant and underlying self-referentiality in his work, in the shape of orchestration of sound and vocabulary and in narrational complexity, that draws his work closer to Joyce's, to Beckett's, and to John Banville's than has been usually acknowledged. The phonological patterning of parts of his novels (for example, the opening paragraph of *The Barracks*) pulls his texts close to poetry, as does the syntactic and lexical parallelism of sections of *The Leavetaking.* The narrational intricacies of *The Dark* remain striking even after thirty years. McGahern's cavalier way with dates in *That They May Face the Rising Sun* is unlikely to be a matter of carelessness but, rather, a subtle reminder to the perceptive reader that this is a story, a fiction, and one shaped by an author's hand. The constant reworking of biographical material, too, is both a statement of his fiction's rootedness in documented and personally authenticated *realia* and also a constant reminder of the operations of the writer's workshop, the rearranging and reworking of a limited number of experiences. His fiction is deeply autobiographical; yet interviews and *Memoir* make clear the degree to which McGahern has transformed experience into art through selectivity and imaginative reshaping. It is McGahern's sly mixing (and the word "sly" seems particularly appropriate) of conventions that gives his work a fascinating and very complex flavor. It is as if he pretends at times to be a much more traditional and simpler writer than he actually is. One sometimes has the impression that he is gently laughing at his readers.

Many complexities, however, have been widely recognized. Although McGahern speaks with his own voice, he draws on a European literary tradition. Commentators constantly compare him to Chekhov, Proust, and Joyce, among others. McGahern writes about Ireland and Irish matters; yet his often restricted worlds are universal in their existential scope and resonance. The French reception of McGahern's work is particularly telling in this respect. His fiction presents individual fates, yet these fates are linked with and interweave with the course of twentieth-century Irish history. They interweave, too, with the course of other countries' histories. The Reegans and Morans, both female and male, and their encounters with history, social change, and patriarchy are recognizable in many non-Irish contexts. McGahern is an acknowledged master not just of the novel but of the short story too, and he has produced some of the most powerful short fiction written in English of the last fifty years of the twentieth century.

For different readers different characters and moments will stand out in his novels—Elizabeth Reegan's facing death, young Mahoney's paralysis at university, the young Irish schoolteacher's edgy responses to London (in *The Leavetaking*), the pornographer's experience of an affair gone sour, Moran's reminiscences of the Anglo-Irish War, Ruttledge's clear-eyed visions of nature and his neighbors. Different aspects of the short stories will stick in one's memory—the unease of "Korea"; the hopelessness yet beauty of "The Wine Breath" and "Swallows"; the economical presentation of history and individuals in history in "Oldfashioned," "Eddie Mac," and "The Conversion of William Kirkwood"; the complexity of individual and community relations in "The Country Funeral." The work as a whole, however, also impresses, and will surely continue to impress, with its richness, its complexity, its artistry, and its humane intelligence.

Notes

Chapter 1. John McGahern

1. Important interviews with McGahern include Julia Carlson, "John McGahern," in *Banned in Ireland: Censorship and the Irish Writer* (London: Routledge, 1990), 53–67; Denis Sampson, "A Conversation with John McGahern," *Canadian Journal of Irish Studies* 17 (July 1991): 13–18; Liliane Louvel, Gilles Ménégaldo, and Claudine Verley, "John McGahern—17 November 1993," in "John McGahern," ed. Jean Brihault and Liliane Louvel, special issue, *La Licorne* 32 (1995): 19–31; Rosa Gonzales Casademont, "An Interview with John McGahern," *European English Messenger* 4 (1995): 17–23; James Whyte, "An Interview with John McGahern," in *History, Myth, and Ritual in the Fiction of John McGahern: Strategies of Transcendence* (Lewiston, Queenstown, and Lampeter: Edwin Mellen Press, 2002), 227–35; Gerd Kampen, "An Interview with John McGahern," in *Zwischen Welt und Text: Narratologische Studien zum irischen Gegenwartsroman am Beispiel von John McGahern und John Banville* (Trier: Wissenschaftlicher Verlag, 2002), 336–42. Biographical essays on McGahern include Michael C. Prusse, "John McGahern," in *British Novelists since 1960,* ed. Meritt Moseley, Dictionary of Literary Biography 231 (Detroit: Bruccoli Clark Layman/ Gale, 2001), 135–45; David Malcolm, "John McGahern," in *British and Irish Short Fiction Writers, 1945–2000,* ed. Cheryl Alexander Malcolm and David Malcolm, Dictionary of Literary Biography 319 (Detroit: Thomson/Gale, 2006), 222–34. McGahern's partial autobiography is contained in McGahern, *Memoir* (London: Faber and Faber, 2005).

2. The award is named for the Irish poet and artist George William Russell [1867–1935], who wrote under the pseudonym Æ, or AE.

3. None of the biographical sources is specifies the date of the collapse of McGahern's first marriage. McGahern himself writes clearly about the marriage's end but without giving precise dates (see McGahern, *Memoir,* 253–55).

4. For McGahern's hesitations about the role of autobiography in fiction, see John Walsh, "Illuminating the Dark Side of the Irish," *Sunday Times* (London), April 29, 1990, H8–9; John McGahern, "Madness/Creativity," in "John McGahern," ed. Jean Brihault and Liliane Louvel, special issue, *La Licorne* 32 (1995): 9–10. James Whyte discusses McGahern's biography and social environment in relation to his work in chapters 1–3 of *History, Myth, and Ritual in the Fiction of John McGahern.* Liliane Louvel's interview with McGahern is published as Louvel, "John McGahern" *Journal*

of the Short Story in English 41 (Autumn 2003): 123–41; see, esp., his comments about *The Barracks* (126).

5. Sampson, *Outstaring Nature's Eye;* Whyte, *History, Myth, and Ritual in the Fiction of John McGahern;* Gerd Kampen, *Zwischen Welt und Text;* Eamon Maher, *John McGahern: From the Local to the Universal* (Dublin: Liffey Press), 2003.

6. Alan Warner, *A Guide to Anglo-Irish Literature* (Dublin: Gill and Macmillan; New York: St Martin's Press, 1981), 245; Liliane Louvel, "John McGahern: La manière noire," in "John McGahern," ed. Jean Brihault and Liliane Louvel, special issue, *La Licorne* 32 (1995): 5; Sampson, *Outstaring Nature's Eye,* xi; O'Dwyer, quoted in Whyte, *History, Myth, and Ritual in the Fiction of John McGahern,* xi; "Noted by the Editors," review of *The Collected Stories, Antioch Review* 51, no. 4 (Fall 1993): 657; Louvel, "John McGahern," 123; Banville, "In Violent Times," review of *Amongst Women, New York Review of Books,* December 6, 1990, 22.

7. Sampson, *Outstaring Nature's Eye,* xii–xiii; Banville, "In Violent Times," 23; Nicola Bradbury, "High Ground," in *Re-reading the Short Story,* ed. Clare Hanson, 95 (Basingstoke and London: Macmillan, 1989); Louvel, "John McGahern," 128; John McGahern, "*Dubliners,*" in *James Joyce: The Artist and the Labyrinth: A Critical Re-evaluation,* ed. Augustine Martin, 64, 65, 67, 71 (London: Ryan, 1990). Neil Corcoran points to Kavanagh as an influence on McGahern in Corcoran, *After Yeats and Joyce: Reading Modern Irish Literature* (Oxford and New York: Oxford University Press, 1997), 71.

8. Corcoran, *After Yeats and Joyce,* 78, 81, 86; James M. Cahalan, *Double Visions: Women and Men in Modern and Contemporary Irish Fiction* (Syracuse, N.Y.: Syracuse University Press, 1999), 108.

9. Sampson, *Outstaring Nature's Eye,* xii; Jürgen Kamm, "John McGahern," in *Contemporary Irish Writers,* ed. Rüdiger Imhof, 187 (Tübingen: Gunter Narr Verlag, 1990); John Banville, "Big News from Small Worlds," review of *The Collected Stories, New York Review of Books,* April 8, 1993, 22.

10. McGahern's depiction of women is a topic that requires a full study. Women are central to many of his novels, including *The Barracks, The Leavetaking, The Pornographer,* and *Amongst Women.* They are peripheral to *The Dark* and *That They May Face the Rising Sun.* The short stories often focus on male protagonists and their relationships with other men, although women are very important in "My Love, My Umbrella," "Peaches," "The Beginning of an Idea," "Along the Edges," "Gold Watch," "Oldfashioned," and "Bank Holiday." Annie May is one of the central figures, and the main loser, in the William Kirkwood stories ("Eddie Mac" and "The Conversion of William Kirkwood"). McGahern usually writes of women from the point of view of a male protagonist, and often these women fulfill, socially and culturally, very traditional roles. However, McGahern is perfectly capable of choosing female protagonists and is a meticulous analyzer of the effects of patriarchy and a patriarchal order on women. Elizabeth Reegan is the central example of a complexly realized female figure, one whose life has resonances beyond itself in terms of women's experience in a particular kind of

social order. *Memoir* is full of vital and powerful female figures McGahern clearly admires greatly.

11. Wolfgang F. W. Schmitz, *Die Darstellung Irlands in der modernen irischen Short Story: Eine Bestandsaufnahme zur thematisch-inhaltlichen Ausrichtung irischer Short-Story-Autoren in den sechziger und siebziger Jahren* (Frankfurt am Main and Bern: Peter D. Lang, 1981), 112; Patrick Goden, "Interview with John McGahern," *Scrivener: A Literary Magazine* 5, no. 2 (Summer 1984): 25–26; Sampson, *Outstaring Nature's Eye,* 11; Kamm, "John McGahern," 180; Anne Goarzin, *John McGahern: Reflets d'Irlande* (Rennes: Presses Universitaires de Rennes, 2002), 10; Claude Fierobe, "John McGahern: Le fugitif et l'éternel," in "Études sur *The Barracks* de John McGahern," ed. Claude Fierobe and Danielle Jacquin, special issue, *Études Irlandaises* (October 1994): 13.

12. Warner, *A Guide to Anglo-Irish Literature,* 245, 250–51; Kampen, *Zwischen Welt und Text,* 8; Sampson, *Outstaring Nature's Eye,* ch. 1; Roger Garfitt, "Constants in Contemporary Irish Fiction," in *Two Decades of Irish Writing: A Critical Survey,* ed. Douglas Dunn, 224 (Cheadle, U.K.: Carcanet, 1975); James M. Cahalan, *The Irish Novel: A Critical History* (Dublin: Gill and Macmillan, 1988), 271; Seamus Deane, *A Short History of Irish Literature* (London: Hutchinson, 1986), 222; Robert Hogan, "Old Boys, Young Bucks, and New Women: The Contemporary Irish Short Story," in *The Irish Short Story,* ed. James F. Kilroy, 193 (Boston: Twayne, 1984).

13. Warner, *A Guide to Anglo-Irish Literature,* 245; Kamm, "John McGahern," 187; Sampson, *Outstaring Nature's Eye,* 12, 243–4, xii; Kampen, *Zwischen Welt und Text,* 341; Cahalan, *The Irish Novel,* 271; Wolfgang Görtschacher, "'The Real Experiment Is a Constant Experiment,'": John McGahern's Short Stories," in *The Legacy of History: English and American Studies and the Significance of the Past,* ed. Teresa Bela and Zygmunt Mazur, 1:335–48 (Kraków: Jagiellonian University Press, 2003); Stanley van der Ziel, "The Aesthetics of Redemption: John McGahern's *That They May Face the Rising Sun," Studies: An Irish Quarterly Review* 93, no. 372 (Winter 2004): 473–86.

14. Terence Brown, "John McGahern's *Nightlines:* Tone, Technique, and Symbolism," in *The Irish Short Story,* ed. Patrick Rafroidi and Terence Brown, 295 (Gerrards Cross: Colin Smythe / Atlantic Highlands, N.J.: Humanities Press, 1979).

Chapter 2. The Land (I)

1. John McGahern, *The Barracks* (New York: Penguin, 2004), 14–16. All subsequent references are to this edition and appear in parentheses in the text.

2. Burgess's and Lodge's reviews are quoted in Sampson, *Outstaring Nature's Eye,* 34. Other texts referred to in this paragraph are: John Cronin, "'The Dark' Is Not Light Enough: The Fiction of John McGahern," *Studies* 58, no. 232 (Winter 1969): 427; Eileen Kennedy, "The Novels of John McGahern," in *Contemporary Irish Writing,* ed. James D. Brophy and Raymond Porter, 116 (Boston: Iona College Press / Twayne, 1983); Fierobe, "John McGahern," 11.

3. McGahern's language in *The Barracks,* including his use of the passive voice, is discussed by Helène Chuquet, "Étude de quelques marqueurs linguistiques de la

distanction chez John McGahern," in "John McGahern," ed. Jean Brihault and Liliane Louvel, special issue, *La Licorne* 32 (1995): 33–53.

4. For a further discussion of cyclical motifs in McGahern's work see: Bernard Cardin, "Un aspect du temps: Le cycle dans les nouvelles de John McGahern," in "John McGahern," ed. Jean Brihault and Liliane Louvel, special issue, *La Licorne* 32 (1995): 179, 182, 184; and Pascale Amiot, "'The Road Away Becomes the Road Back': L'enfermement dans *The Barracks*," in "Études sur *The Barracks* de John McGahern," ed. Claude Fierobe and Danielle Jacquin, special issue, *Études Irlandaises* (October 1994): 45.

5. Gerd Kampen points to inconsistencies in dating (*Zwischen Welt und Text,* 39–40). McGahern himself is vague about the dating of the novel; see Nicole Ollier, "Step by Step through *The Barracks* with John McGahern," in "John McGahern," ed. Jean Brihault and Liliane Louvel, special issue, *La Licorne* 32 (1995): 57.

6. Liliane Louvel, "John McGahern: La manière noire," in "John McGahern," ed. Jean Brihault and Liliane Louvel, special issue, *La Licorne* 32 (1995): 6; Neil Corcoran, *After Yeats and Joyce,* xi–xii. See also: Shaun O'Connell, "Door into the Light: John McGahern's Ireland," *Massachusetts Review* 25, no. 2 (Summer 1984): 255; and Cronin, "'The Dark' Is Not Light Enough," 117.

7. Sampson, *Outstaring Nature's Eye,* 12.

8. See, for example: Kennedy, "The Novels of John McGahern," 116, 118, 119; Alan Warner, *A Guide to Anglo-Irish Literature,* 251; Sylvie Mikowski, "L'expérience fictive du temps dans *The Barracks*," in "Études sur *The Barracks* de John McGahern," ed. Claude Fierobe and Danielle Jacquin, special issue, *Études Irlandaises* (October 1994): 36–38; Cronin, "'The Dark' Is Not Light Enough," 427–28.

9. Sampson, *Outstaring Nature's Eye,* 35.

10. Quoted in Prusse, "John McGahern," 137.

11. Cahalan, *Double Visions,* 113; Whyte, *History, Myth, and Ritual in the Fiction of John McGahern,* 167; Riana O'Dwyer, "'Her Woman's Days,': Gender Roles in *The Barracks*," in "Études sur *The Barracks* de John McGahern," ed. Claude Fierobe and Danielle Jacquin, special issue, *Études Irlandaises* (October 1994): 161.

12. This topic is discussed in Garfitt, "Constants in Contemporary Irish Fiction," 223, and Warner, *A Guide to Anglo-Irish Literature,* 245.

13. Sampson, *Outstaring Nature's Eye,* 36–37; Kennedy, "The Novels of John McGahern," 118–19; Foley is quoted in Warner, *A Guide to Anglo-Irish Literature,* 251; Mikowski, 43; Cronin, "'The Dark' Is Not Light Enough," 427–28.

14. Sampson, *Outstaring Nature's Eye,* 35, 36, 53; Mikowski, "L'expérience fictive," 36–38; Kampen, *Zwischen Welt und Text,* 47–52.

Chapter 3. The Land (II)

1. Kamm, "John McGahern," 180; Sampson, *Outstaring Nature's Eye,* 83.

2. "The Choice" was first published as part of "Coole Park and Ballylee, 1931," in *Words for Music Perhaps and Other Poems* (1932) but published separately in *The Winding Stair and Other Poems* (1933) and thereafter.

3. John McGahern, *The Dark* (New York: Penguin, 2002), 33. All subsequent references are to this edition and appear in parentheses in the text.

4. The extracts are reprinted in *An Anthology from X: A Quarterly Review of Literature and the Arts, 1959–1962,* ed. Patrick Swift and David Wright, selected with an introduction by David Wright, 153–63 (Oxford: Oxford University Press, 1988).

5. The following are reviews of *The Dark:* "Swotting out of the Farm," *Times Literary Supplement,* May 13, 1965, 365; Vivian Mercier, "Growing Up in Ireland," review of *The Dark, New York Times Book Review,* March 6, 1966, 50. See also: "Ireland Intensified," review of *Nightlines, Times Literary Supplement,* November 27, 1970, 1378; David W. Madden, "By the Lake," *Review of Contemporary Fiction* 22, no. 3 (2002): 163; Corcoran, *After Yeats and Joyce,* 88–89.

6. Hedwig Schwall, review *John Banville: Fictions of Order,* by Ingo Berensmeyer, and *Zwischen Welt und Text,* by Gerd Kampen, *Irish University Review: A Journal of Irish Studies,* 22 (March 2003): 221; Kampen, *Zwischen Welt und Text,* 61–62; Corcoran, *After Yeats and Joyce,* 89; Cahalan, *Double Visions,* 110; Kamm, "John McGahern," 182.

7. Kampen, *Zwischen Welt und Text,* 64.

8. Sampson calls the novel's first six chapters "separate scenes, prose poems" (*Outstaring Nature's Eye,* 65).

9. It has become common in English-language literary studies to identify as a bildungsroman any novel that depicts the maturation of young male or female protagonist. This ignores the fact that the genre is specifically a German-language one, rooted in nineteenth-century German, Austrian, and Swiss literary traditions. One wonders how appropriate it is to apply the term in a British, Irish, or U.S. literary context.

10. See, for example, Sampson, *Outstaring Nature's Eye,* 61–63, and Kamm, "John McGahern," 182. Eileen Kennedy argues that the comparison, although valid, between the two texts "should not be pressed" ("The Novels of John McGahern," 120).

11. Cahalan, *The Irish Novel,* 137, 274.

12. Cahalan, *Double Visions,* 125.

13. "Swotting out of the Farm," 365.

14. Sampson describes *The Dark* as "an existential study of a consciousness in an indeterminate state" (*Outstaring Nature's Eye,* 63). He emphasizes that Mahoney's attempts to choose are central to the novel and also that these set him off from his father (63–64, 68). Kamm, however, argues that McGahern's "pessimism" refuses to allow young Mahoney "any constructive form of escape" ("John McGahern," 181–82).

15. James Whyte quotes McGahern on his and his generation's sense of powerless while he was growing up (*History, Myth, and Ritual in the Fiction of John McGahern,* 26).

16. Compare Samuel Beckett, *Waiting for Godot:* "They give birth astride of a grave, the light gleams an instant, then it's night once more" (London: Faber and Faber, 1965, 89).

17. Mahoney is reading Horace's *Carmen 11.*

18. Cahalan, *Double Visions,* 123.

19. Declan Kiberd, "Fathers and Sons: Irish Style," in *Irish Literature and Culture,* ed. Michael Kenneally, 127 (Gerrards Cross: Colin Smythe, 1992).

20. Corcoran, *After Yeats and Joyce,* 88.

Chapter 4. Paralyses

1. Sampson, *Outstaring Nature's Eye,* 88.

2. The following are reviews of *Nightlines:* "Ireland Intensified," *Times Literary Supplement,* November 27, 1970, 1378; David Pryce-Jones, "Nightlines," review of *Nightlines, New York Times Book Review,* February 7, 1971, 30.

3. Antoinette Quinn, "Varieties of Disenchantment: Narrative Technique in John McGahern's Short Stories," *Journal of the Short Story in English* 13 (Autumn 1989): 77–89.

4. See Liliane Louvel, "Introduction—The Art of John McGahern's Short Fiction," *Journal of the Short Story in English* 34 (Spring 2000): 16; Denis Sampson, "The Rich Whole: John McGahern's *Collected Stories* as Autobiography," *Journal of the Short Story in English* 34 (Spring 2000): 25–26.

5. Brown, "John McGahern's *Nightlines,"* 295; D. J. Enright, "Stuck in the Slot," review of *The Collected Stories, London Review of* Books, October 8, 1992, 10; Banville, "Big News from Small Worlds," 22.

6. Quinn, "Varieties of Disenchantment," 77, 78, 83.

7. John McGahern, *Nightlines* (Boston and Toronto: Little, Brown, 1971), 11. All subsequent references are to this edition and appear in parentheses in the text.

8. This aspect of McGahern's language in *Nightlines* is ably discussed by Görtschacher ("'The Real Experiment Is a Constant Experiment,'" 335–48) and by Bertrand Cardin, "Figures of Silence: Ellipses and Eclipses in John McGahern's *Collected Stories,*" *Journal of the Short Story in English* 40 (Spring 2003): 59–60.

9. See Bertrand Cardin, "Un aspect du temps: Le cycle dans les nouvelles de John McGahern," in "John McGahern," ed. Jean Brihault and Liliane Louvel, special issue, *La Licorne* 32 (1995): 179, 182, 184; Sampson, *Outstaring Nature's Eye,* 93–94. There is also an extensive critical discussion of McGahern's use of "symbolism" in his short stories. What critics mean by this is the author's choice of an aspect of empirical reality —the spinning wheel (in "Wheels"), Greenbaum searching amid the rubble (in "Hearts of Oak and Bellies of Brass"), the bouncing tennis ball and the comics (in "Strandhill, the Sea"), the rotting shark and the crushed peaches (in "Peaches")—that embodies and encapsulates a complex or clear vision of the world. In this, McGahern is working within a long established tradition, both in the short story and, indeed, in the novel. See Brown, "John McGahern's *Nightlines,"* 293–94; Sampson, *Outstaring Nature's Eye,* 89; Quinn, "Varieties of Disenchantment," 84.

10. Critics point to a clear parallel in this motif with the inertia of characters in James Joyce's *Dubliners.* See Sampson, *Outstaring Nature's Eye,* 86–87.

11. Alan Warner writes that *Nightlines* "portrays the forces of darkness" (*A Guide to Anglo-Irish Literature,* 249). Brown formulates this aspect of *Nightlines* as "cruelty,

decay, the ritual wheel which breaks all backs as it turns" (297), and Wolfgang Schmitz also addresses the pessimism of vision in *Nightlines* (*Die Darstellung Irlands,* 67).

Chapter 5. The City (I)

1. John McGahern, "Preface to the Second Edition," *The Leavetaking* (London and Boston: Faber and Faber, 1984), 5.

2. The reader only learns the narrator's surname when the priest announces his mother's death (*The Leavetaking* [Boston and Toronto: Little, Brown, 1974], 77). In part 2, the narrator is called Patrick by various characters in London (see p. 123, for example); however, this could be a generic nickname since there is a widespread tradition of referring to all Irishmen by some variety of the name Patrick

3. Julian Jebb, "The Call of the Deep," review of *Leavetaking, Times Literary Supplement,* January 10, 1975, 29; Seamus Heaney, "Shedding the Skin of Youth," *Sunday Independent* (Dublin), January 26, 1975, 9; Sampson, *Outstaring Nature's Eye,* 110, 112; Peter Ackroyd, "The Twilight World," *Spectator,* January 11, 1975, 41; Peter Straub, "John McGahern: *The Leavetaking,*" *New Statesman,* January 10, 1975, 50; Kamm, "John McGahern," 183; Jean Brihault, "John McGahern: Introduction générale," in "John McGahern," ed. Jean Brihault and Liliane Louvel, special issue, *La Licorne* 32 (1995): 13.

4. John McGahern, *The Leavetaking* (Boston and Toronto: Little, Brown, 1974), 49–51, 72–75. All subsequent references are to this edition and appear in parentheses in the text.

5. Other examples occur on pages 21, 34, 45, 63, 69, 76, and 77.

6. Other examples can be found on pages 21, 44, and 57.

7. The second sentence contains a grammatical error—"she who could end it I could not have." This should be "her who." It is probably a sign of an attempt at hyper-correctness leading to an error.

8. The centrality of these features to notions of poetry in English are discussed in chapters 4–6 of Geoffrey Leech's classic study *A Linguistic Guide to English Poetry* (London: Longman, 1969). Poetic aspects of McGahern's prose in *The Leavetaking* are noted by Jebb ("The Call of the Deep," 29).

9. This poeticized prose can be compared with passages in James Joyce's *A Portrait of the Artist as a Young Man* (for example, the seabird girl episode at the end of chapter 4). McGahern discusses the aims behind his use of poetic language in *The Leavetaking* in an interview with Nicole Ollier, "Step by Step through *The Barracks* with John McGahern," in "John McGahern," ed. Jean Brihault and Liliane Louvel, special issue, *La Licorne* 32 (1995): 55–85, esp. 80.

10. See, for example, Sampson, *Outstaring Nature's Eye,* 112–16, 129.

11. Sampson's argument that the reader of *The Leavetaking* participates with Moran in an attempt to understand the pattern of his life is suggestive (*Outstaring Nature's Eye,* 112).

12. Moran's relationship with his mother is contrasted with two other negative relationships with parents—Lightfoot's with his mother (30–31), and Isobel's with her father in part 2 (126–34).

13. One should also contrast Moran and Isobel's love with the physically unsavory motifs that occur elsewhere, especially in part 1: the recurrent savage gulls in the school playground (9, 10, 20, 24); the malodorous school lavatories (10, 24); the sewage outlet in Howth (44); the cat excrement in oats (51); and Moran senior's mother's vomiting into her bag (55)—a vomiting that is paralleled by Kate Moran years later (65).

14. Sampson, *Outstaring Nature's Eye,* 112, 115–16. Intertextual reference is also discussed by kampen, *Zwischen Welt und Text,* 74–75, 85, 89, and by Cahalan in *The Irish Novel,* 274.

15. John McGahern, *The Leavetaking* (London and Boston: Faber and Faber, 1984), 117.

Chapter 6. Deaths

1. Michael Irwin, "Sorrowful Pipings," review of *Getting Through, Times Literary Supplement,* June 16, 1978, 663.

2. Sampson, *Outstaring Nature's Eye,* 162.

3. Irwin, "Sorrowful Pipings," 663; Tom Paulin, "Evidence of Neglect," review of *Getting Through, Encounter* 50, no. 6 (June 1978): 64–71; Sampson, *Outstaring Nature's Eye,* 187; Schmitz, *Die Darstellung Irlands,* 73, 76–77; Claude Maisonnat, "Flux et désir dans 'A Slip-Up' de John McGahern: Incontinence et écriture," *Journal of the Short Story in English* 30 (Spring 1998): 45–56 and "Jeu d'écriture et creation problématique dans 'The Beginning of an Idea,'" in "John McGahern," ed. Jean Brihault and Liliane Louvel, special issue, *La Licorne* 32 (1995): 195–206; Quinn, "Varieties of Disenchantment," 77–89.

4. Sampson, *Outstaring Nature's Eye,* 165; Paulin, "Evidence of Neglect," 64–71.

5. John McGahern, *Getting Through* (New York: Harper and Row, 1980), 62. All subsequent references are to this edition and appear in parentheses in the text.

6. Bartleby is surely a reference to Melville's passive dissident in "Bartleby the Scrivener" (1853). His companion Barnaby suggests Dickens's novel *Barnaby Rudge* (1841), although apart from his marginal status, Dickens's character seems to have little in common with McGahern's.

7. The title's ambiguity is typical in *Getting Through.* What idea has its beginning in "The Beginning of an Idea"? Whose is the error in "A Slip-Up," Michael's or Agnes's? "Faith, Hope and Charity" turn out to be three musicians in the story of that title, not Christian virtues. There are no swallows, as such, in "Swallows," and Sierra Leone is not, at first reading, central to "Sierra Leone."

8. Sampson relates this vital presence of the past, summoned by physical stimuli in the present, to similar motifs in the work of Marcel Proust (*Outstaring Nature's Eye,* 187).

Chapter 7. The City (II)

1. Kampen, *Zwischen Welt und Text,* 96; Sampson, *Outstaring Nature's Eye,* 137; Kamm, "John McGahern," 186; Alice Adams, "Mavis, the Colonel, and Sin Chastised," review of *The Pornographer, New York Times Book Review,* December 2, 1979, 53; Patricia Craig, "Concocting Erotica," review of *The Pornographer, Times Literary Supplement,* January 11, 1980, 46; Deane, *A Short History of Irish Literature,* 223; John Updike, "An Old-Fashioned Novel," *New Yorker,* December 24, 1979, 95–98, reprinted in *Hugging the Shore: Essays and Criticism* (London: André Deutsch, 1983), 388–93.

2. John McGahern, *The Pornographer* (New York: Harper and Row, 1979), 13. All subsequent references are to this edition and appear in parentheses in the text.

3. This formulation is yet another clear echo of Beckett in McGahern's work. See note 16, chapter 2). Compare also, for example, Vladimir's words in *Waiting for Godot:* "Astride of a grave and a difficult birth. Down in the hole, lingeringly, the grave-digger puts on the forceps" (90).

4. Kennedy, "The Novels of John McGahern," 124; Craig, "Concocting Erotica," 46.

5. Other commentators see the motif of pornography in the novel in a somewhat different way. Cahalan sees it as a challenge to and provocation of the Irish censors who had banned *The Dark* (*The Irish Novel,* 275). Fintan O'Toole discusses it as part of a disappointed response in Irish fiction to sexual liberation in the 1960s ("Island of Saints and Silicon: Literature and Social Change in Contemporary Ireland," in *Cultural Contexts and Literary Idioms in Contemporary Irish Literature,* ed. Michael Kenneally, 33–34 [Gerrards Cross: Colin Smythe, 1988]). Craig sees *The Pornographer* as considering the role of pornography in Irish life ("Concocting Erotica,"46). McGahern himself says, in an interview with Gerd Kampen in 1993, that pornography is meant to show a debased view of sex and an inadequate way of writing about it (Kampen, *Zwischen Welt und Text,* 340).

6. In the interview with Kampen, McGahern says: "Like happiness I think that sex can't be written about. Sex has to be written about, but always sideways" (*Zwischen Welt und Text,* 340). However, in *The Pornographer,* he does try, although not when it comes to Nurse Brady.

Chapter 8. Changes

1. Hogan, "Old Boys, Young Bucks, and New Women," 193; Pat Rogers, "Street Wise," review of *High Ground, London Review of Books,* October 3, 1985, 18; Sampson *Outstaring Nature's Eye,* 188, 190–92, 197.

2. Patricia Craig, "Everyday Ecstasies," *Times Literary Supplement,* September 13, 1985, 1001; Rogers, "Street Wise," 19; Joel Conarroe, "Strong Women, Dreamy Men," review of *High Ground, New York Times Book Review,* February 8, 1987, 9; Bradbury, "High Ground," 86–97.

3. See, in this respect, Sampson, *Outstaring Nature's Eye,* 190–91.

4. John McGahern, *High Ground* (New York: Penguin, 1993), 94. All subsequent references are to this edition and appear in parentheses in the text.

5. Bradbury, "High Ground," 86; Paul Gueguen, "'Like All Other Men': Hantisse et nostalgie de l'ordre," in "John McGahern," ed. Jean Brihault and Liliane Louvel, special issue, *La Licorne* 32 (1995): 187.

Chapter 9. The Father

1. Maher, *John McGahern*, 97, 117.

2. Lindsay Duguid, "The Passing of Old Ways," *Times Literary Supplement,* May 18–24, 1990, 535; Banville, "In Violent Times," 22.

3. John Lanchester, "Self-Effacers," review of *Amonst Women, London Review of Books,* May 24, 1990, 18; Fintan O'Toole, "Both Completely Irish and Universal," *Irish Times* (Dublin), September 15, 1990, Weekend section, 5; Robert F. Garratt, "John McGahern's *Amongst Women:* Representation, Memory, and Trauma," *Irish University Review: A Journal of Irish Studies* 35, no. 1 (Spring/Summer 2005): 121.

 4. For Moran's postwar gratuity, see page 129.

5. John McGahern, *Amongst Women* (New York: Penguin, 1991), 8. All subsequent references are to this edition and appear in parentheses in the text. At this point in the novel, Mona is sixteen and Sheila fifteen. Michael is younger. Luke is presumably older than Maggie, although this is never clearly indicated.

6. Sampson, *Outstaring Nature's Eye,* 216–17.

7. One thinks here of canonical British and Irish novels of the 1980s and 1990s: Salman Rushdie's *Midnight's Children* (1980), Alasdair Gray's *Lanark* (1981), Graham Swift's *Waterland* (1983), Angela Carter's *Nights at the Circus* (1984), and John Banville's *The Book of Evidence* (1989). They are technically different from *Amongst Women,* with differing conventions and relationship to literary history.

8. Gerd Kampen writes about McGahern's extensive pruning of the original typescript of the novel (*Zwischen Welt und Text,* 132).

9. The Irish Civil War was fought from June 1922 to May 1923 between those Irish nationalists who accepted the 1921 treaty with Britain and those who opposed it. The treaty gave the southern counties of Ireland dominion status within the British Empire and considerable autonomy. It entailed, however, the partition of the island of Ireland; Northern Ireland was to remain part of the United Kingdom.

10. See note 6, chapter 2.

11. Robert Garratt calls it "the *omphalos* of McGahern Country at least in this novel." See "John McGahern's *Against Women,*" 124n5.

12. Sampson, *Outstaring Nature's Eye,* 221. This is probably correct, although the dating is not wholly coherent in *Amongst Women.* Moran is already in advanced middle age when he meets and marries Rose. Rose is in her late thirties (*Against Women,* 24), and is described as "much younger" than Moran (27). He is in the eighth grade at school when the "Troubles" start (74), and is presumably a young man in his late teens or early twenties during the war against the British. This is one point where one wonders

about the consistency of the dating. What year exactly is he in the eighth grade? It must be 1916 (the year of the Easter Rising in Dublin), for otherwise he could scarcely be a commander of an IRA flying column in the early 1920s. Even supposing 1916 as the date he leaves school, if the novel's dating were consistent, Moran would be a young man during the Anglo-Irish War. After the war, he still has his youth and good looks, but by the time he meets Rose, youth and fame are gone (36–37). This would place his marriage to Rose in the late 1940s or early 1950s. Michael and Nell want to see an Alan Ladd western in Sligo (106), which probably places this part of the novel in the mid-1950s. The terminus ad quem of the novel's present is probably in the mid-1960s. One can argue this because there are no references to the recrudescence of the Troubles in Ulster in 1968, which would probably make a trip to Northern Ireland, such as Rose and Moran make to Enniskillen, different from the way it is presented toward the end of the novel (174).

13. "Teddy Boys" were working-class young men in Britain in the second half of the 1950s who modeled their clothes, to some extent, on early-twentieth-century (Edwardian) upper-class fashions (hence their name). Long jackets, narrow trousers, suede shoes with thick soles, hair worn long and held in an elaborate front quiff by grease à la Elvis Presley—these were among the marks of their tribe. The fashion was less prominent by 1960.

14. Lanchester, "Self-Effacers," 18.

15. It is notable that the Irish Civil War (1922–23) receives only one abrupt reference in *Amongst Women*. After getting rid of the British, McQuaid remarks austerely, "Then we fought one another" (18). The silence relating to the civil war in *Amongst Women* is deafening. One can compare the sparse references to the civil war in Colm Tóibín's novel *The Heather Blazing* (1992), which is contemporary with *Amongst Women* and covers some similar territory.

16. Maher, *John McGahern,* 116.

17. Sampson, *Outstaring Nature's Eye,* 217.

18. *Double Visions,* 122; Sampson, *Outstaring Nature's Eye,* 217.

19. Banville, "In Violent Times," 22.

20. Maher, *John McGahern,* 99.

21. Corcoran, *After Yeats and Joyce,* 90. See also: Whyte, *History, Myth, and Ritual in the Fiction of John McGahern,* 92–93, 226; Maher, *John McGahern,* 108; and Sampson, *Outstaring Nature's Eye,* 11.

22. Banville, "In Violent Times," 22.

Chapter 10. The Community

1. John McGahern, "Introduction," *The Power of Darkness* (London: Faber and Faber, 1991), vii.

2. Nicholas Greene, "John McGahern's *The Power of Darkness,*" in "John McGahern," ed. Jean Brihault and Liliane Louvel, special issue, *La Licorne* 32 (1995): 159–60.

3. McGahern, "Introduction," vii

4. Michael L. Storey, review of *The Collected Stories, Studies in Short Fiction* 31, no. 1 (Winter 1994), 120. *The Collected Stories* are also reviewed by Banville in "Big News from Small Worlds," 22–24, and by Enright in "Stuck in the Slot," 9–10. "The Country Funeral" is discussed in "John McGahern," ed. Jean Brihault and Liliane Louvel, special issue, *La Licorne* 32 (1995): 207–20.

5. Paul Binding, "Welcome to Paradise, County Leitrim," review of *That They May Face the Rising Sun, Independent on Sunday* (London), January 27, 2002, 15; Hilary Mantel, "Getting Through," review of *By the Lake, New York Review of Books,* May 23, 2002, 10–14; Seamus Deane, "A New Dawn," *Guardian* (Manchester), January 12, 2002, Saturday Review 9; Denis Sampson, "'Open to the World': A Reading of John McGahern's *That They May Face the Rising Sun,"* in "John McGahern," ed. John Brannigan, special issue, *Irish University Review: A Journal of Irish Studies* 35, no. 1 (Spring/Summer 2005): 136–46; Eamonn Hughes, "'All That Surrounds Our Life': Time, Sex, and Death in *That They May Face the Rising Sun,"* in "John McGahern," ed. John Brannigan, special issue, *Irish University Review: A Journal of Irish Studies* 35, no. 1 (Spring/Summer 2005): 147–63; Declan Kiberd, "Fallen Nobility: The World of John McGahern," in "John McGahern," ed. John Brannigan, special issue, *Irish University Review: A Journal of Irish Studies* 35, no. 1 (Spring/Summer 2005): 164–74. The reception of *That They May Face the Rising Sun* is discussed by Eamon Maher in *John McGahern,* 121–22.

6. Maher, *John McGahern,* 121. See also van der Ziel, "The Aesthetics of Redemption," 473–86.

7. John McGahern, *By the Lake* (New York: Vintage, 2003), 150, 170. All subsequent references are to this edition and appear in parentheses in the text.

8. Sampson comments on the use of dialogue in *That They May Face the Rising Sun* ("Open to the World," 140).

9. That is not to say that characters do not exert choices and shape their own lives at times. The Shah decides to sell the scrap business. Most notably, the Ruttledges decide to settle by the lake. They refuse Robert Booth's offer of a job in London. John Quinn's new wife abandons an unpromising marriage. However, the novel does focus on many processes that are nonhuman or communal, and even where human agency is involved the text linguistically shifts the focus from that agency to the actions themselves.

10. The problem of time setting in *That They May Face the Rising Sun* is noted by Mantel ("Getting Through," 10). It is possible McGahern is making another, metafictional, point. Novels are fictions; they can compel readers' interest and belief even when they are not consistent by the standards of the empirical world. The metafictional aspects of McGahern's fiction certainly need further research.

11. Sampson, "Open to the World," 136, 139; Maher, *John McGahern,* 122.

12. It is important to note that other characters, in the wider world, also inhabit restricted worlds. Kate's grandfather is an example (226), as is Johnny in London. Ruttledge sees his account of life there as opening up "a small world" (220).

13. Critics write of *That They May Face the Rising Sun* that it constitutes McGahern's "swansong" for rural Ireland (see, for example, Maher, *John McGahern,* 121). If so, this is another motif of death and transience. However, to a non-Irish reader looking at evidence in the novel, this dirge for a passing life is not entirely obvious. The farms of characters in the novel are small but seem viable. Ruttledge uses quite sophisticated farming machinery (119–22, 126–28, 135–42). Lambs are sold and slaughtered in factory-like conditions of efficiency and modernity (152–62). Cattle are sold in a technologically sophisticated manner (248–54). Admittedly, most of the characters in the novel are aging, but that does not mean that their way of life is on the edge of destruction. Large parts of Europe are full of thriving small family farms.

Conclusion

1. Richard Pine, "John McGahern," *Guardian* (Manchester), March 31, 2006, 37. Frances Byrne, who worked with McGahern for BBC radio, writes a brief memory of the author as a conclusion to the obituary in the *Guardian.*

2. "John McGahern," *Daily Telegraph* (London), March 31, 2006, 25.

3. W. J. McCormack, "John McGahern," *Independent* (London), April 1, 2006, 44

4. Ibid.

5. Joseph O'Connor's appreciation of McGahern is appended to McCormack's obituary in the *Independent* (London), April 1, 2006, 44.

Selected Bibliography

Works by John McGahern (in order of publication)

Books

The Barracks. London: Faber and Faber, 1963; New York: Macmillan, 1964.

The Dark. London: Faber and Faber, 1965; New York: Knopf, 1966.

Nightlines. London: Faber and Faber, 1970; Boston: Little, Brown, 1971.

The Leavetaking. London: Faber and Faber, 1974; Boston: Little, Brown, 1975; revised edition, London: Faber and Faber, 1984.

Getting Through. London: Faber and Faber, 1978; New York: Harper and Row, 1980.

The Pornographer. London: Faber and Faber, 1979; New York: Harper and Row, 1980.

High Ground. London: Faber and Faber, 1985; New York: Viking, 1987.

Amongst Women. London and Boston: Faber and Faber, 1990; New York: Viking, 1990.

The Power of Darkness. London: Faber and Faber, 1991.

The Collected Stories. London: Faber and Faber, 1992; New York: Knopf, 1993.

That They May Face the Rising Sun. London: Faber and Faber, 2002; U.S. edition published as *By the Lake.* New York: Knopf, 2002.

Memoir. London: Faber and Faber, 2005; U.S. edition published as *All Will Be Well: A Memoir.* New York: Knopf, 2006.

Selected Nonbook Publications

"The End or the Beginning of Love." *X: A Literary Magazine* 2 (April 1961): 36–46.

"The Image: Prologue to a Reading at the Rockefeller University." *Honest Ulsterman* 8 (December 1968): 10. A brief comment, much reprinted, considered by critics to be a statement of McGahern's own fictional practice.

"*An tOileánach / The Islandman.*" *Canadian Journal of Irish Studies* 13, no. 1 (June 1987): 7–15. A much reprinted essay, considered by many commentators to be a kind of credo by McGahern and to anticipate his aims and aspects of his technique in *That They May Face the Rising Sun.*

"Dubliners." In *James Joyce: The Artist and the Labyrinth: A Critical Re-evaluation,* edited by Augustine Martin, 63–72. London: Ryan, 1990. An invaluable piece of self-commentary, including interesting observations on George Moore, Joyce, and Flaubert.

"The Church and Its Spire." *Soho Square* 6 (1993): 17–27.

"Creatures of the Earth." *Granta* 49 (Winter 1994): 227–43.

"Love of the World." *Granta* 59 (Autumn 1997): 219–50.
"The White Boat." In *New Writing 6,* edited by A. S. Byatt and Peter Porter, 342–72. London: Vintage, in association with the British Council, 1997.

Critical Works on John McGahern

Biographical Works

Malcolm, David. "John McGahern." In *British and Irish Short Fiction Writers, 1945–2000,* edited by Cheryl Alexander Malcolm and David Malcolm, 222–34. Dictionary of Literary Biography 319. Detroit: Thomson/Gale, 2006. This article contains biographical information and focuses on McGahern's short fiction. It contains a bibliography of primary texts and selected critical works and interviews.
Prusse, Michael C. "John McGahern." In *British Novelists since 1960,* edited by Meritt Moseley, 135–45. Dictionary of Literary Biography 231. Detroit: Bruccoli Clark Layman / Gale Group, 2001. An overview of McGahern's life and work up to the late 1990s. It contains a bibliography of primary texts and selected critical works and interviews.

Bibliographies

Kampen, Gerd. "Bibliografie John McGahern." In *Zwischen Welt und Text: Narratologische Studien zum irischen Gegenwartsroman am Beispiel von John McGahern und John Banville,* 292–304. Trier: Wissenschaftlicher Verlag, 2002. This thorough and extensive bibliography lists McGahern's nonfiction, articles and essays on him, and reviews of the novels and short stories through *Amongst Women.*
van der Ziel, Stanley. "John McGahern—an Annotated Bibliography." In "John McGahern," edited by John Brannigan. Special issue, *Irish University Review: A Journal of Irish Studies* 35, no. 1 (Spring/Summer 2005): 175–202. Full and up-to-date, this bibliography lists adaptations of McGahern's work in other media, interviews and profiles, special issues of periodicals devoted to McGahern, reviews, essays, and books. It also lists French translations of the novels and short stories.
Whyte, James. "Bibliography." In *History, Myth, and Ritual in the Fiction of John McGahern: Strategies of Transcendence,* 241–61. Lewiston, Queenstown, and Lampeter: Edwin Mellen Press, 2002. This detailed bibliography lists McGahern's journalism and essays, interviews and profiles, and reviews and criticism. It also lists newspaper articles relating to the scandal over *The Dark.*

Monographs

Kampen, Gerd. *Zwischen Welt und Text: Narratologische Studien zum irischen Gegenwartsroman am Beispiel von John McGahern und John Banville.* Trier: Wissenschaftlicher Verlag, 2002. A study of McGahern in relation to the work of his contemporary and fellow Irish novelist John Banville. It contrasts McGahern's traditionality with Banville's more experimental fiction. It underestimates the degree of self-referentiality and metafictionality in McGahern's work but provides full and insightful discussions of McGahern's work through *Amongst Women.* Contains an extensive bibliography and an interview with McGahern.

Maher, Eamon. *John McGahern: From the Local to the Universal.* Dublin: Liffey Press, 2003. A thorough introduction to McGahern's fiction. The subtitle indicates the work's central thesis. Contains a select but extensive bibliography.

Sampson, Denis. *Outstaring Nature's Eye: The Fiction of John McGahern.* Washington, D.C.: Catholic University of America Press, 1993. This study must be the starting point for any scholarly discussion of McGahern's work. It is a brilliant and detailed discussion of McGahern's fiction. Individual chapters are devoted to each of the novels and the volumes of short stories through *Amongst Women.* Sampson writes, "In most of McGahern's fiction the true adventure consists in the engagement of the imagination with the everyday; he is, in short, a poet who happens to write in the medium of realistic prose" (xii). Sampson also emphasizes the local settings of McGahern's fiction, and the coupling of these with mythic ambitions. An outstanding work of scholarship and analysis to which all those who work with McGahern's fiction are indebted. One's only reservation is that it overaccentuates positive aspects of McGahern's vision.

Whyte, James. *History, Myth, and Ritual in the Fiction of John McGahern: Strategies of Transcendence.* Lewiston, Queenstown, and Lampeter: Edwin Mellen Press, 2002. An attempt to relate McGahern's fiction closely to the writer's biographical experience and to social and cultural trends in the Ireland. Whyte writes that "McGahern's aesthetic, like his view of society is characterized by romantic nostalgia. He looks to an imaginary world of social, cultural and linguistic harmony for a literary form which is characterized by epic simplicity, a unity of expression and representation" (92). There are chapters on McGahern's fiction and religion, the family, and patriarchy. Contains an extensive bibliography and an interview with McGahern.

Books

Cahalan, James M. *The Irish Novel: A Critical History.* Dublin: Gill and Macmillan, 1988. Contains analysis of *The Dark* and *The Leavetaking.*

———. *Double Visions: Women and Men in Modern and Contemporary Irish Fiction.* Syracuse, N.Y.: Syracuse University Press, 1999. Chapter 4 addresses McGahern's place among contemporary Irish novelists, such as Edna O'Brien and Brian Moore.

Carlson, Julia, ed. *Banned in Ireland: Censorship and the Irish Writer.* London: Routledge, 1990. Discusses the complexities of the legal framework of censorship in the Irish Free State and the Irish republic and its consequences. Contains interviews with McGahern and with other writers (Benedict Kiely, Edna O'Brien, Brian Moore, and others) who fell foul of it.

Corcoran, Neil. *After Yeats and Joyce: Reading Modern Irish Literature.* Oxford and New York: Oxford University Press, 1997. Discusses McGahern's work in relation to a wide range of other Irish writers (Patrick Kavanagh, Sean O'Faolain, Frank O'Connor, and others). Contains analyses of McGahern's early fiction and *Amongst Women.*

153

Deane, Seamus. *A Short History of Irish Literature*. London: Hutchinson, 1986. Contains material on McGahern's early fiction. Deane, a major figure in Irish letters, argues for the bleakness of McGahern's vision of things.

Goarzin, Anne. *John McGahern: Reflets d'Irlande*. Rennes: Presses Universitaires de Rennes, 2002. Contains observations on McGahern's work in its relation to the subject of Ireland. Goarzin points to the repetitions in McGahern's fiction.

Schmitz, Wolfgang F. W. *Die Darstellung Irlands in der modernen irischen Short Story: Eine Bestandsaufnahme zur thematisch-inhaltlichen Ausrichtung irischer Short-Story-Autoren in den sechziger und siebziger Jahren*. Frankfurt am Main and Bern: Peter D. Lang, 1981. Perceptive on the subject of McGahern's pessimism, especially in the short fiction.

Warner, Alan. *A Guide to Anglo-Irish Literature*. Dublin: Gill and Macmillan; New York: St. Martin's Press, 1981. Detailed and thorough commentary on the novels and short stories up to the early 1980s.

Collections of Articles

Brannigan, John, ed. "John McGahern." Special issue, *Irish University Review: A Journal of Irish Studies* 35, no. 1 (Spring/Summer 2005). A collection of essays by substantial scholars, such as Anne Goarzin, Patrick Crotty, Eamon Maher, Robert F. Garratt, Denis Sampson, and Declan Kiberd. It examines individual novels (*The Barracks, The Dark, Amongst Women,* and *That They May Face the Rising Sun*) and also contains essays on general topics related to McGahern's fiction, such as children and the Protestant "Big House." It has an extensive bibliography.

Brihault, Jean, and Liliane Louvel, eds. "John McGahern." Special issue, *La Licorne* 32 (1995). A rich collection of useful essays, including pieces on McGahern's language, the motif of the wheel, and on short stories ("Like All Other Men," "The Beginning of an Idea," and "The Country Funeral").

Fierobe, Claude, and Danielle Jacquin, eds. "Études sur *The Barracks* de John McGahern." Special issue, *Études Irlandaises* (October 1994). This collection is an invaluable aid to a study of McGahern's first and greatest novel. It contains essays on identity, time, enclosure, silence, and religion in *The Barracks*. Nicole Ollier puts together a detailed guide by McGahern to the novel.

Journal of the Short Story in English 34 (Spring 2000): 15–85. This section is devoted to McGahern's short fiction and contains several stimulating essays, including a piece by Denis Sampson on McGahern's short fiction and autobiography.

Interviews

These are some of the most commonly referred to interviews with McGahern.

Carlson, Julia. "John McGahern." In *Banned in Ireland: Censorship and the Irish Writer,* edited by Julia Carlson, 53–67. London: Routledge, 1990. Gives McGahern's response to the banning of *The Dark*.

Goden, Patrick. "Interview: John McGahern." *Scrivener: A Literary Magazine* 5, no. 2 (Summer 1984): 25–26.

Heneghan, Grace. "Novel Experiences." *Garda Journal: The Journal of the International Police Association, Ireland Section,* November 1995, 34–38. This interview contains an unusual perspective on McGahern's childhood and youth.

Jackson, Joe. "Tales from the Dark Side." *Hot Press,* November 14, 1991, 18–20.

Kampen, Gerd. "An Interview with John McGahern." In *Zwischen Welt und Text: Narratologische Studien zum irischen Gegenwartsroman am Beispiel von John McGahern und John Banville,* 336–42. Trier: Wissenschaftlicher Verlag, 2002. A wide ranging interview in which McGahern talks of *The Pornographer,* the vision underlying his work, the role of art, and repetition in his work.

Louvel, Liliane, Gilles Ménégaldo, and Claudine Verley. "John McGahern—17 November 1993." In "John McGahern," edited by Jean Brihault and Liliane Louvel. Special issue, *La Licorne* 32 (1995): 19–31. McGahern talks of his upbringing, the Catholic Church, his reading as a child and young man, his development as a writer, his attitude toward the short story and the novel, and narration.

Louvel, Liliane. "John McGahern." *Journal of the Short Story in English* 41 (Autumn 2003): 123–41. McGahern talks of his childhood, his early reading, the beginning of his career, his early life in Dublin, how he writes, and *The Barracks.*

Sampson, Denis. "A Conversation with John McGahern." *Canadian Journal of Irish Studies* 17 (July 1991): 13–18. A well-known interview.

Whyte, James. "An Interview with John McGahern." In *History, Myth, and Ritual in the Fiction of John McGahern: Strategies of Transcendence,* 227–35. Lewiston, Queenstown, and Lampeter: Edwin Mellen Press, 2002. McGahern talks of *The Leavetaking* and *The Pornographer,* religion, Proust, women and the family, *Amongst Women,* and self-expression.

Selected Articles and Chapters in Books

Amiot, Pascale. "'The Road Away Becomes the Road Back': L'enfermement dans *The Barracks.*" In "Études sur *The Barracks* de John McGahern," edited by Claude Fierobe and Danielle Jacquin. Special issue, *Études Irlandaises* (October 1994): 45–64. A discussion of one of the central motifs (imprisonment) of *The Barracks*

Bradbury, Nicola. "High Ground." In *Re-reading the Short Story,* edited by Clare Hanson, 86–97. Basingstoke and London: Macmillan, 1989. Serious, if sometimes opaque, commentary on McGahern's third volume of short fiction.

Brihault, Jean. "John McGahern: Introduction générale." In "John McGahern," edited by Jean Brihault and Liliane Louvel. Special issue, *La Licorne* 32 (1995): 11–17. A brief introduction to McGahern's work.

Brown, Terence. "John McGahern's *Nightlines:* Tone, Technique, and Symbolism." In *The Irish Short Story,* edited by Patrick Rafroidi and Terence Brown, 289–301. Gerrards Cross: Colin Smythe / Atlantic Highlands, N.J.: Humanities Press, 1979. A discussion of McGahern's fiction in relation to Irish narrative traditions.

Cardin, Bertrand. "Un aspect du temps: Le cycle dans les nouvelles de John McGahern." In "John McGahern," edited by Jean Brihault and Liliane Louvel. Special issue, *La Licorne* 32 (1995): 179–86. On the motif of the cycle and repetition in McGahern's short fiction.

————. "Figures of Silence: Ellipses and Eclipses in John McGahern's *Collected Stories.*" *Journal of the Short Story in English* 40 (Spring 2003): 57–68. Deals with an important topic in McGahern's fiction.

Hélène Chuquet, "Étude de quelques marqueurs linguistiques de la distanciation chez John McGahern." In "John McGahern," edited by Jean Brihault and Liliane Louvel. Special issue, *La Licorne* 32 (1995): 33–53. An attempt to discuss McGahern's language and its function in various texts.

Cronin, John. "'The Dark' Is Not Light Enough: The Fiction of John McGahern." *Studies* 58, no. 232 (Winter 1969): 427–32. An early appreciation of McGahern's work.

Fierobe, Claude. "John McGahern: Le fugitif et l'éternel." In "Études sur *The Barracks* de John McGahern," edited by Claude Fierobe and Danielle Jacquin. Special issue, *Études Irlandaises* (October 1994): 11–14. Clear and authoritative judgments on McGahern's work.

Garfitt, Roger. "Constants in Contemporary Irish Fiction." In *Two Decades of Irish Writing,* edited by Douglas Dunn, 207–41. Cheadle, U.K.: Carcanet, 1975. Contains commentary on McGahern's world vision.

Görtschacher, Wolfgang. "'The Real Experiment Is a Constant Experiment': John McGahern's Short Stories." In *The Legacy of History: English and American Studies and the Significance of the Past,* edited by Teresa Bela and Zygmunt Mazur, 1:335–48. Kraków: Jagiellonian University Press, 2003. An original and thorough essay examining poetic aspects of McGahern's short fiction.

Hogan, Robert. "Old Boys, Young Bucks, and New Women: The Contemporary Irish Short Story." In *The Irish Short Story: A Critical History,* edited by James F. Kilroy, 169–215. Boston: Twayne, 1984. Hogan finds McGahern's subject matter limited and doubts if the writer can develop.

Kamm, Jürgen. "John McGahern." In *Contemporary Irish Novelists,* edited by Rüdiger Imhof, 175–91. Tübingen: Gunter Narr Verlag, 1990. Valuable above all for its comments on *The Leavetaking* and *The Pornographer.* Kamm finds McGahern's work bleak and repetitive.

Kennedy, Eileen. "The Novels of John McGahern: The Road Away Becomes the Road Back." In *Contemporary Irish Writing,* edited by James D. Brophy and Raymond Porter, 115–26. Boston: Iona College Press and Twayne, 1983. The commentary on *The Barracks* is insightful. Kennedy reads *The Barracks* as less dark than other critics suggest it is. The essay is also useful with regard to *The Dark.*

Kiberd, Declan. "Fathers and Sons: Irish-Style." In *Irish Literature and Culture,* edited by Michael Kenneally, 127–43. Gerrards Cross: Colin Smythe, 1992. The discussion of the father motif is relevant to a reading of McGahern.

Louvel, Liliane. "John McGahern: La manière noire." In "John McGahern," edited by Jean Brihault and Liliane Louvel. Special issue, *La Licorne* 32 (1995): 5–10. A brief but clear view of McGahern's writing by a major McGahern scholar. She writes of silence and entrapment and the tension in McGahern's work between past and present, lyricism and emotional restraint, childhood and adulthood, the countryside and the city.

————. "Introduction." In "The Art of the Irish Short Story," edited by Liliane Louvel. Special issue, *Journal of the Short Story in English* 34 (Spring 2000): 15–19.

Maisonnat, Claude. "Flux et désir dans 'A Slip-Up' de John McGahern: Incontinence et écriture." *Journal of the Short Story in English* 30 (Spring 1998): 45–56. An original approach to a McGahern short story, based on Freudian and Lacanian concepts, and pointing to a metafictional aspect of the text.

Mikowski, Sylvie. "L'expérience fictive du temps dans *The Barracks*." In "Études sur *The Barracks* de John McGahern," edited by Claude Fierobe and Danielle Jacquin. Special issue, *Études Irlandaises* (October 1994): 27–44. Commentary on time in *The Barracks*.

O'Connell, Shaun. "Door into the Light: John McGahern's Ireland." *Massachusetts Review* 25, no. 2 (Summer 1984): 255–68. A thorough discussion of McGahern's fiction to the early 1980s. He writes that "McGahern is . . . concerned with the latent politics of Irish life: provinciality, family enclosure and Church repression of sexual expression" (257).

O'Dwyer, Riana. "'Her Woman's Days': Gender Roles in *The Barracks*." In "Études sur *The Barracks* de John McGahern," edited by Claude Fierobe and Danielle Jacquin. Special issue, *Études Irlandaises* (October 1994): 147–62. Argues that the novel "represents the conventions of a woman's life, with its restrictions and frustrations, but also interrogates such conventions continually" (164).

Ollier, Nicole. "Step by Step through *The Barracks* with John McGahern." In "John McGahern," edited by Jean Brihault and Liliane Louvel. Special issue, *La Licorne* 32 (1995): 55–85. Almost everything one could wish to know about McGahern's own view of his first novel and its relation to his own life.

O'Toole, Fintan. "Island of Saints and Silicon: Literature and Social Change in Contemporary Ireland." In *Cultural Contexts and Literary Idioms in Contemporary Irish Literature,* edited by Michael Kenneally, 11–35. Gerrards Cross: Colin Smythe, 1988. Contains observations on sexual mores in southern Ireland after the 1960s that are related to McGahern's *The Pornographer*.

Quinn, Antoinette. "Varieties of Disenchantment: Narrative Technique in John McGahern's Short Stories." *Journal of the Short Story in English* 13 (Autumn 1989): 77–89. Insightful readings of McGahern's short stories.

Theil, Alain. "Manifestations et avaries du pouvoir dans 'Christmas' de John McGahern." *Journal of the Short Story in English* 5 (Autumn 1985): 55–64. A reading of a McGahern short story in terms of power and breakdowns of power.

Updike, John. "An Old-Fashioned Novel." In *Hugging the Shore: Essays and Criticism,* 388–93. London: André Deutsch, 1983. A clear analysis and positive evaluation by an eminent novelist.

van der Ziel, Stanley. "The Aesthetics of Redemption: John McGahern's *That They May Face the Rising Sun*." *Studies: An Irish Quarterly Review* 93, no. 372 (Winter 2004):

473–86. An original contribution to the discussion of McGahern's sixth novel. Van der Ziel argues that this novel does not fit into an existing novel tradition. He emphasizes poetic and religious aspects of the text.

Reviews

Adams, Alice. "Mavis, the Colonel, and Sin Chastised." Review of *The Pornographer. New York Times Book Review,* December 2, 1979, 14, 53. A typical bemused review of this novel.

Banville, John. "In Violent Times." Review of *Amongst Women. New York Review of Books,* December 6, 1990, 22–25. A major review by a major novelist. It focuses on *Amongst Women* but also examines McGahern's work as a whole.

———. "Big News from Small Worlds." Review of *The Collected Stories. New York Review of Books,* April 8, 1993, 22–24. Banville is, as always, positive and insightful in his review. He writes of McGahern's literary echoes, the settings of the short stories, language, and the father. He writes that McGahern has "made a great thing out of simple components" (23).

Binding, Paul. "Welcome to Paradise, County Leitrim." Review of *That They May Face the Rising Sun. Independent on Sunday* (London), January 27, 2002, 15. A laudatory review.

Breslin, John B. "Pastoral." Review of *By the Lake. Commonweal* 129, no. 10 (May 17, 2002): 22. Observations on "Homeric" elements in the novel and on Johnny's role in it.

Conarroe, Joel. "Strong Women, Dreamy Men." Review of *High Ground. New York Times Book Review,* February 8, 1987, 9. A thorough review of McGahern's third volume of short stories.

Craig, Patricia. "Concocting Erotica." Review of *The Pornographer. Times Literary Supplement,* January 11, 1980, 46. An intelligent review of McGahern's most difficult text.

Duguid, Lindsay. "The Passing of the Old Ways." Review of *Amongst Women. Times Literary Supplement,* May 18–24, 1990, 535. The author writes of the motif of change in *Amongst Women* and of the novel's universality.

Enright, D. J. "Stuck in the Slot." Review of *The Collected Stories. London Review of Books,* October 8, 1992, 9–10. Sensitive analysis of McGahern's short fiction by an accomplished poet.

"Ireland Intensified." Review of *Nightlines. Times Literary Supplement,* November 27, 1970, 1378.

Irwin, Michael. "Sorrowful Pipings." Review of *Getting Through. Times Literary Supplement,* June 16, 1978, 663. The reviewer admires but does not enjoy the collection, which he describes as melancholy.

Jebb, Julian. "The Call of the Deep." Review of *The Leavetaking. Times Literary Supplement,* January 10, 1975, 29. Jebb notes poetic elements in the text, and argues that the novel shows a broadening of McGahern's fiction.

Lanchester, John. "Self-Effacers." Review of *Amongst Women. London Review of Books,* May 24, 1990, 18.

Maher, Eamon. "Worth the Wait," Review of *That They May Face the Rising Sun. Irish Literary Supplement* 21 (September 22, 2002): 27. This review stresses the elegiac aspect of the novel.

Mantel, Hilary. "Getting Through." Review of *By the Lake. New York Review of Books,* May 23, 2002, 10–14. A major review by a major novelist. Mantel deals with McGahern's sixth novel but also responds to his work as a whole.

Mercier, Vivien. "Growing Up in Ireland." Review of *The Dark. New York Times Book Review,* March 6, 1966, 50.

"Noted by the Editors." Review of *The Collected Stories. Antioch Review* 51, no. 4 (Fall 1993): 657.

Paulin, Tom. "Evidence of Neglect." Review of *Getting Through. Encounter* 50, no. 6 (June 1978): 64–71. Praise for McGahern's short fiction from a distinguished poet.

Pryce-Jones, David. "Nightlines." Review of *Nightlines. New York Times Book Review,* February 7, 1971, 30.

Rogers, Pat. "Street Wise." Review of *High Ground. London Review of Books,* October 3, 1985, 18–19.

Shannon, Elizabeth. Review of *The Collected Stories. Commonweal* 21, no. 1 (January 14, 1994), 38–39. Comments on pessimism and female characters.

Storey, Michael L. Review of *The Collected Stories. Studies in Short Fiction* 31, no. 1 (Winter 1994): 118–20. Commentary on "The Country Funeral."

"Swotting out of the Farm." Review of *The Dark. Times Literary Supplement,* May 13, 1965, 365.

Thompson-Noel, Michael. "When Truth Is More Important Than Facts." Review of *That They May Face the Rising Sun. Financial Times Weekend,* January 19–20, 2002, vii.

Index